LYRIC TIME

Lyric Time

DICKINSON AND THE LIMITS OF GENRE

Sharon Cameron

THE JOHNS HOPKINS UNIVERSITY PRESS / BALTIMORE AND LONDON

This book has been brought to publication with the generous assistance of the Andrew W. Mellon Foundation.

The Johns Hopkins University Press, Baltimore, Maryland 21218
The Johns Hopkins Press Ltd., London

Library of Congress Catalog Number 78-9983   ISBN 0-8018-2171-1
Library of Congress Cataloging in Publication data will be found on the last printed page of this book.

To Carol Baird
and to the Memory of
Louis Briskin
(1889–1976)

Contents

Acknowledgments

ALTHOUGH I conceive the audience for the present study as readers of lyric poetry as well as readers of Dickinson, it is the latter whom I have had most cogently in mind during the writing of the book. I would therefore like to express my gratitude first to those Dickinson scholars and critics whose works continue to school me in the subtleties of Dickinson's poetry; in particular to Charles Anderson, David Porter, and Robert Weisbuch. In the dialogue one frequently imagines during long and solitary writing labors, their voices were loudest and most formidable in my mind, and in fact there are instances in my text where I simply externalize the conversation.

On a more personal level, I am grateful to Kathleen Fitzgerald, Alix Pollack, Jody Millward, and Jacqueline Wehmueller, who helped in the preparation of the manuscript, and to the funds of the University of California, Santa Barbara, which made much of this help possible. Without the patience and scrupulous care of Louise Woods, the index would not exist. I am also grateful to Anna Briskin and Rosaline Cameron, whose financial assistance enabled me to take a year off from my teaching duties to finish the project.

It was from Barbara Herrnstein Smith at Bennington College that I first learned how to ask those questions about poetry which led indirectly but surely to the present study. I have been graced along the way with more than my share of discriminate readers, who offered both the sharpness of their criticism and the magnanimity of their advice, and I would like here to thank Kent Dixon, Mimi Still Dixon, Elizabeth Falsey, William Frost, Albert Gilman, Laurence Holland, Joan Manheimer, Patrick McCarthy, Mark Rose, Herbert Schneidau, Sylvia Sieferman, and Muriel Zimmerman. I am especially grateful to J. Hillis Miller, who gave this project his encouragement when it was barely more than an idea, and who continued to stand by it in the course of several years. Finally, I should like to thank Allen Grossman, friend, teacher, inexhaustible bibliography and primary source in his own right, and Garrett Stewart, whose real dialogue with me and continual willingness to think in depth about the concerns of this book deepen my understanding of generosity.

LYRIC TIME

Introduction
"THE ANGLE OF A LANDSCAPE"

"THERE IS no first, or last, in Forever—," Emily Dickinson wrote to her sister-in-law, Susan Gilbert Dickinson, in 1864, "It is Centre, there, all the time—"[1] (L 288), and, in the same year,[2] to the man to whom she was serving such a bizarre literary apprenticeship, Thomas Wentworth Higginson, "The only News I know/Is Bulletins all day/From Immortality" (L 290). However self-conscious the remarks may be, they effectively draw our attention to a central feature of Dickinson's poetry—its resolute departure from temporal order and its reference to another absent or invisible order that is invoked as "Immortality" or alluded to, in this case, as "Centre." It is hardly surprising that Dickinson's language teases conception, exempting itself as it does from the necessity of acknowledging beginnings and ends and the points that intervene between the two; these are temporal relationships renounced as inferior to the conceptual harmony specified by the permanence of immortality and the promised completion of a center. For underneath words and syntax, at the primary level of thought, we sense Dickinson's belief that to adhere to the exactions of temporal relationship is to relinquish all hope of the immortality that will replace time itself. Nonetheless it remains a paradox that Dickinson's utterances fragment, word cut from word, stanza from stanza, as a direct consequence of her desire for that temporal completion which will fuse all separations into the healing of a unified whole.

Interestingly enough, she conceives of immortality not as morning but as "noon,"[3] and if we investigate the many times the word appears in her poetry, we realize that it implies not only noon, but noon in the middle of summer, not only summer but a summer light whose intensity dazzles to blindness, its glare burning away all but vision of itself. Thus "noon," alchemized into light, comes consistently to stand for the clockless escape from time that would liberate into the longed-for permanence. The pull between time and immortality charges Dickinson's poems. Once she polarized it as follows:

> Some—Work for Immortality—
> The Chiefer part, for Time—
> He—Compensates—immediately—
> The former—Checks—on Fame—
>
> Slow Gold—but Everlasting—
> The Bullion of Today—
> Contrasted with the Currency
> Of Immortality—
>
> A Beggar—Here and There—
> Is gifted to discern
> Beyond the Broker's insight—
> One's—Money—One's—the Mine—   (P 406)

In the imperative world of Dickinson's poems, immortality exists because its absence would be intolerable. There is frequently in the poems a time not present that haunts the present as it haunts the speakers' minds, confusing its dominance in memory or dream with a prediction about the future, mistaking itself for prophecy. The present, then, the "time" of Dickinson's poems, is overwhelmed by the promise of another, more satisfactory, order that will destroy time altogether, replace it by "Slow Gold—but Everlasting—," and this belief in that impossible future is strengthened in direct proportion to how deeply a given speaker is mired in the characteristic deprivations of experience. For many of Dickinson's speakers the world is a landslide of lost things, and their imagining of a future, rectifying providence lurks beneath the surface of the speech, as tenacious a conception as it is a wordless one. Silence serves illusion in such instances, for the dream that revenges itself on an inadequate reality by giving to itself what it will never be given conceals the consolation it knows is not true.

The profound confusion of loss and immortality, in which the presence of one signifies the promise of the other, is permitted, even encouraged, by the way in which both are predicated on the transcendence of the body—in the case of loss, as the body is sacrificed to the outlines of memory; in the case of immortality, as the body is carved to the essence that underlies mortal appearance. In the sharing of the substitution (of spirit for body, image for form), temporal deprivation and immortal recompense are bound to each other by the negation at their center. For immortality as Dickinson dreams it into existence is not simply specified as permanence; it is also presence liberated from the mortal encumbrances of both flesh and language. In P 679, immortality, personified as a bodiless visitor, assumes the prophetic shape of pure essence, and Dickinson's description of it seems to borrow from the central store of a phenomenalist vocabulary she could not possibly have known. "Presence—," she writes, "is his furthest license—." In P 664, she scripts the presence in more personal terms:

> Of all the Souls that stand create—
> I have elected—One—
> When Sense from Spirit—files away—
> And Subterfuge—is done—
> When that which is—and that which was—
> Apart—intrinsic—stand—
> And this brief Drama in the flesh—
> Is shifted—like a Sand—
> When Figures show their royal Front—
> And Mists—are carved away,
> Behold the Atom—I preferred—
> To all the lists of Clay!

As the dream literalizes itself and takes shape, we see it has no shape at all, that it reduces human form to the essence of an "Atom—" that underlies it; elsewhere the flinging away of the body (in P 511 Dickinson had spoken of tossing it away "like a Rind") is feared as well as desired. After the death of Edward Dickinson, his daughter writes: "I dream about father every night . . . and forget what I am doing daytimes, wondering where he is. Without any body, I keep thinking. What kind can that be?" (L 471). Yet however it puzzles conception, immortality purified of all but created soul is what Dickinson professes to want, and she sometimes appears to hoard the losses allotted to her, as if through the holes made by time and space immortality might be glimpsed. Implicit in the utterances on loss is the belief that immortality not only will

replace an inadequate temporal scheme in the future that is promised by
a traditional Christianity (this is the mathematics of recompense about
which I just spoke), but also that it does replace temporality in the
present, as the body is transcended in the phenomena of loss and immortality alike.[4] It is no wonder that Dickinson retreated to her legendary
solitude, for to people her world would have been to forfeit the identification between loss and immortality and to substitute in its stead the
palpable forms that negated both. She did not do it. Her poems juxta-
pose time and immortality with the fervor of a hallucination, and, notwithstanding the simplification of any such statement, the juxtaposition
might be said to underlie all the temporal perplexities that aggravate the
poems and to create as well the great mirages that transform illusion into
something we can only call art, the complex meditations on the terrible
grief of dying.

II

"Tell all the Truth but tell it slant—/Success in Circuit lies," Dickinson
writes in P 1129, and the statement turns our attention to the implied
synonymy between slantness and circuity, even though one is linear,
coming at an angle, and the other curvilinear, working around a circumference. The illogical overlap between obliquity and circuity is a direct
consequence of Dickinson's preoccupation with ineffable centerings. For
however close the lens of a given poem comes to the subject of attention,
to a center, its speaker perceives that subject shift out of the line of
direct vision. To see from a perspective is to see at a slant, as the following poem indicates:

> The Angle of a Landscape—
> That every time I wake—
> Between my Curtain and the Wall—
> Upon an ample Crack—
>
> Like a Venetian—waiting—
> Accosts my open eye—
> Is just a Bough of Apples—
> Held slanting, in the Sky—
> . . . .   (P 375)

In the "Bough of Apples—" forming its own angle, the subject comes to
light readily enough, however deceptively it appears on the wrong side of

the horizon, but most poems are not so quick to distinguish the landscape from the linear displacements of the speaker's angle of vision. At a more subtle level of obliquity, entire landscapes can seem like indirect renderings of something larger of which they are a mere part. Landscapes are thus generally symbolic in the poems, bearers of more meaning than a given speaker can interpret (as in "There's a certain Slant of light"), or they are deficient of meaning, unable to rise to its occasion (as in "A Light exists in Spring"), and this excess or deficit indicates a profound discrepancy between the multitudinous lines of the world and the optics of a central vision that, more often than not, they may be accused of baffling. Thus the horizon, with which a fair number of Dickinson's poems are concerned,[5] is an especially beguiling landscape, because the infinite transformations to which it is subject hint at an ultimate disclosure, the lurking of something behind the visible to which it will shortly give way.

To alter the metaphor, we can distinguish the lines of the characteristic Dickinson angle if we observe that it often brings time and immortality into direct proximity. The angle, then, is a comparative one, but the particular nature of the comparison raises problems: first, because since the immortal world cannot be seen, it must be specified in lieu of any concrete form, discerned in the shape of a formal absence; and second, just because we are at a loss to see the invisible half alluded to, the particularities of the temporal world, when it is invoked, can seem equally inscrutable and, sometimes for lack of any focusing comparative, even arbitrary. Dickinson seems to have the dilemma of an implied but unspecified second world in mind when she writes:

> A Spider sewed at Night
> Without a Light
> Upon an Arc of White.
>
> If Ruff it was of Dame
> Or Shroud of Gnome
> Himself himself inform.
>
> Of Immortality
> His Strategy
> Was Physiognomy. (P 1138)

Here the relationship between what is visible and what is not strains toward formulation in the last stanza, but the polysyllabic abstractions

that link appearance, calculated effort, and an intimated other world
cohere more as a consequence of verbal patterning (the like sound of
words and their arrangement in a sequence suggestive of meaning) than
of any demonstrated semantic connection. The poem advances an analogic relationship between "Physiognomy" and "Immortality"; the
spider's "Arc of White" (the meaning of which cannot be discerned) is
of a piece with the inscrutable web of "Immortality," but the confounding preposition *"Of"* which precedes "Immortality," backs away from
the question of how (are the two connected by an identity of elements,
by shared origin, or is the spider's unfathomable design a mere characteristic of "Immortality"?). Thus the fact of the relationship overtakes
all single explanation of it, and the multiple possibilities hang between
the two terms, a web of the poet's making. We might speculate that the
form of the web is to the spider's conception of it ("Himself himself
inform," as the poem puns)[6] as the web is to immortality, and both the
first and last terms of the analogy remain unspecified, for however close
Dickinson comes to defining the relationship between the embodied
world and the immortal one, she falls short of a satisfactory answer.
"Not 'Revelation'—tis—that waits/But our unfurnished eyes—," she had
written impatiently (P 685), and as if to jar vision from the modesty of
its limitations, her poems spin out new attempts at defining the relationship, each time catching it at a different angle.

   Sometimes the contrast between the embodied world and the immortal one assumes implicit temporal form, as in the following poem:

> A Bird came down the Walk—
> He did not know I saw—
> He bit an Angleworm in halves
> And ate the fellow, raw,
>
> And then he drank a Dew
> From a convenient Grass—
> And then hopped sidewise to the Wall
> To let a Beetle pass—
>
> He glanced with rapid eyes
> That hurried all around—
> They looked like frightened Beads, I thought—
> He stirred his Velvet Head
>
> Like one in danger, Cautious,

> I offered him a Crumb
> And he unrolled his feathers
> And rowed him softer home—
>
> Than Oars divide the Ocean,
> Too silver for a seam—
> Or Butterflies, off Banks of Noon
> Leap, plashless as they swim.   (P 328)

The discrete movements of the first stanzas, introduced by anaphora and rhythmically imitative of the rapid, uneven motions of the bird glimpsed close-up, give way to the sheer verb of flight, irreducible to singularity or sequence. Riding on the brilliance of Dickinson's similes for it, this latter, seamless movement suggests a further implied contrast between diachronic progression and the synchrony that surpasses it, between the mortal world which can be fathomed and the magical one which evades the understanding as it evades the eye. The second inscrutable world establishes its connection to the immortal one, first, because of the leap meaning takes off the metaphoric "Banks of Noon," which, even were this not Dickinson's temporal indication of immortality, would insist on an interpretation beyond all bounds of the finite, and second, because of the extravagant comparative ushered in by the one simile that does describe a finite reality: "And rowed him softer home—/Than Oars divide the Ocean,/Too silver for a seam—." The grammar makes it ambiguous whether it is the ocean that is seamless or the rowing, and the comparative statement poised between the possibilities insists that Dickinson intended this ambiguity, which imitates the indivisibility it talks about by refusing to allow us to separate the two ideas. In fact the poem exemplifies a typical pattern of development in a good number of Dickinson's utterances, as they linger on concrete, often trivial but entirely comprehensible phenomena, and then alter their focus in a tensile shift of the received lines into a shape that utterly perplexes them. Thus the question raised by "A spider sewed at Night" is now posed in the speaker's implicit query of the relationship between sequence and simultaneity, division and seamlessness.

In "The Soul has Bandaged moments," temporal contrast is made explicit, formulated by the soul's transcendence of temporal division:

> The soul has moments of Escape—
> When bursting all the doors—

> She dances like a Bomb, abroad,
> And swings upon the Hours,
>
> As do the Bee—delirious borne—
> Long Dungeoned from his Rose—
> Touch Liberty—then know no more,
> But Noon, and Paradise—

and

> The Soul's retaken moments—
> When, Felon led along,
> With shackles on the plumed feet,
> And staples, in the Song,
> . . . .   (P 512)

The contrast between liberty and bondage is measured best by two lines
that emphasize its antiphonal strains despite the fact that they are not
grammatically parallel: by "And swings upon the Hours," which, borne
into motion by the preceding line, eases the speaker from one temporal
unit to the next as dexterously as if the hours had become partners in
the fluid dance of movement, and by "And staples, in the Song," which
continues the metaphor of music by internalizing it as song and, in its
most complex achievement, drives together through one word, "staples,"
the separate ideas of division and pain. Although the poem presents an
ostensible contrast between "Dungeoned" moments and "moments of
Escape—," it does so partially in order to uncover the underlying dialectic of time and its annihilation (the "deliri[um]" of immortality which
is "Noon").

Many of Dickinson's poems are balanced on such a contrast; others
lean toward one of its extremes. In the following poem, for example,
which envisions a leavetaking of the known temporal world, abstraction
invests utterance with the foreignness of the venture:

> I saw no Way—The Heavens were stitched—
> I felt the Columns close—
> The Earth reversed her Hemispheres—
> I touched the Universe—
>
> And back it slid—and I alone—
> A Speck upon a Ball—

> Went out upon Circumference—
> Beyond the Dip of Bell—   (P 378)

How much language depends upon the conceptual ignorance that underlies it is immediately apparent if we think of the systematic conversion
of everything known into a territorial blank. The dead-end of the poem's
beginning, which closes the speaker off from heaven and then more
dramatically turns the world inside out so that, almost expelled from it,
she is left standing upon a mere rim, the "Circumference—" of the last
lines, is one of the most drastic metaphors for exile Dickinson ever conceived, and the language is giddy with the speaker's disorientation. When
Dickinson's poems go "Beyond the Dip of Bell—," as this one attempts
to do, to excavate the territory that lies past the range of all phenomenal
sense, they are haunted by the terrible space of the venture, as language
is flung out into the reaches of the unknown in the apparent hope that
it might civilize what it finds there. At the other extreme, the temporal
particularities of the familiar world are observed at close range:

> Bees are Black, with Gilt Surcingles—
> Buccaneers of Buzz.
> Ride abroad on ostentation
> And subsist on Fuzz.
>
> Fuzz ordained—not Fuzz contingent—
> Marrows of the Hill.
> Jugs—a Universe's fracture
> Could not jar or spill.   (P 1405)

Even here, however, in the last lines, the unexpected "Fuzz ordained—
not Fuzz contingent—" rescues the bee from the triviality to which
"Buccaneers of Buzz" had almost certainly doomed it. This is not so
much metaphor as it is metaphysics when, from another world, the bee
is invested with priest-like powers. Inversely, at the end of "I saw no
Way," the final image, "Beyond the Dip of Bell—," offers a concrete
temporal sound (however it claims a departure "Beyond" it) to which we
can anchor the preceding descriptions that might otherwise fail to survive abstraction.

As the contrast between "I saw no Way—The Heavens were stitched"
and "Bees are Black with Gilt Surcingles" indicates, Dickinson writes best
about what she must conceptualize, and Archibald MacLeish states this
fact succinctly when he observes that her images are "not always visible

. . . nor are they images brought into focus by the muscles of the eye."[7]
When we recall some of the most typical Dickinson lines ("Pain—has an Element of Blank—" [P 650], "A nearness to Tremendousness—/An Agony
procures—" [P 963]), we note that these lines strain toward conceptual
realization that will replace, as by an effort of mind, what is visible with
depictions that more adequately represent the landscape of the mind.
Sometimes the angle of a poem is formed by the disparity between the
dimensions of the palpable world and those of a less circumscribed
interior. So she writes: "Two Lengths has every Day—/Its absolute
extent/And Area Superior/By Hope or Horror lent—" (P 1295). Sometimes a poem is trained on the divergence of private and public value:
"The Voice that stands for Floods to me/Is sterile borne to some—"
(P 1189). And as I shall be suggesting in the following chapters, the
poems that command the most interest are concerned with certain substitutions that relegate the visible world to the second place accorded it
by the sharper demands of imagination and desire: the substitution of
immortality for temporal progression, the remembered moment for the
immediate one, presence for the language it has dispensed with. These
poems address themselves to the world of absent things, to what is
"Convenient to the longing/But otherwise withheld" (P 1753), and as a
consequence they often become problematic, for, as I have been asserting, when an absent world is alluded to, especially in a comparative
circumstance, the angle of a poem's landscape is frequently difficult to
ascertain.

III

When Dickinson told Thomas Wentworth Higginson that she had not
learned to tell time by the clock until she was fifteen,[8] she must have
shocked him, though like many Dickinson readers after him, he did not
think to explain the disjointed syntax of her utterances or the reluctance
of the words to totalize themselves in a concrete situation by their
author's pull away from time. The poems bear traces of a different shock,
as they are jarred loose and jolted from the requirements of a temporal
world. I shall say more about temporality and Dickinson's poems in a
moment, but I should like first to summarize some of the other, acknowledged critical problems that plague her work—problems of biography,
literary history, and textual history, and those which arise more directly
from a reading of the poems. My intention in these introductory pages is

to characterize the diversity of response to Dickinson and the difficulties of her poetry rather than to recapitulate it in total (for most of these subjects wholly adequate book-length studies exist), and to suggest a framework for my own discussion in the following chapters.

"Biography first convinces us of the fleeing of the Biographied—" (L 972), Dickinson wrote in an assertion her biographers have been fond of ever since, because it seems to offer such compelling justification for the blurred distinctions between fact and fiction that have characterized the attempts to explain her life. Thus in the earliest full-length biography, George Whicher reminds us that we should not "heedlessly disregard Emily Dickinson's warning that the speaker is not herself but a 'supposed person,'" but in the next sentence he adds: "Her romance was not created out of nothing, and the supposed person may often be considered as identical with the author to the extent of voicing her real feelings."[9] And when in *Circumference and Circumstance: Stages in the Mind and Art of Emily Dickinson* Robert Sherwood suggests that an accurate ordering of the poems would show us the specific nature of Dickinson's spiritual crisis,[10] we see that the problem has come full circle: the life is now the primary text, the poems an explication of it. Though biographical studies were supplemented by documentary ones (in 1970 Jay Leyda published his two-volume reference book, *The Years and Hours of Emily Dickinson*,[11] which reconstructed Dickinson's life and the life of the Amherst community by juxtaposing entries from diaries, church records, newspaper clippings, letters, and the like, and in 1966 Jack L. Capps brought out his sourcebook, *Emily Dickinson's Reading*),[12] the demythologizing of Dickinson's personal history was countered from the beginning by the many studies that sought to advance their own myths by offering elaborate theories on the identity of Dickinson's lover(s) and, more recently, by the psychoanalytic speculation of John Cody's *After Great Pain*.[13]

We assume that the penchant for reconstruction and invention is the consequence of a dearth of biographical material. Perhaps, however, the problem is exactly the reverse, for we have those endlessly suggestive letters that are on the one hand held up as literary documents[14] and, on the other, appealed to as if their assertions could command the authority of fact. It is questionable whether anyone's letters should be taken as a reliable form of biography, and Dickinson's letters are particularly suspect, for, as her brother, Austin, claimed, his sister definitely posed in

them. Once, for example, she wrote to Higginson: "Father . . . buys me
many Books—but begs me not to read them—because he fears they joggle
the Mind" (L 261). In the face of Austin's astonishment at the story, we
may speculate that Dickinson was merely literalizing the harshness of an
emotional truth, translating Edward Dickinson's indifference into outright unreasonable severity. It is what we do all the time when we wish
to ground a feeling in the palpable occurrence that would substantiate
it. We say "It was like . . ." if we are scrupulous, and "It was . . ." if
we are not. We lie for the sake of accuracy. In Dickinson's letters we can
observe that the more vested the relationship with the letter recipient,
the more aphoristic, epigrammatic, and explicitly literary the letters
become, almost as if she were calling on distance to temper the disquieting anxieties of unmediated connection, and the letters may, in
fact, tell us more about the postures that replace relationship than about
the relationships themselves.[15] In addition, they share characteristic
features of the poems: many of them are metrical compositions, some
are subject to meticulous revision, and certain phrases, even whole formulations, appear in both letter and poem contexts. Thus as Brita
Lindberg-Seyersted suggests, the letters bear a frank confusion between
the public and the private,[16] and if we have difficulty separating the life
from the poetry, this is aggravated by Dickinson's confusion of the two.
Even Richard Sewall's wonderfully complete two-volume biography
reads like a detective story with a chapter devoted to each of the characters, the details of whose lives we note so that we may better construe
the intricacies of plot. When we are baffled by the poems, we dismiss our
confusion by embracing the myth, ready at hand, of Dickinson the half-
cracked poetess.

If the story of Dickinson's life is unclear, her place in literary history
has been subject to greater uncertainty. Even after literary opinion
warmed to the texts, no longer dismissing them as incompetent or incomprehensible, critics seemed unable to determine Dickinson's relation
to the tradition into which they welcomed her, and it was not until Roy
Harvey Pearce's *The Continuity of American Poetry* was published in
1961 that her connection to Emerson, Thoreau, Melville, and Whitman
was firmly established in a literary history.[17] To this day Dickinson
criticism remains divided between those who regard her as a Romantic
poet and those who see her work firmly rooted in the New England
tradition of an earlier Puritanism. Allen Tate, advancing a compromise
position, maintains that Dickinson stands between a declining theocracy

and a rising industrialism, and that she "probes the deficiencies of the tradition" in which she lives, continuing to enact "the puritan drama of the soul," but now on individual terms.[18] Albert Gelpi, echoing Tate, calls her "a Romantic Poet with a Calvinist's sense of things."[19] But Charles Anderson asserts that she had "less kinship with her romantic predecessors than with Jonathan Edwards,"[20] and Sherwood agrees, insisting that the "conjoining of passion with status that distinguished the Puritans from the enthusiasts they detested . . . separates Emily Dickinson from the Romantic tradition into which Tate would like to place her work."[21] These points of view are, of course, predicated on unstated assumptions about social influence and identity. Elsa Greene argues with them: "[Dickinson] did not, in fact, inhabit the same milieu which influenced Ralph Waldo Emerson and his puritan male forebears; and it is a deadly favor to assume that she did. . . . Emily Dickinson risked psychic and social penalties unknown to her masculine predecessors."[22] Dickinson's place within a literary tradition is thus a problem that invites multiple interpretation, and I shall consider it explicitly in the last chapter when I discuss the relationship between the temporal features of Dickinson's poems and the temporal representations characteristic of both an older Romanticism in England and of a newer, more audacious American Romanticism.

The discriminatory haggling over status and position has gone on at a critical level, too. Yvor Winters writes, "Probably no poet of comparable reputation has been guilty of so much unpardonable writing," and he adds, "One cannot shake off the uncomfortable feeling that her popularity has been mainly due to her vices."[23] And R. P. Blackmur: "One exaggerates, but it sometimes seems as if . . . a cat came at us speaking English."[24] Robert Hillyer defends the idiosyncrasies when he asks "Who, in the presence of these amazing poems, would wish a single twisted syllable straightened to ensure the comprehension of mediocre minds or the applause of pedants?"[25] But while we might agree with him that Dickinson's works will not stand regularizing, the critical bickering suggests problems. These are problems of text, of poetic development, of syntax and diction, of consequent ambiguity, and of the temporal assumptions that underlie these features, and I shall say a few words about each of them.

With the publication of the Johnson variorum in 1955, it became possible to determine whether a given Dickinson piece is a finished poem, a note for a poem, or a prose fragment,[26] but although the textual situation is improved beyond measure, the variorum is less free of editorial interpretation than one could wish, and the reader's edition is even more burdened with it. This is true first because while any hand-written text must suffer the inexact representation (the regularizing) of the printed word, the problem is particularly severe for Dickinson's texts, punctuated as they are with dashes of varying lengths and perhaps of varying meanings.[27] A second and more central textual difficulty arises over the question of the variants. This is stated succinctly by R. W. Franklin in his invaluable book on the editing of the Dickinson manu-scripts: "Scholarly editions are concerned only with authors' sanctioned texts, preferably the latest . . . [but] with Emily Dickinson we do not have the guidance of this principle, for she never willingly committed herself to print."[28] Problems posed by the reader's edition are even more complex, for there one variant must often be arbitrarily selected as representative, a process that is tantamount to editorial completion of the poem in question.[29]

If we could observe changes in the style of the poems, it might be easier to arrive at textual decisions. But, in fact, as most critics agree, there is no development in the canon of poems.[30] The experiences recorded by these poems are insular ones, subject to endless repetition.[31] Indeed it sometimes seems as if the same poem of pain or loss keeps writing itself over and over. Perhaps there is no development in the poetry because development is at least partially the result of influences that mediate the given, and Dickinson never accepted any mediation, even that which she enthusiastically solicited.[32]

The absence of development within the 1775 poems is reflected in the resistance of many individual poems to the rigors and exactions of sequence and progression. For the words in Dickinson's poems often exist outside of a situation and, more disturbing, seem to shrink from the necessity of creating one. In fact many poems contain lines that are memorable in contexts that are not, and the memorable lines are fre-quently the first lines. Of the provocative first lines, Charles Anderson writes, "Not one in ten [poems] fulfills the brilliant promise of the opening words,"[33] and R. P. Blackmur adds, "The movement of the parts is downward and towards a disintegration of the effect wanted."[34] Dickinson herself, hardly blind to the power of initial lines, wrote of another (unidentified) poet, "Did you ever read one of her Poems back-ward, because the plunge from the front overturned you? I sometimes . . . have—A something overtakes the Mind" (PF 30).

Sometimes problems of sequence and structure are apparent at the simplest level of relationship. The feeling after great pain is of "A Quartz contentment, like a stone—" (P 341), but quartz is a stone, and without explanation, the meanings overlap seemingly without purpose. When an entire line is unclear the situation is more baffling yet. "Unit, like Death, for Whom?" P 408 begins, and although we learn from context that the "Unit" alluded to is comprised of death and its victim, the simile in the first line remains perplexing because it presents an identic connection as if it were an analogic one. The relationship between the elements of Dickinson's poems can be difficult to perceive as a consequence of the order in which they are introduced. When we are told that "The difference between Despair/and Fear—is like the One/Between the instant of a Wreck—/And when the Wreck has been—" (P 305), we adjust to the fact that the terms of the simile are presented in inverse order from those of the initial comparison, but I have yet to teach the poem when the adjustment has not been a grudging one.

Frequently, as I have suggested, Dickinson presents us with states of feeling that are severed from the geography that would explain them, and many poems begin with a deliberately unspecified "it," as, for example, "'Tis so appalling, it exhilirates" does, in which we are never quite certain whether the subject is death or a horror so manifestly unspeakable that it evades all attempts at direct naming. Robert Weisbuch attributes the apparent "scenelessness" of Dickinson's poetry to the replacement of scene by analogy:[35] "The poems do not lack a situational matrix—that would be impossible—but mimetic situations are transformed, transported to a world of analogical language which exists in parallel to a world of experience, as its definition."[36] Given this interpretation, poems do not progress in customary sequences, because they are intent on dramatizing the heart of an experience rather than its outward shape. While one could wish Weisbuch had somewhere distinguished between a type of lyric poetry (which he assumes these analogic collections to be) and a problem with it, his study, concerned with poems as analogues and, in a larger context, as types, makes impressive sense of the obscure relationships in Dickinson's poems, and it brings to the critical foreground difficulties of situational coherence, of meanings that break through the surface of a poem and seemingly bear little relation to it, and of the balancing of a poem on its divided loyalties (whether they be to type and antitype, analogue and its reference, this world and the next).

A reader may perceive the problem of fragmentation first at the level of syntax that is often hopelessly involuted, as if in response to the task of representing interior experience. Richard Chase comments on the bizarre syntax when he writes, "It is clear that, however memorable some of her phrases are, she had an exaggerated idea of what could be accomplished merely by tinkering with syntax. This faith in the efficacy of . . . word magic is one of the permanent acquisitions of the period."[37] Thus in Dickinson's poems we often have the impression that the phenomena presented have been subjected to extreme compression—objects elided with each other so that we can no longer observe the totality of their separate shapes, but only the jutting of lines away from an unseen center of convergence. It is almost as though utterance conspires to angle meaning to such a degree that it becomes oblique to the point of invisibility. In the following poem, for example, verbal designation seems to guard the meaning it ostensibly specifies:

> As the Starved Maelstrom laps the Navies
> As the Vulture teazed
> Forces the Broods in lonely Valleys
> As the Tiger eased
>
> By but a Crumb of Blood, fasts Scarlet
> Till he meet a Man
> Dainty adorned with Veins and Tissues
> And partakes—his Tongue
>
> Cooled by the Morsel for a moment
> Grows a fiercer thing
> Till he esteem his Dates and Cocoa
> A Nutrition mean
>
> I, of a finer Famine
> Deem my Supper dry
> For but a Berry of Domingo
> And a Torrid Eye.   (P 872)

The analogues for ravenousness (the "Maelstrom" for the "Navies," the "Vulture" for the "Broods," the "Tiger" for the "Crumb of Blood," and, finally, the speaker for the unspecified object of absence) collapse upon each other, each an illustration of the same thing, except progressively humanized and growing in the extremity of famine.[38] The utterance is not easy to read; everything about it conspires to withhold sense, a fact emphasized by the long single sentence that attenuates meaning, making it wait on the finality of a grammatical completion. The synecdochic process of taking a part for the whole, common to all poetry, is exaggerated in Dickinson's characteristic use of it in which the representative incompletions are placed in a larger context of verbal incompletion, of truncated verb forms ("Till he meet a Man"), of unlike terms disconcertingly coupled with each other ("Crumb of Blood"), and of those off-rhymes that can often seem a paradoxical combination of singsong and dissonance (Man/Tongue, thing/mean, Famine/Domingo)—all pushing utterance dangerously close to a mere word tangle. The utterance is intent on joining two lines of thought that have an unclear relationship to each other, and at the same time the claims made by these thoughts are not fleshed out by any discursive explanation. Thus the whole vision is seen from the vantage of an unspecified perspective (in this case, the relationship between famine and fulfillment) that must be specified before the reader can begin to make sense of it.

Addressing himself to comparable difficulties, David Porter writes, "Here is the verbal equivalent of *sfumato*, the technique in expressionistic painting whereby information . . . on a canvas is given only piecemeal and thereby necessarily stimulates the imaginative projection of the viewer, who, out of his own experience, supplies the missing . . . context."[39] Mention of contextual difficulty in Dickinson's poems runs like a theme throughout the criticism, but the crucial relationship between contextual disorder and temporal conception has never been examined in detail, and in chapters 1 and 2 I shall look closely at words that refuse to totalize themselves in a context and at the shrinking from temporal sequence that underlies such a refusal.

It is easy to assume that the individual words in Dickinson's poems startle as a consequence of their rare usage, but William Howard, in his informative article on Dickinson's vocabulary, tells us that according to statistical study, Dickinson does not have certain favorite or idiosyncratic words. What accounts for the seeming oddness of the diction is her habit of using a word now in a metaphoric context, now in a literal one, with no clear distinction between the two.[40] Austin Warren agrees that "the referent and its metaphoric referend are often difficult to distinguish,"[41] and he reminds us of "There's a certain Slant of light," where death is a metaphor for winter light and winter light is a metaphor for death.[42] I shall have more to say about comparable fusions between death and despair in chapter 3 when I discuss the collapse of figure and thing figured, and underlying, even prompting it, the terror of temporal and spatial difference. The unclear relationship of words to their context and the fusion of metaphor and referent leads predictably to ambiguity. Jay Leyda specifies a further explanation for the ambiguity when he notes that "a major device of Emily Dickinson's writing . . . [is] the 'omitted center,' [t]he riddle, the circumstance too well known to be repeated."[43] While I would want to qualify that assertion by suggesting that in many poems ("A route of evanescence" or "Further in summer than the birds," for example) the center or heart of the experience is presented in lieu of any surrounding context, in chapter 4 I shall look at problems of the omitted center in order to define more explicitly the connection between utterance, absence, and temporality.

Fragmentary lines, the refusal of syntax and diction to subordinate themselves to each other, the subsequent absence of context and progression, the resulting ambiguity and tension—we may conceive of these problems as temporal in origin, for the relationship between the parts of a poem is inevitably a temporal relationship.

IV

All poetry is characterized by problems; put differently, its characteristics, those properties that individuate and distinguish it, also define the specific form of its difficulty. So Yeats's philosophic system is at once a feature of his poetry and a barrier to its accessibility; so the heap of broken images in Eliot's *The Waste Land* asserts an aggressive challenge as well as a method; so Ralegh's *Ocean to Cynthia*, restless in its psychological shifts, presents us with the dilemmas of a fragmentary poem. But to the extent that characteristics become obstacles we must scrutinize them differently; the question of the problematic is really one of degree, and in the next few chapters I shall look more closely at poems that fragment as a consequence of their failure to adhere to the rigors of a temporal scheme. If one reason for investigating these poems is the relationship between problems and characteristics, a second and more theoretical reason is that assessments of the problematic, if they survive scrutiny, have much to tell us about what we imagine to be the model or norm. I am speaking here of fictional models or, to use a more classical term, of mimetic ones, and the subject is a touchy one for many reasons, not the least of which is raised by the old question of whether there is or is not a normative reader with normative expectations of a text that is or is not stable with respect to its hold over us. These questions aside (and I can afford momentarily to put them aside because they have already been partially explored by such writers as Hans-Georg Gadamer, E. D. Hirsch, Stanley Fish, and Richard Ohmann), we wish to know whether a comprehensive picture of actual difficulties in a specific body of poetry will outline the shape of that elusive fictional model on which so many of our assumptions rest unquestioned. Seeing the shape of the problem, might we see double the shape of the form that the problem displaces? The conception here is admittedly Platonic, and if it is exaggerated in its suggestion that good poems conform to one shape, it is useful in its reminder that certain forms of deviation are, for reasons that require investigation, intolerable.

Aristotle spoke of poetry as the imitation of an action; John Stuart Mill specified the action by suggesting it to be one of speech in overheard soliloquy, and we may consider these two assertions as the beginning of a definition of poetic utterance, whose fiction lies in the illusion that someone is really talking. Although we generally believe that how a given speaker talks, or is talked about, will be determined by the ruling assumptions of the fictional world out of which he steps, we are not always sharp to the dramatic implications of that fact. Erich Auerbach, contrasting the different styles of Homeric and Biblical worlds in the unforgettable argument of *Mimesis*, demonstrated that the constructs of a given fictional world impose a reality—they do not mirror it—and these impositions are as various as interpretive possibility permits. One of the largest single differences between Homeric and Biblical worlds is their sense of time. Auerbach writes:

So little are the Homeric heroes presented as developing or having developed, that most of them—Nestor, Agamemnon, Achilles—appear to be of an aged fixed from the very first. Even Odysseus, in whose case the long lapse of time and the many events which occurred offer so much opportunity for biographical development, shows almost nothing of it. Odysseus on his return is exactly the same as he was when he left Ithaca two decades earlier. But what a road, what a fate, lie between the Jacob who cheated his father out of his blessing and the old man whose favorite son has been torn to pieces by a wild beast!—between David the harp player, persecuted by his lord's jealousy, and the old king, surrounded by violent intrigues, whom Abishag the Shunnamite warmed in his bed, and he knew her not. . . . Fraught with their development, sometimes even aged to the verge of dissolution, they show a distinct stamp of individuality entirely foreign to the Homeric heroes. Time can touch the latter only outwardly, and even that change is brought to our observation as little as possible; whereas the stern hand of God is ever upon the Old Testament figures; he has not only made them once and for all and chosen them, but he continues to work upon them, bends them and kneads them, and, without destroying them in essence, produces from them forms which their youth gave no grounds for anticipating.[44]

Auerbach's assertion that each representation of reality is predicated upon a unique understanding of time, history, spatial configuration, and meaning itself is one of the most crucial lessons modern literary theory has to teach us, and the only danger of his stunning examples is that they illustrate the implied contrasts so dramatically that we may mistakenly take them for the exceptions they are not. But narrative predilections (the representation of speech by choral voices or singular ones, as hermetically determined through the interpretations of a censorious narrator, or direct enough to go it without mediation) are an indication of the temporal suppositions that underlie them, and if we doubt the crucial relationship between the ability to speak at all and an indispensable sense of time, we have only to recall the floundering misery of Beckett's Unnamable, whose speech slows to a halt because it is no longer carried by the temporal momentum that would guarantee thought its most rudimentary completion: "The fact would seem to be, if in my situation one may speak of facts, not only that I shall have to speak of things of which I cannot speak, but also, which is even more interesting, but also that I, which is if possible even more interesting, that I shall have to, I forget, no matter. And at the same time I am obliged to speak."[45] Speech falters at a coherent story, even at a complete sentence, because no temporal unity holds the generating conception in the glue of a complete thought. We could say that the Unnamable has no memory of thought's intention beyond the circumscribed present of a given phrase; or, to put it differently, he has no sense of time. Although this is perhaps an extreme example, and although Beckett's work, like that of many other contemporaries, breaks all the generic rules we might specify, it points out the uncompromising relationship between temporal disorder and the ensuing disintegration of speech. Conversely, the narrative generosity of Nabokov's *Lolita* may be explained partly by its central character's desire to transfix the world in the apotheosis of what he calls "minus time-space or plus soul-time,"[46] as, drunk on the nuance of memory, the rapt magnanimous words coax the objects of his descriptions—much as he coaxes the little girl—out of the dull plane of ordinary temporality and into the immutable radiance, the soul-time of that impossible love.

Ideas of temporality perhaps reveal themselves more easily in the complexities of narrative construction, for in narratives problems of linking actions and hence of establishing their relationships in time are necessarily overt. But temporal structures and suppositions are also visible in the imitated action of overheard soliloquy, and if we doubt this we have only to consider the temporal invention of Herbert's "The Sacrifice," or, less conspicuously, of Blake's "Ah Sun-flower," which, caught in the circularity of the lyric cry against time, does not even know how to imagine anything outside of the temporal limitations it desires to overcome. Often, in fact, we cannot perceive the meaning of a given utterance until we understand its speaker's conception of time; this is transparently true in Donne's *Songs and Sonnets*, where temporal advance is countered by the vagaries of terror, however socialized into wit, and in the desperate strategies of Marvell's coy seducer. It is equally true in Eliot's layered speech that would coerce past, present, and future into the sudden illumination of a given moment. It is true in the temporal juxtapositions of Yeats's "Long-Legged Fly," in which greatness is interpreted by the temporal lethargy that fuels its most monumental acts: "Like a long-legged fly upon the stream/His mind moves upon silence," and true also of the multiple possibilities in many of Stevens's poems that express as a sequence what is really a simultaneity ("Thirteen Ways of Looking at a Blackbird" is the most obvious example). It is in fact frequently the case that a poem remains difficult when (or because) we do not understand the temporal suppositions of its speakers, and that this should be so may be explained partially by the fact that a poetic structure (like other mimetic structures, but less obviously because it is shorter) is a complete structure, framed by an end and a beginning (points that are definitively temporal) whose tasks are not only to start and conclude but also, however implicitly, to specify the basis on which speech is begun and ended through the unique particularities of the experience itself.

In *Poetic Closure* Barbara Herrnstein Smith discusses the relationship between fictional totality and the specific context out of which a certain closure is deemed an appropriate one, and she stresses the fact that our ideas about the adequacy of given closure are directly contingent upon how we assess a speaker's situation and motive.[47] Stanley Cavell, writing more philosophically of the temporal-spatial closure that seals a fiction from the hazards of our interruption, points out the consequences of the fact that its characters do not exist in our time and space. Thus the man who rushes to the stage to rescue Othello from the lunacy of his actions only puts an end to the performance: "For that farthest extremity has not touched Othello, he has vanished; it has merely interrupted an evening's work. Quiet the house, pick up the thread again, and Othello will reappear, as near and as deaf to us as ever."[48] And Cavell continues, "We know we cannot approach him, and not because it is not done but because nothing would count as doing it. Put another way, they and we do not occupy the same space."[49] It is precisely because a fiction is housed within the walls of its limitation that we may recognize its characteristics and concerns for what they are, as we are frequently prevented from doing in "real life," where phenomena spill outward, refusing to respect the neatness of any boundaries; precisely because of the intractable adamance of fictional boundaries that we are forced to give over our time and space to the task of true witness. But our ability to do this rests imperatively on the willingness to recognize the fictional world as adjacent to our own, one whose temporal-spatial perspective must first be discerned in the absence of all assumptions except those that are immediately "given."

If a specific fiction is predicated on the unique organization of temporal-spatial reality, it also takes its cues from those generic conventions that spell out the range of the possible alternatives. It goes without saying that how a novel organizes experience (allowing its characters to play out the conflict of their points of view against the backdrop of a narrative authority) is different from how a drama organizes it (liberated as drama is from any visible or embodied unitary perspective), and both novels and drama distinguish themselves from the lyric (whose speaker plots out his concerns in the absence of both action and others), and as my parenthetical qualifications indicate, we tend to cast such differences in terms of narrative technique. All literature attempts to regulate chronology, much literature to defeat it, but the strategic ingenuities of the novel, drama, and lyric regale us variously with the dreams they have wrought. Unlike the drama, whose province is conflict, and unlike the

novel or narrative, which connects isolated moments of time to create a
story multiply peopled and framed by a social context, the lyric voice
is solitary and generally speaks out of a single moment in time. From
the vantage of this distinction certain questions arise: If not by a plurality of characters, how does the lyric represent division, conflict, and multiple points of view? If seeming to defy the social world from which it is
set apart, how is it coerced back into relationship with that world? And
if speech in a poem is not utterance as we talk or think it, what connection does it bear to the less recognizable world of dream and nightmare?
To address these questions, as this book will do, as it considers the relationship between the temporal characteristics of Dickinson's poems and
the temporal characteristics of other lyrics, is to acknowledge their origin
in the problematics of temporality. The heart of the lyric's sense of time
might be specified, at least preliminarily, by its propensity to interiorize
as ambiguity or outright contradiction those conflicts that other mimetic
forms conspicuously exteriorize and then allocate to discrete characters
who enact them in the manifest pull of opposite points of view.

I shall be suggesting that the temporal problems in Dickinson's poems
are frequently exaggerations of those generic features shared by all
lyrics, and that it is precisely the distance some of these poems go toward the far end of coherence, precisely the outlandishness of their
extremity, which allows us to see, literally magnified, the fine workings
of more conventional lyrics. Although I have specified Dickinson's
poems as concerned with "The Angle of a Landscape ," with those
recondite lines and relations that interpret the landscape and often come
to constitute it, most lyrics similarly look under the surface of external
phenomena for the hidden perspectives that organize meaning. And
although I have suggested that Dickinson's lyrics are especially caught up
in the oblique dialectic of time and immortality, we shall see the extent
to which all lyrics oppose speech to the action from which it exempts
itself, oppose voice as it rise momentarily from the enthusiasms of temporal advance to the flow of time that ultimately rushes over and drowns
it. This is a book, then, about time in a particular body of poetry as it
teaches us to be aware of the temporal characteristics of a genre, and my
interest here is unabashedly theoretical. What is a temporal structure?
How is it manifested in the lyric? From what necessity do we engineer
such prodigious rearrangements of time?

The poems I shall look at in the next two chapters present interpretive difficulties as their words come unhinged from all context, and this phenomenon is perfectly consistent with the speakers' desire to shelter themselves from the anxieties of temporal sequence. As much at loose ends as Beckett's Unnamable, they seem to imagine a bitter equation between coherence and completion, completion and an analogic association with death. They will not make sense, will not totalize themselves, for to make sense is to do so in the clutches of temporal finitude. Thus courting distance from the pain of all complexity, the poems discussed in chapter 1 shy away from a dialectical understanding of experience, and sometimes their speakers seem literally stunned to the standstill of a poem's disengaged meanings. In chapter 2 I compare narrative conceptions of temporality with lyric conceptions of it, as I try to account for that group of Dickinson poems in which a story is begun only to be violently broken into and disrupted. Defining life as a series of unviable alternatives, these poems establish the dialectic eschewed by the first group of poems, but only for the sake of dismissing it. They thus end in a similar state of disorder, equally seeming to pin their hopes on the belief that a verbal sabotage of sequence will trigger a temporal one, that, grown sufficiently desperate, the maneuvers of speech can stop time dead. As they straddle the line between utterance and cry, between coherent gesture and mere inarticulate protest, they remain curiously unconscious of the dilemmas they enact.

The poems discussed in the next two chapters examine their recoil from temporality; they do not, as a rule, enact it, and the result is more cohesive as well as more conventionally structured utterances. Their subject, however, is far from conventional. Dreaming time to a halt in the trespass of the proleptic utterances, the speakers in the poems discussed in chapter 3 survive the finality of the grave, and the chapter examines the structure of these death excursions as they fuse the terms of the contradictions they do not know how to dispel—the transcendence of mortal vision and the impossibility of that transcendence, an analogic experience of death and the formidable restrictions of a literal one. The poems discussed in chapter 4, no longer angling for a way out of time and its attendant terminus of death, steel themselves on the grief of the suddenly acknowledged relationship between language, temporality, and loss. At times in the following pages, and in the fourth chapter especially, I shall be suggesting that Dickinson practices a phenomenalist poetics as she argues the connection between presence, its loss, and the restorative labors of language.

Throughout the next four chapters, in order to focus on the specific features of Dickinson's poems, I have relegated general comments about lyric utterance to the margins. These assertions are recovered, explored, and, in some instances, qualified in chapter 5, which, as Dickinson waits in the wings, turns its central attention to more theoretical observations about the temporal features of the lyric and attempts to discriminate between Dickinson's lyrics and the subcategory of lyric utterance that her poems help to define, as both exist against the backdrop of lyric speech in English.

"What, then, is time?" Augustine asks in *The Confessions*,[50] but the following passage precedes his direct query, as the intimation of an absent permanence precedes sudden bewilderment about change:

> [The] heart flutters among the changing things of past and future, and it is still vain. Who will catch hold of it, and make it fast, so that it stands firm for a little while, and for a little while seize the splendor of that ever stable eternity, and compare it with times that never stand fast, and see that it is incomparable to them, and see that a long time cannot become long except out of many passing movements, which cannot be extended together, that in the eternal nothing can pass away but the whole is present, that no time is wholly present? Who will see that all past time is driven back by the future, that all the future is consequent on the past, and all past and future are created and take their course from that which is ever present?
>
> Who will hold the heart of man, so that it may stand still and see how steadfast eternity, neither future nor past, decrees times future and those past? Can my hand do this, or does the hand of my mouth by its little words effect so great a thing?[51]

In the following pages we shall observe the ways in which lyric poems attempt such a stasis, as they slow temporal advance to the difficult still point of meaning. "The Torrents of Eternity/Do all but inundate—," wrote Dickinson in P 1380, but, like Augustine, she was speaking out of desire.

I

Naming as History
DICKINSON'S POEMS OF DEFINITION

The world of the nightmare . . . of bondage and pain and confusion; the world as it is before the human imagination begins to work on it. . . .
—Northrop Frye

FOR EMILY Dickinson, perhaps no more so than for the rest of us, there was a powerful discrepancy between what was "inner than the Bone—" (P 321) and what could be acknowledged. To the extent that her poems are a response to that discrepancy—are, on the one hand, a defiant attempt to deny that the discrepancy poses a problem and, on the other, an admission of defeat at the problem's enormity—they have much to teach us about the way in which language articulates our life. There is indeed a sense in which these poems test the limits of what we might reveal if we tried, and also of what, despite our exertions, will not give itself over to utterance. The question of the visibility of interior experience is one that will concern me in this chapter, for it lies at the heart of what Dickinson makes present to us. In "The Dream of Communication," Geoffrey Hartman writes, "Art 'represents' a self which is either insufficiently 'present' or feels itself as not 'presentable.'"[1] On both counts one thinks of Dickinson, for her poems disassemble the body in order to penetrate to the places where feelings lie, as if hidden, and they tell us that bodies are not barriers the way we sometimes think they are. Despite the staggering sophistication with which we discuss complex issues, like Dickinson, we have few words, if any, for what happens inside us. Perhaps this is because we have been taught to conceive of ourselves as perfectly inexplicable or, if explicable, then requiring the aid of someone else to scrutinize what we are explicating, to validate it. We have been taught that we cannot see for ourselves—this despite the current emphasis on our proprioceptive functions. But Dickinson tells us that we can see. More important, she tells us how to name what we see.

Naming, defining, creating propositions—a significant group of Dickinson's poems are engaged in these strenuous tasks, and fulfill them with varying degrees of perplexity and success. I should add here that I mean "names" and "naming" in the inclusive sense of those words. Thus I will be speaking about names as metonymic equations; of complete poems as designations for experience; of metaphor or figuration as a property of naming; and, finally, of definitions as a specific group of names. How poems go about naming will be the subject of the chapter, but before I turn to it explicitly, I wish to conclude my introductory remarks with a few general comments on the necessity for names, and some speculation on their function.

The most excruciating interior experience, and perhaps the most inherently nameless, is that of pain. If we leave aside for a moment, though it is hardly an irrelevant consideration, the fact that pain is private, not sharable, we see that Dickinson also insists its torture is a consequence of the ways in which it distorts perception. Again and again, she tells us that pain is atemporal and hence dislocating.[2] It jars one's ordinary sense of oneself and the relation of that self to the world:

> Pain—expands the Time—
> Ages coil within
> The minute Circumference
> Of a single Brain—
> . . . .
> (P 967)

And it is dogged:

> It struck me—every Day—
> The Lightning was as new
> As if the Cloud that instant slit
> And let the Fire through—
>
> It burned Me—in the Night—
> It Blistered to My Dream—
> It sickened fresh upon my sight—
> With every Morn that came—

> I thought that Storm—was brief—
> The Maddest—quickest by—
> But Nature lost the Date of This—
> And left it in the Sky—   (P 362)

In consequence, the self suffers separation from its own experience:

> . . . .
> And Something's odd—within—
> The person that I was—
> And this One—do not feel the same—
> Could it be Madness—this?   (P 410)

The experience of the self perceived as other is a central occurrence in Dickinson's poetry, a kind of ritual enactment her speakers survive to tell about. She had called madness "The yawning Consciousness" (P 1323) and spoke of "a Cleaving in my Mind—/As if my Brain had split—" (P 937). In *Disease, Pain and Sacrifice*, referring to such experiences, David Bakan suggests that pain is the imperative to the ego to become whole again: "At the same time, however, the affected part of the body becomes 'other' to the ego. . . . Getting rid of the pain often means getting rid of the affected part."[3] This is perhaps a partial explanation of why, in so many of Dickinson's poems, parts of the body are personified. They are, in the telling, isolated from the rest of the body and hence, metaphorically at any rate, severed from it.

What she needed to survive such experiences was "Pyramidal Nerve" (P 1054), for she knew: "Power is only Pain—/Stranded, thro' Discipline" (P 252). This discipline had naming at its heart, for names specify relationships that have been lost, forgotten, or hitherto unperceived. Dickinson knew, moreover, that the power of names was in part a consequence of their ability to effect a reconciliation between a self and that aspect of it which had been rendered alien. Names were a way of remembering and accepting ownership of something that, by forgetting or refusing to know, one had previously repudiated. Metaphor, then, is a response to pain in that it closes the gap between feeling and one's identification of it. Metaphoric names are restorative in nature in that they bring one back to one's senses by acknowledging that what has been perceived by them can be familiarized through language.

But names are social as well as personal strategies. As Kenneth Burke suggests, a work of art "singles out a pattern of experience that is sufficiently representative of our social structure, that recurs sufficiently often *mutatis mutandis* for people to 'need a word for it' and to adopt an attitude toward it. Each work of art is the addition of a word to an informal dictionary."[4] While in some respects metaphor and analogy are a last resort, they are also often all we have. In lieu of direct names we improvise or we do without. Such improvisation of course has rules, since language is in the public domain and what we have to work with is a vocabulary that is, more than one might suspect, "given."[5] Thus, finding new names for interior experience is an ambivalent process, for on the one hand by the very insistence upon its necessity, the invention of a new name defies the social matrix. On the other hand, since articulation is a matter of social coherence, it must make reference to that matrix. Hence, naming is in need of precisely that thing which it deems inadequate.

II

Up to this point I have spoken about naming as an act that performs a function both social and personal, and I have gone so far as to make hyperbolic claims for its efficacy. But there are problems with naming in Dickinson's poetry. The names Dickinson gives us for experiences are frequently the most striking aspect of her poetry, and they occur often, as one might expect, in poems of definition. The problem they ask us to consider is precisely their relationship to the context in which they occur. Definitions in Dickinson's poems take two forms. The first group of statements contain the copula as the main verb, and their linguistic structure is some variation of the nominative plus the verb "to be" plus the rest of the predicate. The characteristics of the predicate are transferred to the nominative, and this transference becomes a fundamental aspect of the figurative language, as the following examples indicate:

> God is a distant—stately Lover—   (P 357)
> Mirth is the Mail of Anguish—   (P 165)
> Crisis is a Hair/Toward which forces creep   (P 889)
> The Lightning is a yellow Fork/From Tables in the sky   (P 1173)
> Safe Despair it is that raves—/Agony is frugal.   (P 1243)
> Water, is taught by thirst.   (P 135)
> Utmost is relative—/Have not or Have/Adjacent sums   (P 1291)
> Faith—is the Pierless Bridge   (P 915)
> Drama's Vitallest Expression is the Common Day   (P 741)

The previous assertions are global in nature, encapsulating the totality or whole of the subject under scrutiny. The following group of assertions attempt to establish a single aspect or identic property of the thing being defined:

> A South Wind—has a pathos/Of individual Voice—   (P 719)
> Pain—has an Element of Blank—   (P 650)
> Remembrance has a Rear and Front—   (P 1182)

Or they personify characteristic actions and attributes of the subject under consideration, distinguishing and so defining them:

> The Heart asks Pleasure—first—   (P 536)
> Absence disembodies—so does Death   (P 860)
> The Admirations—and Contempts—of time—/Show justest—
>   through an Open Tomb—   (P 906)

Many of these assertions are frankly aphoristic:

> A Charm invests a face/Imperfectly beheld—   (P 421)
> Perception of an object costs/Precise the Object's loss—
>   (P 1071)

for in both groups, feeling and experience are abstracted from the context that prompted them, and from temporal considerations; the words are uttered in the third person present tense and may lack definite and indefinite articles, all of these strategies contributing to the speaker's authority, as they make a claim to experiential truth that transcends the limitations of personal experience. The distinctions between the two groups may seem to exist more in formulation than in function. Nonetheless, given a range of utterance, the former assertions lie at the epigrammatic extreme and occur with more frequency in the poems (it is thus with them that I shall be most concerned); the latter assertions, which appear with increased frequency in the letters, by their very admission of partiality, come closer to confessing their evolution from a particular incident or context.

The function of a successful formulation, one that says reality is one way and not another, is that it have no qualification; that it be the last word. The problem in many of Dickinson's poems is that it is the first word. It was Emerson who called proverbs "the literature of reason, or the statements of an absolute truth without qualification,"[6] and there is a sense in which statements like "Capacity to Terminate/Is a Specific

Grace" (P 1196) or "Not 'Revelation'—'tis that waits/But our unfurnished eyes" (P 685) preclude further statement because any statement
will qualify them.

Hobbes, in *The Leviathan*, makes the following observation about
names and definitions:

> Seeing then that truth consists in the right ordering of names in our
> affirmations, a man that seeketh precise truth had need to remember
> what every name he useth stands for . . . or else he will find himself
> entangled in words, as a bird in lime-twigs. . . . And therefore in geom-
> etry (which is the only science which it hath pleased God hitherto
> to bestow on mankind), men begin at settling the significations of
> their words; which settling of significations they call *definitions*,
> and place them in the beginning of their reckoning. (part I, chapter
> IV)

Geometric constructions are not, however, metaphoric ones, and it is
important to note that in poems such definitional knowledge is credited
best when it occurs at the end of a speaker's reckoning. Perhaps this is
because, unlike Hobbes, we believe that, at least in poems, definitions
are neither arbitrary nor conventionally agreed-upon assignations.
Wrested from experience, they imply a choice whose nature is only made
manifest by its context.[7]

But Dickinson's names and definitions not only posit themselves at
the beginning of poems, they also shrug off the need for further context,
for it is difficult to acknowledge the complexity of a situation while
stressing its formulaic qualities—unless the point of the formulation is to
reveal complexity. In fact, definitions are often predicated on the
assumption that experience can be expressed summarily as one thing.
The detachable quality of some of Dickinson's lines receives comment as
early as 1892 when Mabel Loomis Todd writes:

> How does the idea of an "Emily Dickinson Yearbook" strike you?
> . . . My thought is that with isolated lines from the already published
> poems, many of which are perfect comets of thought, and some of
> those wonderful epigrams from the *Letters*, together with a mass of
> *unpublished* lines which I should take from poems which could never
> be used entire, I could make the most brilliant year-book ever issued.
> . . . If I do not do it, some one else will want to, because ED abounds
> so in epigrams—.[8]

One of her first biographers, George Whicher, comments: "Her states of mind were not progressive but approximately simultaneous."[9] R. P. Blackmur summarizes the situation less charitably when he speaks of Dickinson's poems as "mere fragmentary indicative notation,"[10] and in a statement cited only in part in the Introduction, he explains himself: "The first thing to notice—a thing characteristic of exercises—is that the order or plot of the elements of the poem is not that of a complete poem; the movement of the parts is downwards and towards a disintegration of the effect wanted. A good poem so constitutes its parts as at once to contain them and to deliver or release by the psychological force of their sequence the full effect only when the poem is done."[11] For how a poem tells the time of the experience it narrates directly determines the crucial relationship between what we might distinguish as the mechanism of that poem's closure and its true completion, which would be perceived as a "natural" end even were the utterance to continue beyond. We have different modes of reference to the movement that leads to the coincidence of closure and internal completion within a given poem. We speak of a poem's progressions, of emotions if not of actions, of its building. We are thus presuming that a poem has development, a sense of its own temporal structure. When a poem remains innocent of the knowledge of an ordering temporality, the poem and its meaning are problematic.

These problems are notable at the simplest level of relationship. In essays dealing with aspects of aphasia, or language disturbance, Roman Jakobson makes a distinction between the two opposite tropes of metaphor and metonymy. Assuming that language is predicated upon modes of relation, he distinguishes between the internal relation of similarity (and contrast), which underlies metaphor, and the external relation of contiguity (and remoteness), which determines metonymy. Jakobson concludes that any verbal style shows a marked preference for either the metaphoric or metonymic device.[12] Now Dickinson's predilection for the metonymic device is clear. That preference becomes significant when we note that Jakobson's description of a contiguity disorder (the language impairment that affects the perception of context) offers a fairly accurate picture of many of Dickinson's problematic poems.[13] "First," he writes, "the relational words are omitted."[14] Then:

The syntactical rules organizing words into higher units are lost; this loss, called agrammatism, causes the degeneration of the sentence into a mere "word heap." . . . Word order becomes chaotic;

the ties of grammatical coordination and subordination . . . are dissolved. As might be expected, words endowed with purely grammatical functions, like conjunctions, prepositions, pronouns, and articles, disappear first, giving rise to the so-called "telegraphic style."[15]

Jakobson's description resonates against a similar, albeit less technical, comment on Dickinson's poems made by Louis Untermeyer: "The few lines become telegraphic and these telegrams seem not only self-addressed but written in a code."[16] When Jakobson further explains that the type of aphasia affecting contexture tends to give rise to one-sentence utterances and one-word sentences, we recall how many of Dickinson's poems are single sentences.[17] Again, in a less clinical assertion, Donald Thackery writes of Dickinson's "shorthand vocabulary": "One notices how many of her poems seem less concerned with a total conception than with expressing a series of staccato inspirations occurring to her in the form of individual words."[18] In addition, Jakobson asserts that aphasics of this type make frequent use of quasi-metaphors which are based on inexact identification, and his description of that identification is reminiscent of the definitional poems about which I have been speaking. Jakobson concludes: "Since the hierarchy of linguistic units is a superposition of ever larger contexts, the contiguity disorder which affects the construction of contexts destroys this hierarchy."[19] We recall Gelpi's words: "The very confusion of the syntax . . . forces the reader to concentrate on the basic verbal units and derive the strength and meaning largely from the circumference of words."[20]

I have mentioned the Jakobson studies with hesitation, for it would be a mistake to assume that we could diagnose such a disorder from Dickinson's poems. Perhaps the primary reason for citing Jakobson is not to make a brash connection between disease and poetic style, but rather to query the curiosity of relationship between statements so essentially alien: literary criticism of a particular poet, and the description of a linguistic disorder. For one is obliged to note that the predilection for definitional statements, many of which are of a quasi-metaphoric nature, the frequent omission of words that perform grammatical functions, and the absence of contextual clarity bear a striking relationship to Jakobson's description of a contiguity disorder, and that his description brings together and clarifies many of the earlier critical assertions about the poems. Insofar as poetic speech is a violation of the linguistic status quo, it should come as no surprise that such speech deviates from the ordinary configurations that bear our meanings out. That the deviations take these particular forms, however, is a fact that invites interpretation even as it mystifies any summary conclusions.

III

In the following pages I shall consider the problems that arise when a poem's beginning is more forceful than its conclusion; when the name or definition it contains bears no relation or a problematic relation to its context; when a word in such a poem lacks adequate contextual specification. I shall then examine a group of poems in which definitions successfully require their contexts, temporal or otherwise; which exist in an effort to clarify an internal state or to clear up an external confusion; which open rather than close the issues they consider; and in which the complexity of definition is revelatory of the complexity of the speaker's situation and the need for its exegesis.

There are frequent instances in Dickinson's definitional poems where the poem's conclusion follows poorly from its beginning. Sometimes, as in the following poem, it is redundant and hence gratuitous:

> Hope is a subtle Glutton—
> He feeds upon the Fair—
> And yet—inspected closely
> What Abstinence is there—
>
> His is the Halcyon Table—
> That never seats but One—
> And whatsoever is consumed
> The same amount remain—   (P 1547)

The second stanza glosses the first. It explains the fact that Hope's table is prosperous (a restatement of line 2), and that Hope's consumption in no way depletes the fare of reality, since Hope feasts only in supposition (an idea contained in the last two lines of the first stanza). The problem with the restatement is that it is not particularly interesting. Similarly, the opening of the following poem has an exactitude that its conclusion lacks:

> Longing is like the Seed
> That wrestles in the Ground,

Believing if it intercede
It shall at length be found.

The Hour, and the Clime—
Each Circumstance unknown,
What Constancy must be achieved
Before it see the Sun!   (P 1255)

Similes recognize that we fail at direct names because we fail at perfect comprehension, and that certain experiences evade mastery and hence definition—the best we can do is approximate or approach them; a simile is an acknowledgment of that failure and contains within it the pain of imperfect rendering. What is evocative about the simile in P 1255 is the way in which it gets the verb to enact the tension between being, which is manifest, and presence, which is hidden. This tension is precisely the essence of longing, and externalizing it reveals the conflict: it can never be perfectly rendered because, half-hidden with its object, it can never be perfectly apprehended. Dickinson is using the word "intercede" to suggest that surfacing of longing which would be tantamount to its acknowledgment, its open coming between the speaker and an instigating source. What might be "found" at such a moment is not simply the shape of the buried feeling, but also its object, which, one presumes, is similarly absent or unavailable. In the poem's following lines, however, both the representation of tension between presence and being and the recognition that it is this tension that makes longing so difficult to represent are abandoned, and the simile is "extended" with little regard for the significance of its original distinction. Here, then, as in the previous poem, the most complex part of the assertion is the name itself. In such an instance, an explanation of, or rationale for, the genesis of the name after the fact of it cannot help but affect the reader as gratuitous.

As in the following poem, the definition exists for the purpose of dismissing the situation with which it purports to deal:

Remorse—is Memory—awake
Her Parties all astir—
A Presence of Departed Acts—
At window—and at Door—

Its Past—set down before the Soul
And lighted with a Match—
Perusal—to facilitate—

Of its Condensed Despatch

Remorse is cureless—the Disease
Not even God—can heal—
For 'tis His institution—and
The Complement of Hell—   (P 744)

The emphasis in the first two stanzas is on the excruciating sense in which we can be inhabited by a past that will not stay still. Remorse awakens memory and memory prevents calmness (perhaps literally prevents sleep, as the metaphor in the first line suggests) by lighting our minds with unwanted thoughts. Remorse (for that is the match) illuminates the past so that the flash revealed to us is simply accusatory. If we did not distort the past by condensing it, if we knew not to simplify, the accusation would be less clear. The speaker is defining a situation in which our experiences play upon our minds in such a way that we cannot doubt them to be ours, yet robbed of their specificity, we cannot see them as they in fact happened to us. The hell of remorse is that it blinds us to the real meanings of our experiences and simultaneously convinces us that the distortion we are seeing in place of that meaning is reality.

Our sense of the speaker in the first two stanzas is that of someone who is naming or defining an experience in order to achieve mastery over it. But in the third stanza, control is secured as a consequence of ascribing blame, so the focus of the poem narrows to exclude experience. The definitions in the first two stanzas are concerned with the quality of remorse. In them the speaker makes clear the way in which remorse is experiential hell. The definition in the third stanza is concerned with its cause. There we are told about the way in which it is a complement of theological Hell. That remorse is God's institution may be a matter of fact or, more important, a matter of belief, but it shifts the speaker's role in the experience by predicating an agent for the affliction. A relationship exists between these two factors but the poem is not positioned with respect to that relationship.

In the following poem, a disjunction between the initial naming in line one and the lines that follow it leads the reader to interpretive despair, for there is no way to figure the confusion that ensues:

Doom is the House without the Door—
'Tis entered from the Sun—

> And then the Ladder's thrown away,
> Because Escape—is done—
>
> 'Tis varied by the Dream
> Of what they do outside—
> Where Squirrels play—and Berries die—
> And Hemlocks—bow—to God—   (P 475)

If the statement in line one is literal, it perhaps refers to the grave. But it need not be literal, perhaps cannot be literal, as line two suggests. Maybe then the speaker is using "Doom" as a metaphor for an inevitability one may come to dwell in (like a house) but be unaware of (and therefore enter like a doorless house). The second stanza, far from clarifying these concerns, only confuses them, for the shape of the two realities implicitly being compared remains too ambiguously sketched for the reader to see a coherent picture.

The lack of explicit connection between the statements in a definitional poem sometimes results in speech that is almost unintelligible:

> Experience is the Angled Road
> Preferred against the Mind
> By—Paradox—the Mind itself—
> Presuming it to lead
>
> Quite Opposite—How Complicate
> The Discipline of Man—
> Compelling Him to Choose Himself
> His Preappointed Pain—   (P 910)

The distinctions are so coiled here that it is difficult to understand them. One way of interpreting the first stanza is to assume that experience is chosen above the mind (preferred against it) even though (and this is the paradox) the mind itself states its preference for experience. But it is not clear what the mind presumes experience will "lead/Quite Opposite [to]," since the line breaks in the middle of the thought. If we infer that the object of the implicit preposition is "pain," this is still awkward sense, and it is certainly awkward syntax. The real problem, however, is that the focus of the poem shifts in stanza two. There "The Discipline of Man," an idiosyncratic but in no way interesting (because not made relevant) periphrasis for the mind, is called "Complicate," and this is then stated as the reason man chooses his "Preappointed Pain," itself an unexplained paradox. "Preappointed," moreover, has resonances of a final judgment, though whether of salvation or damnation is not clear. These resonances come from the word itself and our inferences about how Dickinson might be likely to use it rather than from the poem's context. While there is too little linguistic specificity to substantiate inference, one wonders if the speaker is choosing between the immediacy of this world and the promise of the next only to discover that any choice must confront the inevitability of pain. The problem with my reading is that while the mind has been rendered as complex, it has not been so rendered in terms of these specific issues. The problem with the poem and particularly with that suggestive last phrase is that it insinuates my reading without confirming it.

The poems about which I have been speaking have become progressively more difficult to understand, and the efforts at understanding them progressively less rewarding. In "Hope is a subtle Glutton" we found that the poem repeated without elaborating upon its initial name; in "Longing is like the Seed" and "Remorse is Memory awake" that complex situations were stated only to be dismissed by the poems' conclusions; in "Doom is the House without the Door" and "Experience is the Angled Road" that context and conclusion bore such an ambiguous relation to the initial names that we literally could make no sense even of the names themselves. The problem with these poems and with the many like them is twofold. First, they raise the question of the point in an experience at which one's awareness of it yields a name. For whether a name seems gratuitous or appropriate is contingent upon its relationship to the rest of the experience being narrated. Second, there is the problem of how a given speaker manifests the need of, or reason for, the name at which she arrives. It is not here my intention to theorize on criteria for fictional coherence, but it ought to be obvious that one credits speech in direct presence, and no less in poems, that issues out of a discernible and describable situation and that is functional in nature. In a discussion of the following poems, I will examine the quite specific and complex tasks that naming and definition-making can perform.

IV

Sometimes the point of a definition can be to reveal the speaker's knowledge of its inadequacy, as, for example, in the following:

A Coffin—is a small Domain,
Yet able to contain
A Citizen of Paradise
In it's diminished Plane.

A Grave—is a restricted Breadth—
Yet ampler than the Sun—
And all the Seas He populates
And Lands He looks upon

To Him who on it's small Repose—
Bestows a single Friend—
Circumference without Relief—
Or Estimate—or End—   (P 943)

The first stanza, at least nominally, answers the question of what space a person inhabits after death. It is notable, therefore, that the second stanza should return to that question. Maybe the speaker returns to the literal facts of death in order to anchor herself in a reality that is not speculative, as if the positive assertiveness of the first stanza were more bravado than belief. We know further that the reason she is not free of her initial question is that her manner of dealing with it has not spoken to the anxiety implicit in its insistence.

So the definitional voice comes back like the voice of reality: "A Grave—is a restricted Breadth—." Because in stanza one the limited space of the coffin has been juxtaposed to the infinity of the dead person's new dwelling place, we might suppose the speaker is again minimizing the grave's size in order to point to the spaciousness of an afterlife. But the infinity to which she now refers is inside of her and is of the everlastingness of loss. Similarly overwhelmed, another of Dickinson's speakers has spoken of "a Wilderness of Size" (P 856). The shift in definition has been occasioned by the shift in the speaker's perspective, for this is a poem in which awe discovers its origin and its proper object. It discovers that its object is not elsewhere at the supposition of another life, but rather here at the fact that this one is mortal.

Definition, then, can be a way of coming to terms with a discrepancy between what one believes and what one feels, of growing knowledgeable about one's feeling.[21] For the first definition is insufficient not be-

cause it is untrue, but rather because it is irrelevant. In the following
definitional poem, renunciation is the strategy for coming to terms with
loss:

> Renunciation—is a piercing Virtue—
> The letting go
> A Presence—for an Expectation—
> Not now—
> The putting out of Eyes—
> Just Sunrise—
> Lest Day—
> Day's Great Progenitor—
> Outvie
> Renunciation—is the Choosing
> Against itself—
> Itself to justify
> Unto itself—
> When larger function—
> Make that appear—
> Smaller—that Covered Vision—Here—   (P 745)

This poem, unlike "A Coffin is a small Domain," begins with the tone of
a voice aware of the situation's complexity. It is the tone of someone
trying to convince herself of something she finds both difficult and imperative to believe—that renunciation is a virtue; that it is piercing she
knows. The pain of the conflict is woven into the first three lines and
enacted in the direct discourse of "Not now—." The force of the imperative moves the speaker back to a more bounded place where she can
more safely (because the danger of capitulation is less real) define renunciation with specificity: "The putting out of eyes—/Just Sunrise—."
Sight must be avoided at all costs because it will inform her that day
surpasses "Day's great Progenitor—." Of course the very presumption
that if she could see God's light it would be judged dim compared to the
light of day is itself a judgment. In 1885 Dickinson had written to Maria
Whitney: "I fear we shall care very little for the technical resurrection,
when to behold the one face that to us comprised it is too much for us,
and I dare not think of the voraciousness of that only gaze and its only
return" (L 969). And almost twenty years earlier, to the Hollands: "If
God had been here this summer, and seen the things that *I* have seen—
I guess that He would think His Paradise superfluous" (L 185). More

soberly, she had expressed the belief that the reason earthly bliss does not last is that, if it did, "'Twould supersede the Heaven—" (P 393). "I have never believed [Paradise] to be a superhuman site," she had insisted (L 391).

At the point in the poem at which the speaker exhibits a clear preference for this world, a second definition is formulated, perhaps as an explanation for why she is opting for what she does not want. The syntax of lines ten to thirteen is convoluted because the idea that renunciation is a matter of one's best interest is a convoluted idea involving, as the lines literally do, several iterations of the concept of self: the sense in which renunciation is an act that violates the self; the sense in which it is an act that legitimates the self; and the sense in which the self stands as ambivalent arbiter between the two. The diction of the last three lines lacks the precision of the rest of the poem, but, to paraphrase what I believe to be the speaker's conclusion, she is saying: "My act of renunciation will be justified when the vision of God makes this world appear insignificant." Though she concedes that God's revelation will dwarf that of this world, she clearly indicates that with the eyes she now has, a presence looks better than an expectation. The speaker's last word is "Here," for the most significant fact about this world is its presence.

The relationship between renunciation and loss remains tentative throughout the poem, as I suspect it remained tentative throughout Dickinson's life. In 1882, she had written to James D. Clark, "No Verse in the Bible has frightened me so much from a Child as 'from him that hath not, shall be taken even that he hath'" (L 788), and we can speculate that the speaker's willingness to give up this world is contingent upon her recognition of the requirement of doing so. Definition here, then, is a way of teaching the will to desire what a force external to it has deemed necessary.

The following definitional poem establishes familiarity with a subject about which we ordinarily feel profound and disquieting ignorance:

> Death is the supple Suitor
> That wins at last—
> It is a stealthy Wooing
> Conducted first
> By pallid innuendoes
> And dim approach

But brave at last with Bugles
And a bisected Coach
It bears away in triumph
To Troth unknown
And Kindred as responsive
As Porcelain   (P 1445)

One of the most striking characteristics of this utterance is the speaker's awareness that while death is always with her, his relationship to her is always changing. Therefore the definition takes the form of a progression. Isolating the steps in the process is a strategy for asserting knowledge over something, half of whose threat lies in its insistence that we cannot know it. Though we are told about death's activities, and not about the speaker's, the poem is itself a telling insofar as it is clear by the second line that the speaker is repelled by the suit. If death is company of which the speaker cannot be rid, then the speech is uttered in his presence the way an insult would be.

Once in an effort to define the "Porcelain" quality of death to which she here refers, Dickinson found words for the terrible transformation she witnessed:

'Twas warm—at first—like Us—
Until there crept upon
A Chill—like frost upon a Glass—
'Till all the scene—be gone.

The Forehead copied Stone—
The Fingers grew too cold
To ache—and like a Skater's Brook—
The busy eyes—congealed—

It straightened—that was all—
It crowded Cold to Cold—
It multiplied indifference—
As Pride were all it could—

And even when with Cords—
'Twas lowered, like a Weight—
It made no Signal, nor demurred,
But dropped like Adamant.   (P 519)

In the space created by the words, at the center of which lies recognition (as in the space created by the lowering of the corpse, at the center of which lies grief), definition is by default.

The effort to understand the incomprehensible frequently depended upon definitions that took scrupulous note of the progressions of experience whose totality evaded the grasp. If one could at least chart the stages whereby a thing passed into incomprehensibility, one might come to terms with the fact that process itself and the loss with which it concludes is not sudden, as it appears, but has stages. Here the person neutered by death becomes unrecognizable in direct proportion to the speaker's perception of his/her loss of feeling. " 'Twas warm—/at first—like Us," but the ultimate abdication of human life is the numbing and final absence of sensation, interpreted from a mortal perspective as "Pride": the power to remain unmoved. Dickinson had observed a related progression when she noted: "The Living—tell—/The Dying—but a Syllable—/The Coy Dead—None—" (P 408).

Definitions that had their genesis in the stages of a situation were useful precisely because, through their recapitulation, a speaker might perceive a relationship between the first and final steps of a phenomenon that seemed otherwise of inexplicable origin. The definition of such a phenomenon was thus a reconstruction of its history:

> Crumbling is not an instant's Act
> A fundamental pause
> Dilapidation's processes
> Are organized Decays.
>
> 'Tis first a Cobweb on the Soul
> A Cuticle of Dust
> A Borer in the Axis
> An Elemental Rust—
>
> Ruin is formal—Devil's work
> Consecutive and slow—
> Fail in an instant, no man did
> Slipping—is Crashe's law.   (P 997)

Here we are told that the beginning of a process contains and predicts its conclusion. Though in retrospect we are capable of understanding the relationship between one part of an experience and another, at the time they may seem radically disconnected. Effecting a connection often comes, as in the following poem about disillusionment, only after it is too late:

Finding is the first Act
The second, loss,
Third, Expedition for
The "Golden Fleece"

Fourth, no Discovery—
Fifth, no Crew—
Finally, no Golden Fleece—
Jason—sham—too.   (P 870)

In this case the step past the final one is really the step upon which
all other deceptions are predicated. Jason is mentioned last as something
absolutely unforgettable would be. We note, too, that his deception cannot be formulated serially; it is too large. It is because Medea made this
discovery last that she was not saved from making the other, earlier discoveries.

V

In my discussion of the preceding poems, I have wished to emphasize
the history-making function of names and definitions. To tell the story
of the self and its experiences is necessarily to posit a history for that
self: a temporal structuring of the elements that comprise its meanings.
As psychoanalysis knows, this is a complex business, perhaps more complex than it seems, for it depends upon the recognition that one's names
for a given experience are comprehensible only in terms of their history.
"Of our first Creation we are unconscious," Dickinson had written to
Higginson (L 575), but presumably the later creations—the constructions
and reconstructions of meaning—were in need of scrutiny. Hence one's
account of how a name comes into being, if it is a genuine account, is
also an interpretation of it.

If we return for a moment to Blackmur's complaint that the movement of parts in a poem is downwards, towards a disintegration of the
effect wanted, it becomes clear that in the poems to which he refers, the
names or definitions have disengaged themselves from their contexts or
have never sufficiently discovered them. The space between the history
of a definition and the fact of it perhaps explains why Jakobson's description of contiguity disorder seems to characterize these poems. That
meaning should be so contingent upon one's perception of temporal
order is something of a curse, for the struggle for meaning involves, at

the very least, the arduous effort to know how relationships evolve in time. The excruciating pain (the "Tomahawk in my side" [L 248]) to which her poems give faithful testimony left Dickinson with a radically dislocated sense of time, and sometimes with the illusion of its cessation. In P 1159 she had written of a universe with no temporal laws:

> . . . Epoch had no basis here
> For Period exhaled.

In P 937, in despair:

> The thought behind, I strove to join
> Unto the thought before—
> But Sequence ravelled out of Sound
> Like Balls—upon a Floor.

And in P 443, of the ultimate horror, herself as a broken clock:

> And yet—Existence—some way back—
> Stopped—struck—my ticking—through—

Thus the mere presence of pain demands an interpretation its manifestations prohibit. For, to recall Bakan, since there is no distance between pain and the self that suffers it, the perception of that self is reduced to the perception of pain.[22] At the same time, insofar as we try to rid ourselves of pain, we seek to repudiate that self with which, in our minds, it has become identical. Hence pain blinds us, not only to the external world, but also to the true nature of the self. In such a situation one might say that there is not enough room between experience and its agent for knowledge to take shape. "Existence . . . stopped . . . my ticking"; "Existence . . . struck . . . my ticking"; "Existence . . . struck—my ticking—through—." No matter which word one emphasizes, it is clear that existence stops itself and its agent in the simultaneity of ambiguous grammar. The sense of being apprehended by—caught at the center of—the various aspects of one's experience that refuse one the singleness of interpretation (for interpretations depend upon the hierarchy or ordering of phenomena, which in turn depends upon one's ability to achieve momentary distance from them) is perhaps the central dilemma that confounds Dickinson's speakers and, at times, Dickinson's poems. Bound to the moment (without memory or imagination, that is, without concept of time), the spatial dimensions of the world overwhelm, for they alone determine and delimit one's place in it. The heightened awareness of

one's body at such moments and the way in which that body experiences
the tug of contradictory forces is made palpable in Donne's Holy Sonnet I:

> Thou hast made me, And shall thy worke decay?
> Repaire me now, for now mine end doth haste,
> I runne to death, and death meets me as fast,
> And all my pleasures are like yesterday;
> I dare not move my dimme eyes any way,
> Despaire behind, and death before doth cast
> Such terrour, and my feeble flesh doth waste
> By sinne in it, which it t'wards hell doth weigh;
> Onely thou art above, and when towards thee
> By thy leave I can looke, I rise againe;
> But our old subtle foe so tempteth me,
> That not one houre I can my selfe sustaine;
> Thy Grace may wing me to prevent his art
> And thou like Adamant draw mine iron heart.

Notwithstanding the differences between the two poets, differences revealed in part by Donne's ability to imagine an alternative to his dilemma, this poem shows us the shape of an experience about whose center
Dickinson spent her life writing. Perhaps its most harrowing moment
comes with that admission, "I dare not move my dimme eyes any way"
(a line that is the metaphoric equivalent of "Existence—some way back—
/Stopped—struck—my ticking—through—"), for with the moment severed
from that which precedes and follows it and the eyes of the self having
nowhere to look but inward, literally having no world, the self falls back
on itself and finds that it is nothing. In the Donne sonnet, negation lies
at the intersection of despair and death in one direction and hell and
absence in the other. At the cross of these forces what is needed is outside presence; Donne called it "Grace," for the self is at one with its
insufficiency. "Leave" to "look" outward, leave to see connection, is
redemptive for both poets, for the eyes forced inward by the absence of
all else is equivalent to psychic annihilation. Without such connection,
Dickinson had written ". . . Being's—Beggary—" (P 377).

It is, in fact, a function of poems that they provide us with connections that, incapable of making ourselves, we can at least recognize. One
of the tasks poetry accomplishes is the creation of a vocabulary in which
we can see those experiences that (despite all our knowledge) we thought
were only ours. I am not speaking about the kind of experience we

validate by observing another's actions and noting that they resemble
our own. I am speaking about experiences that do not show in others'
actions, or that show only indirectly. In poems I see something I can
ordinarily never see unless I am observing myself: I see a self alone. What
is affirmed by that sight is the perception that not only is the world
always changing, but we are changing in it, and our own transformations
are often as incomprehensible to us as those that lie outside us and that
we have the obligation to call "other." These interior transformations,
the ones we are supposed to know about and be in control of because
they are ours and happen inside us, we frequently fail to know precisely
because they are ours and happen inside us. Dickinson, without the aid
of her own poems, suffered the same confusion. "Your thoughts dont
have words every day," she remarked (P 1452). When she did have them,
they sometimes came to her with violence, for cognition unacquainted
with its own history is liable to blow itself up. The attempt to know
something could thus result in the act of wrenching it apart. "Split the
Lark—and you'll find the Music—" (P 861), she had written, but like her
"Sceptic Thomas," in those instances, what she too often found was a
"Scarlet Experiment"—not music but blood.

I shall conclude this chapter with a look at two poems that present
experiences that are traditionally nameless and in which the speakers' incomprehension is a direct result of the lapsed connection between experience and its history or context. The speaker can exemplify experience
but never interpret it. Meaning, then, resists knowledge and asserts itself,
if at all, only at the level of intimation:

> The Soul's distinct connection
> With immortality
> Is best disclosed by Danger
> Or quick Calamity—
>
> As Lightning on a Landscape
> Exhibits Sheets of Place—
> Not yet suspected—but for Flash—
> And Click—and Suddenness.   (P 974)

As in "'Twas warm at first like Us," the subject here lurks in the connections between the words, elusive and perceived indirectly. The source of
the terror conferred by the revelation is unclear, though the fact of it is
indisputable. Its violence; the hugeness of its scope coupled with the

suspicion that it affords vision without sight ("Sheets of Place—" is no landscape we recognize, but is empty of specificity and is deliberately, terrifyingly, ambiguous); the unmistakable connection between "Flash," "Click," "Suddenness," and death—these are partial explanations. Perhaps what is most appalling is the discrepancy between the enormity of the revelation and the blankness of our comprehension of it. For if it imparts an intimation of what we have previously not known, that intimation tells us such knowledge is not forthcoming. We will be annihilated before we understand. Perhaps annihilation without benefit of meaning is what we are meant to understand. "Had we the first intimation of the Definition of Life," Dickinson had written to Mrs. Holland, "the calmest of us would be Lunatics!" (L 492).

It is unclear whether the inability to interpret exterior experience is less disquieting than the failure to understand the working of one's own mind. I would hazard a guess, however, that when our feelings resist interpretation, when we know neither the source, size, nor scope of those feelings, consciousness goes begging for meaning. Then truly the landscape of the mind is as harrowing as the landscape revealed in the previous poem, and more inescapable:

> It was not Death, for I stood up,
> And all the Dead, lie down—
> It was not Night, for all the Bells
> Put out their Tongues, for Noon.
>
> It was not Frost, for on my Flesh
> I felt Siroccos—crawl—
> Nor Fire—for just my Marble feet
> Could keep a Chancel, cool—
>
> And yet, it tasted, like them all,
> The Figures I have seen
> Set orderly, for Burial,
> Reminded me, of mine—
>
> As if my life were shaven,
> And fitted to a frame,
> And could not breathe without a key,
> And 'twas like Midnight, some—
>
> When everything that ticked—has stopped—

And Space stares all around—
Or Grisly frosts—first Autumn morns,
Repeal the Beating Ground—

But, most, like Chaos—Stopless—cool—
Without a Chance, or Spar—
Or even a Report of Land—
To justify—Despair.   (P 510)

It is Dickinson's great achievement here that she is able to create the fiction of disorientation while rescuing the reader from the fact of it. The source of the speaker's affliction is that she cannot identify it. "It was not Death," the poem begins, and concludes implicitly, "it was Despair." Even this inference, however, is one the speaker cannot quite make. Unable to order the experience temporally, and lacking relevant outer criteria for it, she is imprisoned in the chaos of her feelings as muteness or inexpressiveness is an imprisonment.

It is no accident that words for Dickinson's two most crucial subjects, despair and death (exemplified here by "'Twas warm at first like Us" and "It was not Death for I stood up"), should have been indirect ones, shaped in both cases by inferences about the elusive "it." These poems evade metaphor and explicit naming, and their evasion is the point, for insofar as names involve distance from and interpretation of what has been apprehended, they are precisely what certain experiences—perceived in complexity and multifaceted—will not yield. These experiences defeat names. They flood conception, overwhelm it, so that it gives way to tenuous, incomplete, and multiple representation. For when experience stops a speaker by striking her through, her report of it will of necessity be fragmentary. At the center of her subject and hence unable to see its totality, she is often at a loss to know what it is. Hence she can only define by negation and simile, strategies that are acutely conscious of inaccuracy in the one case and imperfection in the other. Thus in "It was not Death," words are aware of the limitation of words. In search of meaning and skeptical of it, they acknowledge the fact that equative assertions are false ones. Even negative equations collapse under scrutiny, for while equations are correct in stipulating that meaning is manifested by connection, they err in assuming that such connection is identic. Not death, nor night, nor frost, nor fire—yet the negations are equivocal, not only because they are retracted in the third stanza ("And yet, it tasted, like them all"), but also because even their own terms are based on inaccurate inference. "It was not Night," the speaker asserts, "for all the Bells/Put out their Tongues, for Noon"; but since chimes at noon sound indistinguishable from those at midnight, the lines betray the speaker's confusion. She cannot tell one state from the other, perhaps because of the sudden relationship she perceives between them—and indeed she finally concedes, "And 'twas like Midnight, some—." Similarly, the initial assertion, "It was not Death," is complicated by the depiction of the corpse to which the speaker compares herself in the third stanza, the cessation of time, and Autumn's quite literal repudiation of life in the fifth.

The power of these negations is revealed in how firmly they stake out the territory of the known until all that is left is the vague and terrifying inference that this state is worse than physical death because, having most of its attributes, it is denied any of its reliefs: outside of time, it does not end. The violence that is "Stopless" is thus the violence that strikes one through, the paralysis of movement and the compulsion to it a cross at the center of which the speaker stands. From that spot she, like Donne's speaker, has no leave to look outward, no leave to see connection. A "Report of Land—" would "justify" despair in the theological sense of absolving the speaker from it, and would also make sense of despair, for in this poem despair is the one feeling that has lost touch with its antithesis and is hence meaningless. If in other poems Dickinson had asserted that knowledge of something is contingent upon its equative representation, she seems here to find such a solution inadequate. Despair cannot be named or even known because it will not recognize its context or history, because it has been severed from those surrounding and indeed opposite feelings that constitute its meaning.

It is, in fact, in those instances in which Dickinson is blind to the problem of opposites and to an understanding of dialectical knowledge that her poems falsify the experiences they represent. Such poems involve linear or equative visions of experience, and they are trivial to the extent that they master experience by severing it from its roots, from the tangle of contradictory elements. Dialectical knowledge is, of course, only one aspect of complexity, but perhaps it is the most primary aspect and, for the problem of naming, the one on which all the more subtle complications of relationship are predicated. For to the extent that our response to a given experience acknowledges its own ambivalence, we falter at designation. Perhaps this is why, in many of Dickinson's other utterances, the whole issue of naming is recognized as unmanageable and

is explicitly avoided. Her effort there is directed away from definition
and toward description of those temporal moments in a given experience
that chart its boundaries. Thus poems like "I felt a Funeral in my Brain,"
"Because I could not stop for Death," and "I heard a Fly buzz when I
died" are manifestly structured by their temporal progressions ("this
happened . . . then this . . . then this . . .") and are equally distinguished
by our inability to determine the precise nature or status of the experience being represented, our inability to name it. Real or imagined death,
psychosis or the memory of an actual funeral—we are so deeply sunk
into the interior of these experiences that their external shape eludes us.
A poem like "It was not Death," however, mediates between those
poems that despair of the task of naming and those poems that simplify it.

"It was not Death," insists on the problematic features of the doubleness of names and insists, also, that it is this doubleness that has the
power to liberate us. For dialectical knowledge in which experience is
put in touch with its antithesis involves the mind's ability to construct,
through memory, a connection between that which is not present at a
given moment in time and that which is. Such knowledge frees the mind
of the constraints of the moment by making it conscious of those elements of its own experience that, if they were not hidden, would transform it. Fredric Jameson writes, "From the physical intimidation of the
Fascist state to the agonizing repetitions of neurosis, the idea of freedom
takes the same temporal form: a sudden perception of an intolerable
present which is at the same time, but implicitly and however dimly
articulated, the glimpse of another state in the name of which the first
is judged."[23] The claim that an experience has antithetical aspects and
that one's knowledge of it depends upon the confrontation of those
aspects is founded upon a profound insight into the nature of identity.
Herbert Marcuse spoke of identity as "the continuous negation of inadequate existence."[24] Much earlier, Hegel had expressed the fundamental importance of antithesis by asserting that thinking itself lies in the
ability to negate that which is immediately before us. Freud, discussing
the double consciousness that is a result of the fact that each of our conceptions is acquired in contrast to its opposite, writes of the way in
which names reflect such negations: "If everything that we can know is
viewed as a transition from something else, every experience must have
two sides; and either every name must have a double meaning, or else
for every meaning there must be two names."[25] To the extent that

dialectical knowledge remains in touch with the totality of its own experience, the representation of that experience will be comprehensive and complete.

A dialectical sense of experience (and hence of our names for it) is also a historical one, for experiences evolve in time and are modified by it. When equative names are blind to their historical evolution—do not acknowledge that they are generated by the needs of the moment, which are particular needs—these names both simplify and fragment experience. Like the poems in which they occur, such names or definitions lack integrity; they achieve a comment upon experience only by removing themselves from it. Poems with multiple names or definitions (as "A Coffin is a small Domain") or with multiple meanings constituting the name or definition (as in "Renunciation is a piercing Virtue"), or poems like "It was not Death for I stood up," which confront, even if they are confounded by, the problem of antithesis, recognize the fact that experience involves a struggle between opposites. The revelation of such a struggle within a poem, which is also its enactment, makes a statement not only about an individual experience but also about the process of knowing itself. David Cooper writes, "Dialectical knowledge of objects is inextricable from knowledge of dialectical knowledge . . . the dialectic is not only an epistemological principle, a principle of knowing about knowing, but also an ontological principle, a principle of knowing about being."[26] For to see the moment in its context is to see it as both passing and partial and to recognize perception itself as incomplete. Such an insight suggests that the effort to sum something up, to name experience, must always be frustrated by one's knowledge of all that complicates and contradicts the name. In this respect, our words distort our thoughts by expressing them one at a time, as if their contradictory elements were progressive rather than simultaneous. In the absence of choice, conception tolerates such simplification. For if one tries to give voice to the strains of contradiction at once, the result is not language but a cry.

Freud taught us that dreams reduce opposites to a unity or represent them as one thing. Awake, the representation is more complex yet. For the point in an experience at which one attempts to externalize one's perception of it lies somewhere between its antithetical extremes. We memorialize that point by giving it a name, but the name must never lose sight of the fact that it arises out of a specific relationship between opposites whose first principles are ones of struggle and flux.

It is the relationship between hope and despair upon which "It was not Death" closes and between which, in retrospect, it has balanced. Such a relationship lacks a name, or else the *poem* is its name as it has been its articulation. The poem's central discovery lies in its connection of seemingly opposite states: day and night, life and death, hope and despair, time and timelessness. Riddled with qualification, neither simply identic nor simply opposite, such connections are painful, for they remind us that each of us is neither identical to nor opposite of any other. Our connection to each other, if it exists at all, is thus not equative, but must be in the form of relationship, taking shape within the space between absolute sameness and absolute difference. Similes are both the acknowledgment of this space and, since it cannot be overcome, the effort to make connections within it.

When Dickinson's speakers do not know and cannot say, the history of the experience is recorded as part of its name, for at such moments the history is all she can tell us. That a name has a history, has a moment in time that it can acknowledge and, in the telling, transcend, is redemptive. For telling changes, externalizes, puts one outside of and beyond. Telling implies knowledge of a listener who is drawn into relationship with the events being narrated and whose presence alters them. That presence provides boundaries for the words of the story. No longer identical with the teller on the one hand and, on the other, no longer spilling into the space of the whole world, the story hovers between teller and listener, discovering and inhabiting its proper space. It breaks the spell of stasis and sets existence in motion again, for relationships exist only in time. Names are thus in search of their moment in time—a moment that is not "struck through" and "stopped," but that is fluid. For as the self tells its story it moves beyond and wins freedom from it. The process of telling is then another story, *itself* in need of naming.

In the next chapter we shall look at poems that directly oppose the rendition of stories, and we shall see that when a speaker eschews the totality of her own story, it is often because of a feared association between the contradictions of the dialectic which will complete that story and the final completion of death itself. The source of the pain suffered by Dickinson's speakers is often, then, paradoxically, the existence of the very temporality that, in the definitional poems, seems to be denied them. This explanation can look curiously circular—temporality identified as the source of pain, pain as numbing all sense of temporality. The circle opens, however, at the recognition of how readily in the complex arena of our mental life desires may come illusorily to masquerade as dreads, and how sometimes, in the form of an inevitability of which consciously we would be rid, those desires are, in fact, diabolically granted. Given the logistics of this inversion, a complicated displacement occurs, and the pain *at* temporality becomes no less than that which precludes it. In the next chapter I shall say more about the reasons for wanting time stopped, as I discuss poems that fashion their stories around a dialectic, but only for the purpose of breaking out of and subverting its implicit temporal structure. Thus we shall see that the sacrifice of temporal order that so far we have observed to be a consequence of pain becomes, in the poems discussed in the next chapter, a defiance of it.

Given the nature of the problem with which she was wrestling, Dickinson's success in "It was not Death" and elsewhere is particularly remarkable. Since the necessity for names becomes most apparent at those moments when they fail us, we may at other times forget that the connection between thought and articulation is not always instantaneous. Thus, how to consider the complex process of naming is, in fact, one of its attendant dilemmas. On this issue, Wittgenstein gives us important advice: "The axis of reference of our examination must be rotated," he writes, "but about the fixed point of our real need."[27] Literary criticism, linguistics, psychology offer diverse investigations of naming. Their studies refer variously to the fact that to externalize meaning so that it is visible requires separating it from one's person, publicizing it, and that process, like the process of any severance, is painful. Independent of us, meaning (particularly names that are interpretive of it) assumes temporal existence, takes shape, in our eyes or in those of another. Once we have words for an experience we are no longer bound to it by solitude. "Silence is all we dread," Dickinson had written, and added, "There's Ransom in a Voice—" (P 1251).

The process I have described, however, is one of which we have reason to despair. We often assume, as a corollary to the painful recognition of our separateness from others and the consequent understanding that they cannot know our inner experiences, that *we* cannot fail to know them. We would do well to be wary of such a fantasy. Our minds produce images for which there are no verbal equivalents; more impenetrable than the images are vague intimations; words are absent or lost. Unable to say what we mean, we also fail to know it. We haven't names for our experiences, and after a while we haven't even the experiences.

What at times Dickinson's poetry suffers from is, in fact, what we all suffer from. Her achievements in wresting meaning from the elusive territory of the mind therefore offer us a powerful example. "I only said the Syntax—/And left the Verb and the pronoun out," Dickinson wrote (P 494)—it is not quite clear whether in apology or boast. Her own description notwithstanding, her words rarely lacked specific designation, even if the object of it lay inside. Did she perhaps think when she confessed the omission of pronoun and verb, we would mistake the invisibility of certain experiences for their absence? Tentative, crude, necessarily indirect, the syntax told a history. With it, she left us names for what might otherwise be unspeakable.

II

"A Loaded Gun"

THE DIALECTIC OF RAGE

The storyteller . . . is the man who could let the wick of his life be consumed completely by the gentle flame of his story.
   —*Walter Benjamin*

> *All men are heroes*
> *By the simple act of dying*
> *And the heroes are our teachers.*
>   —*Nicanor Parra*

STORIES are time- and space-bound phenomena, structured by plots that, as Aristotle pointed out, have beginnings, middles, and ends. The narrator does not tell his character's story all at once; incident or event (indeed, like language itself) reveals its meaning gradually, in slow and often painful unraveling. In that time, certain confrontations occur. Perhaps the most central of these takes place between the individual character and the demands of the world to which he must accommodate himself. Stories are the working out of such accommodations, and we value them partly for their insistence that the world's demands, albeit difficult, can be complied with. The fair lady must guess Rumpelstiltskin's name to be saved from his demands; Sir Gawain confront the Green Knight; Dorothea Brooke win freedom from Casaubon, Don Quixote from his illusion, and for each of these imperatives only a limited time is allotted. Most stories show characters coming to the world's terms or suffering because they have failed to do so. In this respect, stories are astonishingly moral. Stories both enact chronology and insist that it is chronology that has the power to save us. Time will sanction reversals, permit insights, provide space for action, or so we are assured.

Such generalizations about stories, which I must leave, for the moment, incomplete, lead me directly to my subject, which is not stories at all but rather poems, and specifically a group of Dickinson poems that retreat from the telling of stories; from chronology; and sometimes even from coherence. These poems, like those which "name" experience by exempting themselves from it, are patterned by their refusal to make the sort of accommodations described above; they seek a way out of time, a reprieve from it. As such, they raise questions not only about themselves but also about lyric poems as we are going to want to distinguish them from narratives or stories proper. My concerns in the following pages then, will be twofold: first, with a specific group of Dickinson's poems, and second, with the insights they shed on lyric poetry generally.

The Dickinson poems about which I shall be speaking tell a story predicated on a dialectic: this life versus the next; the pleasures of love and sexuality versus a more chaste and bodiless devotion; the demands of the self versus their capitulation to the world's otherness. The dialectic, as my examples suggest, is based on sacrifice (and on protest at its necessity), and it therefore appears to fit into my description of the way in which stories reveal the world as schooling individual expectations. The conflict in the poems, put simply, seems to be between forces of sexuality and forces of death; the poems schematize experience for the explicit purpose of preventing the convergence of sexuality and death, of avoiding the acknowledgment that the two join each other in time, and that the self comes to its end at their meeting. A third voice, intervening in the dialectic, which takes its passion from the knowledge of sexuality and its vengeance from the knowledge of death, is often one of rage.

Rage is a way of preventing the convergence of sexuality and death, albeit momentarily and albeit in full and painful awareness that the two can be kept apart only conceptually and only one step removed from experience. This third voice (the one breaking into the established dialectic in order to complicate it) is a complex one, for its existence, its presence, effects the stopping of time by framing the dilemma in words that exempt themselves from the very process against which they rage and to which they must inevitably return. Thus, if we were to chart the three voices, the two dialectical ones would appear along the same linear plane, although distanced from each other. The third, disruptive, voice would place itself erratically above that linear progression, in defiance of it. Its position in relation to the two dialectical points against which it was lodging its protest would of course determine the specific nature of the poem.

Often protest in the poems I shall discuss takes the form of a speaker's recoil from the eminence of her own insights. When the refusal to know is an unconscious one, Dickinson loses control over her subject, and seems afflicted by the same paralyzing despair that prohibits coherence as her speakers are. If, to simplify matters, we look first at a poem not structured explicitly by the triad of voices but one in which, nonetheless, the subject matter invites distraction, we will see the disruptive consequences of knowledge that dares not scrutinize itself:

> I got so I could take his name—
> Without—Tremendous gain—
> That Stop-sensation—on my Soul—
> And Thunder—in the Room—
>
> I got so I could walk across
> That Angle in the floor,
> Where he turned so, and I turned—how—
> And all our Sinew tore—
>
> I got so I could stir the Box—
> In which his letters grew
> Without that forcing, in my breath—
> As Staples—driven through—
>
> Could dimly recollect a Grace—
> I think, they call it "God"—
> Renowned to ease Extremity—
> When Formula, had failed—
>
> And shape my Hands—
> Petition's way,
> Tho' ignorant of a word
> That Ordination—utters—
>
> My Business, with the Cloud,
> If any Power behind it, be,
> Not subject to Despair—
> It care, in some remoter way,

> For so minute affair
> As Misery—
> Itself, too vast, for interrupting—more—   (P 293)

The first three stanzas, with their fusion of agonizing physical and emotional pain, are clear enough. The remembered transport of agony, the marriage of excruciation and ecstasy, the subsequent mastery of emotion—and the speaker's distancing of all of these in the past tense— lead us to expect a peripety. Control recollected may be control that has suffered a collapse; and the stress on the past-tense nature of the control at the beginning of the initial stanzas suggests that the space between the stanzas, to which the speaker's mind temporarily reverts, is occupied by a less manageable present that will eventually overwhelm even memory. But instead of the collapse of control with which the poem tantalizes us, we get a distraction from it: an appeal to God that becomes a way of avoiding feeling, and the poem ends not with passion, as we might expect, but rather with passion defended against. For passion would need to acknowledge directly the attendant circumstance of its loss, the "him" whose most palpable fact is absence.

Thus in the last stanza, confounded by the requirements of the present, utterance is most in disarray. There the speaker seems to be suggesting she would have commerce with a cloud *if* she could be sure a God were behind it, and, in addition (for "be" in the stanza functions as the verb for two subjunctives), that, could she determine such a power were not itself subject to despair, she would cease petitioning it for relief from an affliction that, failing to understand experientially, it could not mitigate. As my paraphrase suggests, the pronoun referent, like the reason for speech itself, is a matter of confusion. Though "It [would] care" refers grammatically to the cloud, the pronoun would be a less enigmatic "He" if the speaker had any confidence in the power behind it. But although the fifth stanza claims to invoke a God, it is clear by the last stanza that the speaker does not know to whom she is talking, does not know whether she wishes to be talking, and ignorance finally gives way to the acknowledgment that, in such a state, no more can or must be said. For the breaking off of utterance comes at a point when "more" would be an affront not only to God, who may or may not be attending from a distance, but also to the speaker, who acknowledges, albeit covertly, that she has herself become distanced from her subject.

Indeed, what begins as the endurance of great feeling turns into blasphemy on two counts, first with respect to the earthly lover and second with respect to the God who displaces him, for the poem's initial line suggests a pun on "taking His name in vain." To take it in vain is to take it without comprehending its significance, and this the speaker does initially when his name (the lover's) fails to tap the current of meaning, and later when His name (God's) becomes a denomination so remote in significance that it can barely be summoned, and, once recalled, is attributed to someone else ("I think, they call it 'God'—").

Though the reduction of the experience is attributed to God, "remote-[ness]" is a psychological remedy, not the divine cause. Put briefly, God is a way out, an object of simple projection. To the extent that Dickinson fails to know this and does not, I maintain, intend it, we have a complex hermeneutic situation here. Meaning breaks off, dissolves, goes under, at the moment when it is perceived as too painful, and that fact is attended by the rhythmic transformations in the last three stanzas: full rhyme disappears, the common particular meter established in the first three stanzas gives way to variation, as does the regular four-stress line. Such rhythmic change also counterpoints the paraphrasable sense of the lines. The message of the words (their meaning insofar as it can be figured) is "God does not understand and hence cannot care." The rhythmic message of the last three stanzas, however, is "I myself no longer wish to understand and therefore, of course, you must not either." Such a proposition may be arguable, but it makes experiential sense. It is, in fact, the only explanation that makes sense of the abrupt and rather elaborate confusions with which the poem concludes. Agony—in fact all meaning—goes dead on the speaker when she summons distance from her experience and, in so doing, relinquishes it. The poem, though not, I suspect, intentionally, is about what it is like to trivialize feeling because, as is, feeling has become unendurable. Better to make it nothing than to die from it.

The disjunction between the two parts of "I got so I could take his name" is revelatory of narrative breakdown, not of controlled narrative transformation. The speaker is not in possession of her story, or rather she is in possession of two stories, the bringing together of which points to a fundamental ambivalence and an attendant obfuscation of meaning. As a consequence of the ambivalence, meaning becomes symptomatic, breaks out into gesture where it cannot be fully comprehended and where it often expresses feelings that seem antithetical to the earlier intention of its speaker or author—it is difficult to distinguish adequately between the two in such instances, since both are victims of the same confusion.

Stories are comprehensible because of the connections, implicit or otherwise, that exist between their respective elements. Freud saw health in such connection and in the intelligibility that connection implies. The severing of connection, the gaps in chronology, the faulty memory—it is these psychoanalysis claims to treat so that the end result is nothing less than a complete story that is, in Freud's words, "intelligible, coherent, unbroken."[1] I bring this up here because Stephen Marcus's description of such a coherent story offers an important insight into the problematic aspects of Dickinson's poems when they resist knowledge:

> It is a story, or a fiction, not only because it has a narrative struc-
> ture but also because the narrative account has been rendered in
> language, in conscious speech, and no longer exists in the deformed
> language of symptoms, the untranslated speech of the body. At the
> end—at the successful end—one has come into possession of one's
> own story. It is a final act of self-appropriation, the appropriation
> by oneself of one's own history. This is in part so because one's own
> story is in so large a measure a phenomenon of language, as psycho-
> analysis is in turn a demonstration of the degree to which language
> can go in the reading of all our experience.[2]

Poetry, one might say, acknowledging the substitution, is a demonstration of the degree to which language can go in the reading of all our
experience. When it fails, erupts into gesture, becomes "untranslatable,"
or when its rhythmic manifestations grow so distracting as to convey a
separate meaning of their own, we may want to ask why devastation is
preferable to coherence, how knowledge threatens the self so that it
forgets its own story or falters in the telling of it.

Recognizing that the poems often resist cognitive enclosure, we may
want to seek another way of understanding them, or we may modify our
conception of what a successful poetic statement is. Jerome McGann,
writing of Swinburne's poetry, speaks of poetic speech that conveys "its
most moving insights at a level below or beyond the limits of customary
discourse."[3] McGann continues, "Swinburne deliberately puts meaning
beyond the grasp of the cognitive faculties by creating immensely difficult poetic systems or relations; and . . . he simultaneously presents
those systems as perfected enclosures which, though they do not define a
comprehensive meaning, represent the fact and the idea of wholeness."[4]

While Dickinson's and Swinburne's poetry lie distant from each other in almost every respect, McGann's description could well apply to the poems about which I shall be speaking. Like "I got so I could take his name," the poems that present the triad of voices are problematic ones. In them, it is easy enough for the reader to follow the story established by the dialectic. What is not so easy to interpret is the disruptive third voice, which often finds direct language inadequate.

In the first group of poems I shall consider, we will be dealing with that third voice, the one that interrupts a poem's conclusion and, in so doing, hints at a story other than the one propounded by the ostensible narrative. In the second group of poems, the third voice makes its appearance earlier and more openly by breaking into the center of the narrative and suggesting an outright criticism of the story, which it then revises. In the first instance, disruption of the story renders meaning ambiguous; in the second instance, disruption becomes meaning.

Both groups pose questions about how voice or presence (terms that I shall use synonymously) exists in contradistinction to action, consequence, and even story, and in both groups voice seems to fight against coherence, because it assumes coherence means consequence and consequence, death. Speech in the poems, then, is not the end of, or a response to, emotion, but rather its eruption, and this defense against completion (which, as we shall see, is in fact a defense against death) is exactly opposite to the one employed by the definitional poems. There we observed meaning to be trivialized, winnowed from its own complexity. In the following poems, however, we are dazzled by the confusions of complexity, by multiple meanings often contradictory. The profusion of meaning, the simultaneous posing of its antitheses, does not arise from the dialectic, as we might expect, but rather from the conversation between the dialectic and the third voice, which wishes to subvert it. The dramatic manifestations of such speech indicate that these utterances are neither tranquil nor recollected. Caught in the moment, they draw the reader into the net of their own irresolutions, and, if he does not look sharp he, or his comprehension at any rate, perishes there.

II

"Repetition and recollection are the same movement," Kierkegaard wrote, "only in opposite directions: for what is recollected has been, is repeated backwards, whereas repetition, properly so called, is recollected forwards."[5] Kierkegaard continues: "When one does not possess the categories of recollection or of repetition, the whole of life is resolved into a void and empty noise."[6] In possession of them, however, one takes the universe to task for failing to sanction the categories it has prescribed as requisite for meaning. The following poem is generated by the insight that this world must not be allowed to duplicate the next, lest the latter be found superfluous:

> I should have been too glad, I see—
> Too lifted—for the scant degree
> Of Life's penurious Round—
> My little Circuit would have shamed
> This new Circumference—have blamed—
> The homelier time behind.
>
> I should have been too saved—I see—
> Too rescued—Fear too dim to me
> That I could spell the Prayer
> I knew so perfect—yesterday—
> That Scalding One—Sabachthani—
> Recited fluent—here—
>
> Earth would have been too much—I see—
> And Heaven—not enough for me—
> I should have had the Joy
> Without the Fear—to justify—
> The Palm—without the Calvary—
> So Savior—Crucify—
>
> Defeat—whets Victory—they say—
> The Reefs—in old Gethsemane—
> Endear the Coast—beyond!
> 'Tis Beggars—Banquets—can define—
> 'Tis Parching—vitalizes Wine—
> "Faith" bleats—to understand!   (P 313)

By the end of the poem it is manifestly clear that what "they say—" is different from what the speaker knows, for the concept of too much salvation is a horrifying, if not nonsensical, concept. Yet God, far from abjuring sameness, seems to require it: the pattern of the speaker's life must duplicate the Savior's lest the "little Circuit" of this life outclass the "new Circumference—" of the next. If there is a threat prompting the implicit denials, it is inherent in the thought that God does not permit "The Palm—without the Calvary—." Although we might regard the last line as continuous with the poem—considering it only proper for one of the flock to assert that faith must "bleat" its comprehension of God's demands for sacrifice—the quotation marks suggest that this member of the flock who tries to utter the truisms finds herself instead speechless with rage. Thus the implicit grammar of the last line is altered slightly by its juxtaposition to the rest of the poem. The speaker is not saying that faith would have to bleat in order to understand, but rather that faith shakes off human utterance and is roused to animal fury precisely because it cannot. The cry of outrage disrupts the complacent irony that had seemed to structure the initial dialectic, for since "Faith" is the designation for every assertion that has preceded it, at the moment we perceive quotation marks enclose it, the entire poem is suddenly cast into quotation marks.

Although the poem is about excess and the prohibitions against "too much—," it must itself be seen as an extravaganza of protest, enacting the very "too-muchness" that it claims has been prohibited. "Too glad," "too lifted," "too rescued," "too much"—the repetition defies (and not very subtly at that) the injunction against duplicating experience. The syntactic repetitions are equally attention getting ("I should have had the Joy," "My little Circuit would have shamed"); and also attention getting, all the choral expressions of insufficiency ("too dim," "not enough," "without the Calvary—"). Both the common particular meter and the rhyme scheme remain regular throughout, and the poem employs a number of exact rhymes with an insistent repetition that renders their presence didactic, even harsh. It is just the regularity or monotony of sound which seems charged with the fury that will explode at the poem's conclusion.

Thus far my analysis might suggest the poem is an example of what Booth would call "stable irony,"[7] the discrepancy between the content of the words and the tone of their delivery intimating that all is not what it says. But since the reader is overwhelmed by the resonances of verbal and syntactic repetition *before* he understands their significance, and since the poem will ultimately subvert implication entirely, we must distinguish it from a purely ironic statement in which there is a balanced discrepancy (accorded by the simultaneity of perception) between the content and tone that always remains implicit. Here, although the poem seems to move between the dialectical terms it has established—this world versus the next, defeat versus victory, the Palm versus Calvary, words of acceptance versus words of denial—there is neither balance nor distance. The speaker cannot echo the words Christ said in Gethsemane, "not as I will, but as Thou wilt"; she cannot echo any words at all. Insofar as fury is the foundation of the poem, it threatens to rupture the walls of each stanza and to dissolve, as it finally does, into the "bleat[ing]" of incomprehension. At that moment, there is only the fluency of rage, whose true language, as the poem's conclusion attests, leaves words in its wake.

The third voice, then, finds direct language inadequate. The inadequacy is exposed by the neat dialectics, for a dialectical understanding of experience here seems to be a way of simplifying it. Underlying the dialectic, inarticulate but fulsome in its power, is the generative force of rage, an alternative voice that concludes the poem by disrupting or redefining its established meaning. Such a conclusion suggests that even irony, which, in other circumstances, we might have trusted as a mirror for the truth, is an evasion of feeling. The ironic story, no less than the one "told straight," is subject to the revisions that passion cannot contain.

If the conclusion of "I should have been too glad I see" is a readily comprehensible demonstration of the way in which rage grows louder than story until it finally submerges the latter, the conclusion of the following more troubled poem makes it necessary to observe that, although sense is to be found, it is not in the telling of the story:

> My Life had stood—a Loaded Gun—
> In Corners—till a Day
> The Owner passed—identified—
> And carried Me away—
>
> And now We roam in Sovereign Woods—
> And now We hunt the Doe—
> And every time I speak for Him—
> The Mountains straight reply—
>
> And do I smile, such cordial light
> Upon the Valley glow—
> It is as a Vesuvian face
> Had let its pleasure through—

And when at Night—Our good Day done—
I guard My Master's Head—
'Tis better than the Eider-Duck's
Deep Pillow—to have shared—

To foe of His—I'm deadly foe—
None stir the second time—
On whom I lay a Yellow Eye—
Or an emphatic Thumb—

Though I than He—may longer live
He longer must—than I—
For I have but the power to kill,
Without—the power to die—   (P 754)

I should like to offer two conventional paraphrases of the poem, which I shall then suggest are inadequate. In the first, picked up by God, the speaker becomes His marksman: the mountains resound with the echoes of her shots; those bursts of gunfire are as "cordial" as the eruption of a volcano; with the threat of more gunfire, she guards him at night, imagining her power to be total. Alternatively, if "Owner" is a term that suggests a deity, "Master" may suggest a lover (a theory prompted by the "Master" letters). In this reading, the speaker receives identity when she is carried off by the earthly lover whom she thereafter guards with murderous and possessive fury, anxious to protect him from his enemies and preferring, it seems, to watch over his bed than to share it with him; preferring, that is, violence to sexuality. But the problem with the poem is that it makes sense neither as religious allegory—the speaker's service to God does not involve the killing of the unrighteous— nor as the depiction of an erotic relationship. For either paraphrase, once it confronts the last stanza, faces its own inadequacy.

While the last stanza plays with the connections between life and death in a joke of comparative terms, those terms fail to make sense when applied literally to human beings (how could they have the power to kill without the power to die?) and make such obvious sense when applied to the inanimate gun (it goes without saying, and therefore it is unnecessary to say, that guns can kill but not die) that something further seems intended. The seepage of additional meaning, resonances of more complicated intention, infect the experience of the whole poem so that on the first reading we reject a superficial interpretation—the poem depicts neither the relationship between a man and his gun—nor one between a woman and her God or between a woman and her lover. Meaning bearing down on us and, at the same time, eluding us casts doubt on our ability to identify what we are reading, and this mystification is partly a consequence of the way in which the conceit draws attention to its own transparency. In stanza one, for example, it is unclear whether we are to imagine the speaker as gun or as person, and the revealing taint of human presence continues in stanza two, where the echoes returned by the mountain might as easily be those of a voice as of a gun. Likewise in the third stanza, the speaker's smile, however provisional, conceivably takes place on a human countenance—the Vesuvian face that admits, albeit reluctantly, of pleasure. In the next stanza, the implicit alternatives of sexuality and death are clearly human alternatives. In the next, the human parts of the body are so fused with, and completed by, the parts of the gun, that our attention is drawn to the speaker's thumb rather than to the hammer it cocks.[8]

The fusion of gun and person, force and identity, possessor and possessed defines the central problematic features of the poem as well as the central problematic dilemmas of its speaker. The central trope—life as a loaded gun belonging to someone else that, when claimed, goes off—once it is figured, still leaves many questions unanswered, the most crucial of which is: What imaginable relationship can be explained by such violence?[9] I shall begin to address these questions by suggesting that "identity" in the poem is conceived of as violence, just as life is apparently conceived of as rage. The poem is thus the speaker's acknowledgment that coming to life involves accepting the power and the inescapable burden of doing violence wherever one is and to whomever one encounters. But that interpretation, if is a true one, is also terrifying, for violence turned upon the world can be returned by it. It is to guard herself against this return that the speaker imagines herself immortal. For the most foolproof protection from violence against the self is the denial of death. Although my interpretation may sound extreme, it is prompted by the enigmatic last stanza, which makes a shambles out of any conventional interpretation of what precedes it. In the stanza, the focus shifts to the speaker's scrutiny of her own fury, and suggests, as we might have suspected, that this was the real subject after all. The speaker-gun is viewed as the agent of death and not (as the person for whom it stands would be) the object of it. Or, in other terms: fury grown larger than life disassociates itself in terror from the one who feels it and fantasizes its own immortality. The problem with the poem, then, is not that it is devoid of meaning but rather that it is overwhelmed by it (a problem exactly opposite to the one we witnessed in the definitional poems, though related to it, because both are prompted by the same retreat from both partiality and ending). Its phenomena surpass, seem larger than, their explanations. This fact suggests that any explanation will be inadequate, and it therefore draws our attention away from explanation and toward something else.

A similar distraction occurs in the following poem of anonymous authorship, believed to have been written in England around 1784:

> There was a man of double deed
> Who sowed his garden full of seed.
> When the seed began to grow
> 'Twas like a garden full of snow,
> When the snow began to melt
> 'Twas like a ship without a belt,
> When the ship began to sail
> 'Twas like a bird without a tail,
> When the bird began to fly
> 'Twas like an eagle in the sky,
> When the sky began to roar
> 'Twas like a lion at the door,
> When the door began to crack
> 'Twas like a stick across my back,
> When my back began to smart
> 'Twas like a penknife in my heart,
> And when my heart began to bleed
> 'Twas death and death and death indeed.

Although the poem employs a rigid logical structure—the pairing of life and death images, one of which generates, by association, the first term of the next pair (as "melt" suggests "ship," "sail"/"bird," "roar"/"lion," etc.)—the connections that link the images and seem to anticipate their own conclusions are themselves thrown off balance by the shock of death, for which no anticipation can prepare the speaker. Hence, as we read, our experience is not primarily one of the logical relation between incidents, for, like the speaker, we are diverted from logic by the swiftness with which it flashes by us.

In "The Man of Double Deed," as in "My Life had stood a Loaded

Gun," it is death that breaks out of the metaphor or allegory at the poem's conclusion. Metaphor and allegory collapse and give way to a more inescapable reality—death "indeed," which in the one poem is recognized as inevitable and in the other is defended against as impossible. In both poems, however, there is a rapid progression toward terror. That progression is set in motion by forces that are as incomprehensible as they are sudden, triggered in the one case by the "Owner's" appearance and, in the other, by the planting of a seed that bears not fruit but snow. The release of power—in each case destructive: power to kill, power to be killed—corresponds to and becomes no less than the speaker's identity. Who each speaker is, then, is presented strictly in terms of the force that annihilates him or by which he annihilates others. All the storytelling conventions ("This happened, then this, then this") are a thin disguise for the deeper story, which is elegantly simple in its assertion that human life gains its identity when it encounters death. Death "indeed" snaps the conventions of the ordinary and raises man to the dimensions of the hero. The real connections, the likenesses that shoot us through a dizzying sequence of events whose specific content matters less than our inability to order or perceive its shape, inform us that the only defining experience that does not admit of ambiguity is death. Putting an end to experience, death also reveals its shape. It specifies who we are. Despite Shakespeare's adage about cowards who die a thousand deaths, it is those experiences which prefigure death by imitating it that also prepare us for it. Our concern with that preparation is a partial explanation for why we read. For when we read, at least when we read novels, what we read are completed stories: stories whose characters have come in touch with their own ends, or who perceive a stopping point to incident that implies a closure akin to death.

Death makes incident finite and one can best order or assert meaning over that which has both a beginning and an end. At the moment of death, therefore, experience not only becomes knowable, it also assumes transmittable form. Commenting upon the relationship between a storyteller's power and his knowledge of a character's death, Walter Benjamin writes, "Death is the sanction of everything that the story can tell. . . . In other words, it is natural history to which [the teller's] stories refer."[10] Benjamin elaborates:

"A man who dies at the age of thirty-five . . . is at every point of his

life a man who dies at the age of thirty-five." Nothing is more dubious than this sentence—but for the sole reason that the tense is
wrong. A man . . . who died at thirty-five will appear to *remem-*
brance at every point in his life as a man who dies at the age of thirty-five. In other words, the statement that makes no sense for real
life becomes indisputable for remembered life. The nature of the
character in a novel cannot be presented any better than is done
in this statement, which says that the "meaning" of his life is revealed only in his death. . . . The novel is significant, therefore, not
because it presents someone else's fate to us, perhaps didactically,
but because this stranger's fate by virtue of the flame which con-
sumes it yields us the warmth which we never draw from our own
fate. What draws the reader to the novel is the hope of warming his
shivering life with a death he reads about.[11]

Only autobiographical novels, as Scholes and Kellogg remind us,[12] cannot find their resolution in the protagonist's death and must substitute
a stasis of insight for a stasis of action. Indeed, this is also true for the
lyric, which casts off its knowledge of remembered life, driving past and
future apart and away with the wedge of the eternal now. Thus one
crucial difference between most lyric poems and most novels is that the
former do not ordinarily yield the representation of completed lives.
Epic poems do so—Adam's expulsion from paradise is perhaps the greatest story of the first end. Narrative poems can do so—Browning's "Childe
Roland to the Dark Tower Came" not only posits an end for its protagonist, it is also obsessed by the proper interpretation of that end. But
lyric poems catch their speakers in isolated moments and off guard. Insofar as they record a history, it is not the history of a life but rather of a
moment. In fact, as the following assertions are meant to imply, the
lyric's premise of temporality bears obvious similarities to the temporal
assumptions of the poems discussed in these two chapters, though
Dickinson's exaggeration of that premise may distort it past all recognition.

Concerned neither with ends nor with beginnings, concerned with
etiologies only on occasion and sometimes, then, by chance, the context
of the experience narrated in a lyric will need to be reconstructed from
the particularities of the moment. It is its speaker's words that matter,
not her past or future. For the configuration the lyric speaker presents
is usually a static one; not because nothing happens in it but rather

because what does happen is arrested, framed, and taken out of the flux of history. One might almost go so far as to say that in lyric poems history gets sacrificed to presence, as if the two were somehow incompatible. Hence poems often begin in the middle of an action ("I struck the board and cry'd, No more") or in direct address ("Batter my heart, three person'd God"), with an injunction ("Do not go gentle into that good night") or a complaint about a specific relationship ("They flee from me that sometime did mee seek"). No matter how expansive or elaborately philosophical their implications, they frequently withhold physical geography, or if one exists, it seems shockingly limited ("I walk through the long schoolroom questioning"). Experience, then, is unitary in these worlds and it is incidental, although the incident is curiously independent of both time and place. Lyric poems insist that coherence be made of isolated moments because there is no direct experience of an alternative. They suggest, too, that meaning resides neither in historical connection nor in the connection between one temporal event and another. Meaning is consciousness carved out of the recognition of its own limitations. They insist that meaning depends upon the severing of incident from context, as if only isolation could guarantee coherence. The lyric's own presence on a page, surrounded as it is by nothing, is a graphic representation of that belief. If there is a victory in the form of the lyric—the stunning articulation of the isolated moment— despair underlies it. It is despair of the possibility of complete stories, of stories whose conclusions are known, and consequently it is despair of complete knowledge. In its glorification of the revelatory moment, the lyric makes a triumph of such despair.

To return now to "The Man of Double Deed" and "My Life had stood a Loaded Gun," with which we began, it is clear that those poems do tell stories and that the stories they tell are concerned with the way in which death confers both knowledge and power. In "The Man of Double Deed," death can be neither anticipated nor known; it can only be experienced, and before it is experienced, the life of the poem comes to a halt. In the Dickinson poem even the anticipation of death is denied the speaker, though what could put an end to violence (violence turned against the self) would also explain it. Without a foreseeable end, with the fantasy of immortality, there is also no interpretation. The poem thus plays with the idea of death as explanation and concludes by despairing of both death and explanation. Its power is a direct consequence of the explosion that hovers over the individual incident each

stanza narrates, and provides a counterstrain to it. One final, parallel
example, Marvell's "The Mower's Song," may help to illustrate how the
threat of violence (here, the fact of violence) dominates, as an obsession
dominates, and actually obscures the progressions in each stanza:

I

My Mind was once the true survey
Of all these Medows fresh and gay;
And in the greenness of the Grass
Did see its Hopes as in a Glass;
When *Juliana* came, and She
   What I do to the Grass, does to my Thoughts and Me.

II

But these, while I with Sorrow pine,
Grew more luxuriant still and fine;
That not one Blade of Grass you spy'd,
But had a Flower on either side;
When *Juliana* came, and She
   What I do to the Grass, does to my Thoughts and Me.

III

Unthankful Medows, could you so
A fellowship so true forego,
And in your gawdy May-games meet,
While I lay trodden under feet?
When *Juliana* came, and She
   What I do to the Grass, does to my Thoughts and Me.

IV

But what you in Compassion ought,
Shall now by my Revenge be wrought:
And Flow'rs, and Grass, and I and all,
Will in one common Ruine fall.
For *Juliana* comes, and She
   What I do to the Grass, does to my Thoughts and Me.

V

And thus, ye Medows, which have been
Companions of my thoughts more green,
Shall now the Heraldry become

> With which I shall adorn my Tomb;
> For *Juliana* comes, and She
> What I do to the Grass, does to my Thoughts and Me.

The refrain of Marvell's poem, like the concluding stanza of Dickinson's poem, brings the narrative up short with omnipresent and present-tense violence. It is as if conception can tolerate nothing further than violence that shifts curiously enough from past to present tense, in both poems, and defies historical connections by reversing them: "*Juliana* came" but now she "comes." In "My Life had stood a Loaded Gun," the distinction between the pluperfect and the present tense is somewhat less abrupt, but the insistence upon the recurrent present baffles progression in a similar manner: the story we first thought past tense, first thought over, cannot, does not know how to, conclude. Thus the act of annihilation that is promised and prophesied in every stanza of both poems never comes to pass or never ceases coming to pass. "None stir the second time—," but the fact that the killing must be repeated, albeit with a different object, suggests that violence is never done until life itself is done.

Different as the traditions are that shaped Marvell's and Dickinson's poems, and easy to understand as "The Mower's Song" is in comparison, the source of their magic is similar. The "Owner" in Dickinson's poem reveals no presence; all that we know of him is contained in the speaker's response. Although Juliana in "The Mower's Song" is a more conventional figure (the cruel lady of courtly love), she bears analogies to the "Owner" in that she is not so much an individual as a force: she appears precipitously, cuts down life as the mower cuts grass, disorders the natural world and transforms it into a decorative heraldry for his tomb. Though in the poem's beginning Marvell's speaker is victim rather than murderer, the fourth stanza makes clear how thoroughly "Revenge" dissolves the distinction between those terms and how ineffective either posture is against the mysterious otherness of the world. For threaten as he may, Juliana still "comes," and murder as Dickinson's speaker will, she is nonetheless "Without—the power to die—." The real otherness, then, in both poems (represented by Juliana in one and by the "Owner" in the other) is the world, in whose service one engages one's powers. It is against the world or for it (the distinction barely seems to matter) that one does battle, a world whose identity is, at best, shadowy and is, at most, a projection of the force against which, or for which, one fights, and whose power is finally inexorable.

"My Life had stood a Loaded Gun," like "The Mower's Song" and "The Man of Double Deed," is a story that is both without an ending and cognizant of where that ending lies. Held up against the world's otherness and deriving identity in its service, the meaning of the speaker's experience remains hidden in the future of its defeat. The relationship between meaning and death, ending and interpretation—the hero who will not die in Dickinson's poem, and the one who will not stay dead in Marvell's—reminds us of Freud's assertion that the person asleep never dreams of his own death. For the speaker in these poems, as for Freud's dreamer, death is a reality that escapes completion. Huger than life and eventually overtaking it, it lurks meantime in the underlying rhythm of all action.

III

When death is the center to which "Each Life Converges" (P 680), the semiotic distractions it creates will be discernible below the surface of the poem's meaning and will erupt only at its conclusion, as we have seen in "My Life had stood a Loaded Gun." There death's static is perceived as an undercurrent, for the cause of the static is precisely death's failure to manifest itself. Always threatening exposure, it ceases to counter the signs of life only at that moment when it overwhelms them. With this explanation in mind, we can perhaps better understand why the apparent sense of "My Life had stood a Loaded Gun" is threatened by resonances or undertones that are not entirely audible. When, however, the situation is reversed so that death is viewed directly as so omnipresent and continuous a force that it suffers a rupture only brief enough to admit life, the disruptions will themselves break into the center of the space that has been cleared for them. "Human life," Geoffrey Hartman writes in "The Voice of the Shuttle," ". . . is an indeterminate middle between overspecified poles always threatening to collapse it. The poles may be birth and death, father and mother, mother and wife, love and judgment, heaven and earth, first things and last things. Art narrates that middle region and charts it like a purgatory, for only if it exists can life exist."[13] In the following poem, which provides a clear demonstration of Hartman's insight and an important definition of those poems I shall discuss in this section, the speaker is that middle term whose presence pushes eternity and immortality apart and, by so doing, creates the space of life:

Behind Me—dips Eternity—
Before Me—Immortality—
Myself—the Term between—
Death but the Drift of Eastern Gray,
Dissolving into Dawn away,
Before the West begin—

'Tis Kingdoms—afterward—they say—
In perfect—pauseless Monarchy—
Whose Prince—is Son of None—
Himself—His Dateless Dynasty—
Himself—Himself diversify—
In Duplicate divine—

'Tis Miracle before Me—then—
'Tis Miracle behind—between—
A Crescent in the Sea—
With Midnight to the North of Her—
And Midnight to the South of Her—
And Maelstrom—in the Sky— (P 721)

"Eternity" and "Immortality" are literally out of this world. Free of
both beginning and end ("Dateless") and unbroken by event ("pauseless"), they escape real characterization or comprehension. "Midnight"
echoes "Midnight," "Miracle" "Miracle"; even dawn suggests death, so
closely does it resemble twilight. Meaning stuck in the same groove becomes nonsense. Divinity duplicated is thus nothing but an absence, our
world drained of all its meaning. For while the second stanza, which
elaborates on "Immortality," might at first be mistaken for a reverential
expression of dogma, the vacancy of the internal rhyme ("Son of
None—") and the insistence on establishing these facts as suspect ("they
say—") are clear indications of scorn. Were Christ humanly fathered, we
might recognize Him. But perfection rules out both recognition and discrete identity. "Eternity" and "Immortality" seem like mirrors hung on
opposite walls, with barely anything between. Except, as the last stanza
insists, there is something between, which is the speaker's presence. Her
existence disrupts order, is a movement rising out of the sea, shot upward, finally, in chaos ("Maelstrom—in the Sky—"). As Charles Anderson
notes in his provocative comment on the poem, the east-west axis of
eternity-immortality is entirely different from the referential poles of the

speaker's life.[14] In the concluding stanza, the switch in pronouns from the first to the third person suggests that even the speaker's vision of her own life has been redefined and objectified. As she presses against the poles of eternity and immortality with the force of life's disorder, we know that the price of her collapse, the disappearance of the middle term, is not only personal extinction but the omission of life itself, leaving mirrors that reflect the diversity of nothing.

The disruption in the poem, then, is literally the story the speaker has to tell about life. What can be chronicled, what, in other words, has both beginning and end, also has identity. But while the speaker in "My Life had stood a Loaded Gun" shies away from the knowledge that her story has an end (because she equates its end with her own annihilation), this speaker turns her attention elsewhere; here value is wedded to the fact of action as it can be seen to survive its origins and to shake off or, at any rate, stall, its consequences. Value is disruption and disorder: it lies in the volatile middle term.

It must by now be clear that the poems about which I have been speaking enact a tug of war between life and death. The equanimity with which the speaker in "Behind Me dips Eternity" holds at bay the surrounding forces that converge on her is, however, rare. Indeed, a poem like "Behind Me dips Eternity" is marked by its competence in managing the upstart forces of both life and death; even "Maelstrom—in the Sky—," as presented to us, is not especially threatening. But the quiescence of the middle term vanishes when we see it no longer in a definitional context, but now in active engagement with those forces that threaten its existence. In the following two poems, life is also represented as a disruption of stasis. But the disruption here seems more like an outbreak around which control keeps trying, unsuccessfully, to close:

> I tie my Hat—I crease my Shawl—
> Life's little duties do—precisely—
> As the very least
> Were infinite—to me—
>
> I put new Blossoms in the Glass—
> And throw the old—away—
> I push a petal from my Gown
> That anchored there—I weigh
> The time 'twill be till six o'clock

> I have so much to do—
> And yet—Existence—some way back—
> Stopped—struck—my ticking—through—
> We cannot put Ourself away
> As a completed Man
> Or Woman—When the Errand's done
> We came to Flesh—upon—
> There may be—Miles on Miles of Nought—
> Of Action—sicker far—
> To simulate—is stinging work—
> To cover what we are
> From Science—and from Surgery—
> Too Telescopic Eyes
> To bear on us unshaded—
> For their—sake—not for Ours—
> 'Twould start them—
> We—could tremble—
> But since we got a Bomb—
> And held it in our Bosom—
> Nay—Hold it—it is calm—
>
> Therefore—we do life's labor—
> Though life's Reward—be done—
> With scrupulous exactness—
> To hold our Senses—on— (P 443)

Here, in two places, meaning disrupts both vacuous action and the sententia in which such action takes refuge: first, in the lines acknowledging that, if one were to admit it, life would be seen to have come to a dead halt:

> And yet—Existence—some way back—
> Stopped—struck—my ticking—through—

and second, in the suppositional statement that plays with the possibility of exploding the "Bomb [be]got[ten]" by the speaker's fury at life's loss of meaning:

> We—could tremble—
> But since we got a Bomb—
> And held it in our Bosom—
> Nay—Hold it—it is calm—

but steadies itself ("Nay—Hold it—"), rejecting such an explosion. For in order to "hold [her] Senses—on—" course or, more simply, "on" (intact), she thinks fury must tolerate repression.

From its similarity to other Dickinson poems in which the speaker's loss of love is not accompanied by the loss of her life, we can infer that "the Errand" she "came to Flesh—upon—" is both incarnation and carnal destination, the general effort to wrest meaning from experience and the more particular effort to gratify the desires of the flesh. The ticking of existence, the heart, stops not because death overtakes it, but rather because vengeance at the inevitability of loss overtakes it, transforming it into a bomb, as love suffers a metamorphosis into fury. Though the speaker asserts that there is nothing to help and everything to hide, that science and surgery would be "start[led]" by this transformation, it is for purposes of self-protection that calm is maintained, as the last stanza makes eloquently clear. For fury let loose would explode the very reason of the poem: it would blast holes in reason as the lines I have pointed to blast holes in the narrative. Here again, then, life is represented as fury coming to terms with sexuality, and both are subject to the efforts of repression.

If "I tie my Hat—I crease my Shawl" makes an oblique acknowledgment of sexuality and its loss, the following poem rises to the occasion of explicit statement and finally to heresy, and the consequence is not rage but rather ecstasy. Although its catechism is one of renunciation, we must scrutinize the poem carefully to see how renunciation can be so resonant with the presence of what has been given up:

> I cannot live with You—
> It would be Life—
> And Life is over there—
> Behind the Shelf
>
> The Sexton keeps the Key to—
> Putting up
> Our Life—His Porcelain—
> Like a Cup—
>
> Discarded of the Housewife—
> Quaint—or Broke—
> A newer Sevres pleases—
> Old Ones crack—

I could not die—with You—
For One must wait
To shut the Other's Gaze down—
You—could not—

And I—Could I stand by
And see You—freeze—
Without my Right of Frost—
Death's privilege?

Nor could I rise—with You—
Because Your Face
Would put out Jesus'—
That New Grace

Glow plain—and foreign
On my homesick Eye—
Except that You than He
Shone closer by—

They'd judge Us—How—
For You—served Heaven—You know,
Or sought to—
I could not—

Because You saturated Sight
And I had no more Eyes
For sordid excellence
As Paradise

And were You lost, I would be—
Though My Name
Rang loudest
On the Heavenly fame—

And were You—saved—
And I—condemned to be
Where You were not—
That self—were Hell to Me—

So We must meet apart—
You there—I—here—

> With just the Door ajar
> That Oceans are—and Prayer—
> And that White Sustenance—
> Despair—   (P 640)

With the exception of the second and third stanzas, which digress both
from the form of assertion established elsewhere and from the patterned
recital of facts, the poem is structured as a list of criteria that would
make union impossible. In most stanzas we hear two voices: one that
renounces the earthly lover and another that explains the need for renunciation, the foremost explanation being the imminence of a divine rival.
But the comparison between earthly and divine, and the rhythm of statement and counterstatement established by the pairing, is broken into by
the even stronger, more subversive force of sexual energy. The energy is,
in part, revealed in the colloquial speech rhythms that disrupt the more
formal and laconic litany of renunciation (I cannot live with You—/It
would be Life—) in order to qualify it ("And I—Could I stand by/And
see You—freeze—/Without my Right of Frost—"). The intimacy of
address, with its tone of patient explanation and its scrupulous concern
for accuracy ("For You—served Heaven—You know,/Or sought to—"),
warms to its subject and becomes impassioned by it in its testimony of
what finally keeps the lovers apart.

Interestingly enough, what prohibits union seems to be the fact that
it has already occurred. The injunction, then, cannot be to avoid union
but must be rather to guard against its repetition. For although "Because
Your Face/Would put out Jesus'—" seems suppositional, two stanzas
later the event is echoed, explained, and located not in the future at all,
but rather in the past:

> Because You saturated Sight—
> And I had no more Eyes
> For sordid excellence
> As Paradise

The lines here are rich with the pride of acknowledged sexuality, and in
their acknowledgment of supremacy they demote paradise from its conventionally unrivaled estate. The speaker is not only saying "I had no
more eyes for *such* sordid excellence *as* Paradise," but also, more radically, "I had no more eyes *to see* sordid excellence *as* Paradise." The

lover, in this latter interpretation, not only occupies vision but also, apparently, purifies it. Thus, while we are expecting the notion of paradise to be rivaled by love, we are not expecting it to be revised by it, and the revision constitutes much of the power of the lines. A similar transformation occurs two stanzas later where we expect to hear:

> And were You—saved—
> And I—condemned to be
> . . . [In] Hell

and what we hear instead is a new definition of Hell prompted not by God's judgment but rather by the lover's absence, and half-echoing Milton's "Myself am Hell":

> And were You—saved—
> And I condemned to be
> Where You were not—
> That self—were Hell to Me—

To return to the earlier stanza, even the lover's excellence is seen as sordid because it is excessive. Indeed, it is precisely the absoluteness of the lover's excellence, his uncontested supremacy, against which the denomination "sordid" makes its puritanical outcry. For the excess of pleasure is the real force that drives the two lovers apart, notwithstanding the more superficial reasons reiterated by the closing stanzas, which are fashioned around all the external prohibitions against union: the difference in age (implied by the fifth and sixth stanzas), in religious status (implied by the eighth and eleventh stanzas), etc. Although the poem attempts to recover its composure, the stanzas I have spoken about remain too dazzling to be dismissed as containing just a number of good reasons for the lovers' separation. Even their syntactic introductions ("Because Your Face/Would put out Jesus'—," "Because You saturated Sight—"), with their direct announcement of explanation and their implicit accompaniment of passion, insist we consider their centrality.

Despite the "Door ajar," which leaves a distance commutable only by ocean or prayer, and which we might suppose would produce tension, there is a curious quiet to the concluding lines, and two extra lines to the stanza that seem to insist on the enlarging space between the two lovers. The resolution of tension is a consequence of the fact that the renunciation the speaker has predicted as inevitable has been accomplished. The sustenance she now lives on (she calls it "Despair—," but perhaps it is memory drained of detail) is "White" because it has been purified of presence and sexuality. The rhythms of "Oceans" and "Prayer" are calm, all the passion of life has slowed to them. Thus, while the voice of implicit sexuality is quelled utterly in the last stanza, the poem's conclusion offers a resolution, not of the passion, for which there is no resolution, but rather of the less problematic series of statements and counterstatements that have served to divert speaker and reader from passion's verbal enactment throughout the poem.

"To lose what we never owned might seem an eccentric Bereavement but Presumption has its Affliction as actually as Claim—," Dickinson wrote in L 429. But loss also legitimates the desire for possession by freeing desire from all illusion that its object will be granted, and a speaker then affirms her absolute claim to what has absolutely been denied her. As I suggested in the Introduction, in such instances the bodily absence of both loss and immortality associates the two states as if in an identity, and utterance is charged with the task of the pouring of form into what has no form, shape into the hollows of absence. In the service of the reconstruction, memory can be so delusively persuasive that, like the speaker in the following poem, we are swayed into confusing it with actual presence:

> I live with Him—I see His face—
> I go no more away
> For Visiter—or Sundown—
> Death's single privacy
>
> The Only One—forestalling Mine—
> And that—by Right that He
> Presents a Claim invisible—
> No Wedlock—granted Me—
>
> I live with Him—I hear His Voice—
> I stand alive—Today—
> To witness to the Certainty
> Of Immortality—
>
> Taught Me—by Time—the lower Way—
> Conviction—Every day—
> That Life like This—is stopless—
> Be Judgment—what it may—   (P 463)

There is something incantatory about the poem's tone, which suggests that its meaning is positive, that immortality has been discovered in the presence of the earthly lover. But what makes the tone sound so positive is also what makes it sound suspicious. To "see His face—," to "hear His Voice—" is to know the lover by his absence, through memory or longing rather than in fact, for the insistent affirmations (his voice, his face) offer proofs that compensate in the absence of the whole. And as if to reveal the pain of such a memory, its perpetuity is designated by the word "stopless—," familiar to us from "It was not Death for I stood up," and customarily used by Dickinson to indicate despair. The poem, then, is structured to produce a reversal of what it first leads us to expect, and only on a second reading do we really see what is being said.

In the first stanza, we are told that the speaker retreats with the memory of her absent lover in otherwise perfect isolation for, in context, "I live with Him—I see His face—" is the cry of vision estranged from presence. In the second stanza, the pronoun reference switches from the lover to death. Only death, the second stanza informs us, can exact a more imperious solitude; its demand is the only one powerful enough to "forestall" the speaker's vision by canceling her life. But the speaker's life, once canceled by the absence of the earthly lover, leaves little more for death to negate. Sufficient proof of endlessness, loss is the only certainty, the unconditional "given" of human existence. Any other judgment, even death itself, as the grammar of the last stanza reminds us, seems weak as an untested hypothesis. And, if proved, redundant.

"For fear of which hear this thou age unbred," Shakespeare wrote, flaunting the mortality of the friend. Dickinson, acquainted with a more harrowing vision of mortality, one whose consequences were inevitably only personal, faced time with less bravado. If "I tie my Hat I crease my Shawl," "I cannot live with You," and "I live with Him I see His face" all create worlds where vacancy postdates meaning, in the latter poems the speaker insists on its reconstruction. In this case, reconstruction is tantamount to memory—the invention of presence where not to have it would leave the world absent even of pain. The speaker here will not reduce the world to nothing. Only death can relieve the world of meaning; only death can wipe it clean like a slate. And after death? In another one of Dickinson's poems the speaker, anticipating a meeting with God, can only say half drolly and half in disappointment, "Savior—I've seen the face—before!" (P 461).

IV

Holding to one's course, and the evenness of rhythm therein implied, might be defined as the inability to feel, the pulse that refuses to quicken, or so Dickinson suggests in the following poem:

> Through the strait pass of suffering—
> The Martyrs—even—trod.
> Their feet—upon Temptation—
> Their faces—upon God—
>
> A stately—shriven—Company—
> Convulsion—playing round—
> Harmless—as streaks of Meteor—
> Upon a Planet's Bond—
>
> Their faith—the everlasting troth—
> Their Expectation—fair—
> The Needle—to the North Degree—
> Wades—so—thro' polar Air!   (P 792)

Convulsion is "Harmless," however, only when not experienced. But what constitutes convulsion? What elements of sexuality and death and in what relationship? For it is these elements in combination that characterize every poem I have spoken about in this chapter. Only the martyrs in the above poem, seemingly not subject to the force of sexuality, give the illusion of escaping the force of death, for when sexuality is not even there to be overcome, life assumes death's shape. In poems other than this one, however, a choice has been made against sexuality and for death. The consequence of the choice, since it is an unwilling one, is rage that is speechless ("I should have been too glad I see") or subverted by ecstasy ("I cannot live with You") or explicitly repressed ("I tie my Hat I crease my Shawl"), or that escapes repression by protest ("I live with Him I see His face") or defines life as disorder ("Behind Me dips Eternity"), or that erupts openly into violence ("My Life had stood a Loaded Gun").

Insofar as rage constitutes a tear in the established fabric of the narrative, it exists in relation to that narrative very much as Todorov describes the supernatural's relationship to the narrative and with the same important "coincidence": "We see, finally, how the social and the literary functions coincide: in both cases, we are concerned with a transgression of the law. Whether it is in social life or in narrative, the intervention of the supernatural element always constitutes a break in the system of pre-established rules, and in doing so finds its justification."[15] Like the supernatural, rage, too, is a transgression of the social, of the agreed-upon laws that ritualize life and sometimes render it immobile. Both contain outbreaks of sexuality that would not be sanctioned in the main-stream of the narrative or in the mainstream of social action out of which it is woven. "Sexual excesses will be more readily accepted by any censor if they are attributed to the devil," Todorov writes,[16] and indeed the same claim might be made about the scapegoat function of rage. For rage is a kind of devil that bears the burden of all our disapprobation: it is that which, no less than primitive sexuality, we are socialized out of. And significantly it is what, when it overtakes us, we make responsible for all our expressions of will and desire. As Kent reminds us in *Lear*, "Anger hath a privilege." Rage is the great disclaimer, the feeling that puts us beyond ourselves, and in so doing puts us in touch with all the social and private dictates that vie against one another for the dominance of the self. Recognition becomes sanction at precisely that moment when the alternative is seen in its death-dealing context: existence "struck-through" and "stopped." At such a moment, speech itself is a protest against the status quo. The speaker elects words rather than silence, mediation rather than stasis, disruption rather than death.

Ultimately, of course, election is complicated by inadequate alterna-tives. In one of Dickinson's central utterances, the acknowledgment of inadequacy, of the poverty of both literal and imaginative terms, leads the speaker to a despair rich with the sense of life pressing against its own limitations:

> Title divine—is mine!
> The Wife—without the Sign!
> Acute Degree—conferred on me—
> Empress of Calvary!
> Royal—all but the Crown!
> Betrothed—without the swoon
> God sends us Women—
> When you—hold—Garnet to Garnet—
> Gold—to Gold—
> Born—Bridalled—Shrouded—
> In a Day—

> Tri Victory—
> "My Husband"—women say—
> Stroking the Melody—
> Is *this*—the way?   (P 1072)

My reading of the poem is hypothetical by default, for its syntax alone, not to mention the elliptical progressions and the rapid transformation of pronouns, insists upon respect for its difficulty. What we can ascertain is that the speaker is comparing the life of the heavenly bride to that of the earthly one. The woman exalted in the first half of the poem is royal by virtue of what she does not have. Without the sign or ring legitimating marriage and without the swoon of sexuality, this woman, seemingly self-elected, is dangerously close to Plath's "Lady Lazarus," who will also insist upon "Acute Degree—" and who will carry the claim of suffering one step further into hyperbole than Calvary. This miracle—a woman without the swoon, divine by virtue of its absence—makes us hunger for a more generous world where salvation is not had at the expense of life. It is the other world we think we are getting when we read of "the swoon/God sends us Women—/When you—hold—Garnet to Garnet—/Gold—to Gold—." But the transition is strangely enough no transition; deprivation is here not absent, it is simply of another order. "When you—hold—Garnet to Garnet—/Gold—to Gold—" (in the secular context of the earthly wedding ceremony), what you get is death ("Born—Bridalled—Shrouded—/In a Day—"). The shift in pronouns is a shift to the colloquial "you," almost as if in talking implicitly about sexuality the speaker had to cast attribution as far from herself as possible. But in the very process of distinguishing herself from the wealth of the earthly alternative, she temporarily allies herself with it, with the swoon "God sends us Women—." In the fusion and confusion of these lines, both options funnel to death, the contraction of the self into its own ashes. For the birth of the wife becomes the death of the woman. Upon such sacrifices, the gods themselves throw incense. The problem is that both alternatives require sacrifice.

Between the nothing that is the self and the nothing to which the self gets reduced when it capitulates to another, we see our options clearly. While it is true that the jewels in the poem suggest the blessing of the earthly wife, the lines, coming as they do in the middle of the poem (as a manifestation of its transition from divine to earthly), are a half-implied metaphor for the necessary complement of divine and earthly wife, for each by herself is inadequate. Thus although the lines tell us that garnet is held to garnet and gold to gold (each alternative able to assess only itself), the proximity of the lines requires us to see the colors (and the choices they represent) held against each other, as if the speaker's vision of impossibility momentarily enabled its transcendence.

"Stroking the Melody—" is perhaps a metaphor for the very impossibilities delimited by the poem. For the need to get a hold on sound, to imbue it with physical dimensions, reminds us that we have a metaphoric world to console us for the impoverishment of the physical world. Like Lear's desire to "sweeten the imagination" or to wipe the hand "of mortality," Dickinson's phrase suggests that simultaneous perception of loss and compensation that grips the mind at such moments of imaginative invention, as, in the process of calling wishes into being, the speaker inevitably acknowledges their status as wishes, not subject to fulfillment in reality. If only one could "sweeten the imagination" or "Strok[e] the Melody." So utterance grows out of desperation and registers violence at its fact.

Yet options exist because we must take them. We cannot, as Sartre pointed out, not choose. This recognition is the moment the poem records. For the speaker, from the vantage of Calvary, looks enviously at the earthly alternative and finds that it is nothing. Previously she thought she could imitate in name, if nothing else, the title of the earthly wife. Now it is apparent that the imitation is purposeless. She could not have it if she wanted it, and if she had it, she sees now that she would not want it. Her title, then, like the earthly wife's, is empty, the "Melody—" sought after but finally strained once it is acknowledged that any possession is by itself inadequate.

The problem of otherness perceived as death; the problem of otherness for lack of which there is death: the alternatives in these poems are stark ones. Yet the poems themselves are not stark, are, in fact, loaded with energy that is, as I have been suggesting, close to explosive. And it is the energy that needs accounting for, fed as it is by the fuel of sexuality on the one hand, and death on the other, by that combustible that ignites into rage. In the poems presence seems manifested *as* rage and, in particular, as rage at all that is temporal, all that has a history whose requirement is sacrifice and choice. If narrative is that thing which carries a story to its conclusion, presence disrupts the continuity of narrative by holding its moments apart so that its outrageous demands relax their grip on the speaker, as she scrutinizes at leisure and rejects at will the alternatives to which she must eventually capitulate, and this is quite different from the passive protest against temporality as we observed it in the definitional poems. We might say that here protest requires rage because only rage can provide a sufficient stronghold against each of the two terms that threaten to reclaim the speaker. Voice at cross-purposes with conflicting forces, coherence purchased at the expense of continuity, is a central phenomenon in all lyric poems, as I suggested earlier. What is important about the Dickinson poems that I have discussed is that we see the dynamics of this ordinarily hidden triad more explicitly and hence with greater clarity.

It is a commonplace, albeit a sophisticated one, that speech in poems exists across time and space, that a poem never happened or that it happens every time it is read. The commonplace becomes important when we acknowledge its consequences for annihilating process, for Yeats's vision of Byzantium or Keats's of the Grecian Urn. Yet these latter poems are conscious gestures, controlled rejections of the world replaced by the artful vision. The rejection of process is neither as conscious nor as stable in the Dickinson poems I have discussed. True, the world is envisioned as a dead-end, eternity and immortality, for all practical purposes, one and the same. Yet presence or voice breaks into and disrupts the dreaded sequence of moments that follow so rapidly on one another that their very movement blurs to the illusion of stasis. Voice cannot be in a poem except in contradistinction to action. Voice gives way, exhausts itself, at the recognition that it cannot make a difference, that it cannot *be*, except removed from time, also static. So prose wears a poem's guise at last.

If these poems counsel that we must return to what kills us, they also console us by revealing that reading, no less than speaking, offers us a reprieve. For when we read, we are no longer engaged in the world of action: we have set aside those concerns that drive us, willingly or not, to shape our own ends. Like the speaker in the poems, we have agreed that action requires reprieve—because it hurries by, fails to take adequate account of the self entangled in the web of its own inevitabilities. Voice (or as I have been calling it, presence) breaks through the linear sequence of events, disrupts it, offers a temporary escape by refusing the only alternatives, alternatives that are, at the same time, inadequate ones. Yet the temporary escape that is really no more or less than presence afforded the provisions that guarantee its existence—unbounded by event, free of both past and future—suffices, and in the next chapter we shall see how poems take the escape from temporality as their explicit subject (as they have not done in the utterances discussed in these last two chapters) and dare to dream themselves into the structure of the defiant death excursions.

We cannot change the story of our lives. We cannot undo or do again, and if we could, we would not always do better. Even the future takes its shape beyond us. All that we have to make good on is the space of the present. Freud suggested that to be in possession of a story is somehow to be reconciled to it. But no knowledge is sufficient to permit us to forgive the exigencies of a world whose demand for sacrifice is absolute. And, as comedy teaches, without forgiveness, there is no reconciliation. It is not knowledge that saves us but rather the recognition that salvation is a luxury our lives will not purchase. Salvation might mean that our lives could be shaped with the coherence of written stories, well authored and progressing with deliberation toward the promised end. In lieu of this, we accept the space left vacant by the abandoned idea of salvation. Like Keats's "Negative Capability," this space is liberated from the strictures of certainty, closure, and conclusion, all those inevitable first laws of action. Presence occurs at the moment when the self absents itself from the flow of action because comprehension of it requires a slowing and temporary halt of the momentum that, blurring past, present, and future, renders them indistinguishable. These occasions of presence gain the self the only immortality it will ever know, for in a very real sense they lie outside of time and do not "count" in (are not counted by) it. Thus, the absence of consequence that we might once have greeted with despair, we come finally to understand as a consolation. At a distance from experience, presence comes to know its own mind. It shakes off the imperatives of past and future, self and other, sexuality and death, by learning its responses to them and by learning, too, that action, however inexorable, cannot do away with response. Presence then is action's corollary. It is action's "other," and its wisdom consists in what it comes to know of experience once it has been freed of the compulsion for consequence. Purified of event, presence summons up all that is representative of untempered vision, what Yeats called "the foul rag-and-bone shop of the heart."

Yet though severed from experience, presence remains in touch with experience's dilemmas and in touch, too, with the fact that it must inevitably vacate its privileged position and rejoin the stream of action.

As we shall see, even in the proleptic utterances, the speaker's freedom from this world prescribes the limits that return her to it. The hope is that once the self is returned to event, it will know better what to do in it. The poem is like a breathing space, a necessary "time out." The aside to oneself, the soliloquy to an audience, the rush of adrenalin in the actor the moment before the play begins, or simply the man alone pausing before his options—these are analogies. Ultimately, of course, the world will not wait. It catches the speaker up in its momentum again and exerts its authority to insist he make choices. As I have been suggesting, in Dickinson's poems, if choice involves the resolution of conflict, rage represents the refusal to choose: the splitting of impossible infinitives. Vitalized by this refusal, presence meets conflict head-on. Heroic in its "power to kill,/Without—the power to die—," presence is not yet weakened by the realization that immortality is an illusion. In its dissociation from action, its repudiation of necessity, lies strength, a redemptive counter to the dutiful complicity that characterizes our lives.

III

Et in Arcadia Ego
REPRESENTATION, DEATH,
AND THE PROBLEM OF BOUNDARY

The events of the unconscious are timeless, that is, they are not ordered in time, are not changed by the passage of time, have no relation whatever to time.
   —Sigmund Freud

. . . the fact is that consciousness deteriorates as the result of any cerebral shock. Merely to faint is to annihilate it. How then is it possible to believe that the spirit survives the death of the body?
   —Marcel Proust

THE PROBLEM of boundaries is integral to some of our most profound concerns. What is the relationship between self and other, interior and exterior, literal and figural, past and present, time and timelessness? Were they not so crucial these questions would be pedestrian, and indeed how we answer them, whether we are able to answer them, is often an indication of the way in which we lead our lives. Jean Starobinski has recently pointed out that the connection we often make between history or past and interiority or depth is seductive precisely because it avoids the acknowledgment that some boundaries (in this case the one between past and present) render experience irrecoverable: "Making the most remote past coefficient to our most intimate depth is a way of refusing loss and separation, of preserving, in the crammed plenum we imagine history to be, every moment spent along the way. . . . To say that the individual constructed himself through his history is to say that the

91

latter is cumulatively present in him and that even as it was elapsing, it was becoming internal structure."[1] Such a conception may be regarded as a way of mediating between the absolute severance of past and present and their absolute fusion. For if the past is "inside us" rather than attending us, it is no longer necessarily subject to our conscious repossession. To be experienced again it must be re-presented. The past can be conceived, then, as having a diachronic progression that, once it comes into being, assumes synchronic structure. Such a conception both frees the self for future action by asserting that the past is safely contained behind or below the present, and simultaneously binds it by the selfsame fact of that containment. Like it or not, boundaries are not so easy to establish. While we frequently construe past and present by wedging a boundary between the parameters of each, as often in our conception of present and future, we hope to annihilate the severity of such boundaries, for could this be finessed, the present might be relieved of the indeterminacy that awaits it, and simultaneously gifted by the exhilarations of desired change.

I raise these issues in order to provide a context for, as well as to suggest the preliminary complexity of, characteristic problems of temporal boundary in Dickinson's poems. The most eschatological indication of boundary or division is, of course, death, and it is hence no accident that Dickinson's utterances hover around this subject with as much perseverance as the fly in one of her more noted poems. Indeed we might regard death as a special instance of the problem of boundary, representing the ultimate division, the extreme case, the infuriating challenge to a dream of synchrony. On the border of conception, the limits of experience, death both epitomizes the problem of boundary and offers itself as its severest manifestation. It is in this context that we shall examine Dickinson's death utterances, asking how the straying of a poem across impossible limits leads inevitably to the collapse of other boundaries, namely those that set themselves up as walls between figure and thing figured, between literal meanings and metaphoric ones. For if the problem Starobinski discusses may be construed as one of constructing boundaries, in Dickinson's death utterances, on which this chapter will focus, the problem is often one of destroying them. In the following pages, however, we shall see that the relationship between construction and destruction is a complex one—objects slip from one side of a line to another with the ease of a thought falling out of consciousness and rising back into it. And, as with consciousness, whose goal is to enlarge its own area of being, so with the life-space occupied by a poem that pushes with all its might against the line of death, in the hopes that it can, by however scant measure, enlarge its territory.

In part 2 of this chapter I shall examine poems in which the question "Is death literal or figural?" does not admit of a simple or certain answer, in which death is neither a clearly phenomenological fact nor a clearly psychic phenomenon. In such instances we will see that it is difficult to distinguish between figure and thing figured because of their complex relationship to each other. In part 3 I shall turn briefly to poems that purport actually to mark the boundary between life and death and shall look, in conclusion, at those poems that trespass beyond it. I shall tentatively suppose that fusions between the literal and the figural (often represented in Dickinson's poems in terms of death and despair) are related to, and perhaps generative of, the temporal fusions that exist in larger scale in those poems where it is not clear on which side of the grave the speaker's utterance takes place. Finally, in examining these poems I shall want to ask how such fusions obscure the fact of death, blur its edges so that its future threat is undercut by the implicit assertion of its presence or prefigurement, and alternately to ask whether this prefigurement, ultimately subverted, throws death's outlines into sharper relief precisely by its distance from what, in the end, can only be intimated.

II

In many of Dickinson's poems, the relationship between death and despair is complex, not only because one may be the generative occasion for the other, but also and more significantly, because one is liable to be confused with the other. Thus in the following poem, while it is clear enough that the speaker has been reprieved from literal death, the psychic turmoil of its anticipation—or, in simple terms, the torture—so overwhelms the significance of what it anticipates that we are thrown off balance and can no longer specify the shape of the poem's predicament. Such a perplexity is acknowledged by the speaker herself, as the final question of the poem testifies:

> 'Twas like a Maelstrom, with a notch,
> That nearer, every Day,
> Kept narrowing its boiling Wheel
> Until the Agony

Toyed coolly with the final inch
Of your delirious Hem—
And you dropt, lost,
When something broke—
And let you from a Dream—

As if a Goblin with a Gauge—
Kept measuring the Hours—
Until you felt your Second
Weigh, helpless, in his Paws—

And not a Sinew—stirred—could help,
And sense was setting numb—
When God—remembered—and the Fiend
Let go, then, Overcome—

As if your Sentence stood—pronounced—
And you were frozen led
From Dungeon's luxury of Doubt
To Gibbets, and the Dead—

And when the Film had stitched your eyes
A Creature gasped "Reprieve"!
Which Anguish was the utterest—then—
To perish, or to live?   (P 414)

The anonymous creature who in the final analogy orders the halting of
the death process seems, like the speaker, to be wrought to the breaking
point; he is nothing akin to the demons who in calm "Toy coolly,"
practically, with the victim. Nor is he akin to the God whose calm borders on indifference. He seems rather to mediate between the two, as
if only mediation could distinguish them. In fact it is not insignificant
that the power which orders the reprieve should be of uncertain source,
for the affliction is of uncertain source, and that uncertainty is reflected
in the poem's diction, which rocks back and forth from one connotative
sphere to another, as unsettled in its vocabulary for the experience as it
in the experience itself. This lack of clarity is illustrated in the initial
image of the whirlpool. While it steers in the speaker's direction, we note
that the "boiling Wheel" and the "notch" are both parts of the same cosmic machine whose complete shape is blanked out. As in a dream (and
perhaps it is the dream feeling in the first stanza that prompts the

explicit acknowledgment of dream in the next) the synecdochic distortion that isolates and magnifies is frightening precisely because it lacks a context. Disjoint, the only parts that can be seen are vengeful, annihilative. In stanza two the speaker is held upside down ("delirious") just perceptibly by the hem of her clothes, remaining only marginally in existence. What "breaks" in the stanza subsequently are the connections to that existence, and the speaker is delivered from the dream of this death, but delivered into what is unclear.

In the next four stanzas, the attempt to recapitulate a story whose meaning the speaker still does not know is laden with confusions of the earlier rendition. The impulse to tell and retell the same story has a quality of hysteria to it, for the implicit belief that to tell the story over will insure getting it straight is proved wrong. In the final lines the poem's focus shifts from the anticipation of death to a question about its status. If life is "like a Maelstrom, with a notch," and if what is being measured is human endurance, then "To perish" would at least end it. But the poem concludes, as it has been borne along, by the waves of its own exhaustion at the pervasiveness of psychic distress. The speaker may have been rescued from actual death but she seems as a consequence condemned to suffer the same torture to whose stages the poem's stanzas, we would have thought, promised her a terminal point.

While "'Twas like a Maelstrom with a notch" explores the border between life and death—its most articulate denomination of that border contained in the harrowing image of the eyes almost "stitched" permanently—it also raises the question of whether death is a metaphor for the torture or whether the torture is only a prelude to death. Insofar as the poem's final question relocates its subject or, at any rate, calls it into question, we not only ask with the speaker which anguish is most extreme, we also question our prior understanding of the generative experience for the representation. The entire poem, beginning with the second word, understood as a series of analogies by necessity, casts its subject into doubt. The fact of death and the psychic anguish that anticipates it are really no longer separate. In effectively annihilating the boundary between the two, Dickinson forces us to transcend a line that we know, in reality, it is impossible to transcend. With this verbal fusion she perhaps harbors the illusion that she has gained knowledge of what lies over the border. For an implicit, if secondary, assumption of the poem is that the unsurpassable psychic anguish will guarantee her safe or, at any rate, unsurprised passage to death.

If actual death can best be conjured by descriptions of acute pain, Dickinson frequently reverses the representational fusion by summoning psychic anguish in the explicit terms of death and burial:

> I felt a Funeral, in my Brain,
> And Mourners to and fro
> Kept treading—treading—till it seemed
> That Sense was breaking through—
>
> And when they all were seated,
> A Service, like a Drum—
> Kept beating—beating—till I thought
> My Mind was going numb—
>
> And then I heard them lift a Box
> And creak across my Soul
> With those same Boots of Lead, again,
> Then Space—began to toll,
>
> As all the Heavens were a Bell,
> And Being, but an Ear,
> And I, and Silence, some strange Race
> Wrecked, solitary, here—
>
> And then a Plank in Reason, broke,
> And I dropped down, and down—
> And hit a World, at every plunge,
> And Finished knowing—then—   (P 280)

We may speculate that the poem charts the stages in the speaker's loss of consciousness, and this loss of consciousness is a dramatization of the deadening forces that today would be known as repression. We may further suppose that the speaker is reconstructing—or currently knowing—an experience whose pain in the past rendered it impossible to know. We note that part of the strangeness of her speech lies in the fact that not only is the poem grammatically past tense, but it also seems emotionally past tense. It illustrates the way in which one can relate experience and, at the same time, suffer a disassociation from it. Of course in this case the experience itself is one of disassociation. Since the speaker adds no emotive comment to the recollection, it is as if even in the recounting the words did not penetrate the walls of her own understanding. That the poem is about knowledge and the consequence of its repression is clear enough from the poem's initial conceit, for people do not feel funerals and certainly not in the brain. In addition, as a consequence of the persistent downward motion of the poem, we see that the funeral is rendered in terms of a burial, and this fusion or confusion points to a parallel confusion between unconsciousness and death. The burial of something in the mind—of a thought or experience or wish—the rendering of it unconscious, lacks an etiology; its occasion and even content here remain unspecified. As a consequence our attention is fixed on the process itself.

Examining the conceit, we can speculate that the mourners represent that part of the self which fights to resurrect or keep alive the thought the speaker is trying to commit to burial. They stand for that part of the self which feels conflict about the repressive gesture. "Treading—treading—," the self in conflict goes over the same ground of its argument with itself, and sense threatens to dissolve, "break through—," because of the mind's inability to resolve its contradictory impulses. In the second stanza, on a literal level the participants of the funeral sit for the service and read words over the dead. On a figural level the confusion of the mind quiets to one unanimous voice issuing its consent to the burial of meaning. But the mind's unanimity, its single voice, is no less horrible. The speaker hears it as a drum: rhythmic, repetitious, numbing. In the fourth stanza, the repressive force lashes the speaker with retaliatory distortion: the "Heavens" and the cosmos they represent toll as one overwhelming "Bell"; "Being" is reduced to the "Ear" that must receive it. No longer fighting the repressive instinct (for the "Mourners" have disappeared, "Being" and "I" are united), the self is a victim passively awaiting its own annihilation. When the "Plank in Reason," the last stronghold to resist its own dissolution, gives, and the speaker plummets through successive levels of meaning (an acknowledgment that repression has degrees), the result is a death of consciousness. As J. V. Cunningham remarks, the poem is a representation of a "psychotic episode" at the end of which the speaker passes out.[2]

But if we agree that the poem is not about actual death, why is the funeral rendered in such literal terms, terms that might well lead a careless reader to mistake its very subject? Paul de Man, distinguishing between irony and allegory, provides a suggestive answer. Allegory, he writes, involves "the tendency of the language toward narrative, the spreading out along the axis of an imaginary time in order to give duration to what is, in fact, simultaneous within the subject."[3] The structure of irony is the reverse of this form—the reduction of time to one single moment in which the self appears double or disjoint. Irony, de Man writes, is "*staccato* . . . a synchronic structure, while allegory appears as a successive mode capable of engendering duration as the illusion of a continuity that it knows to be illusory."[4] Irony and allegory, he concludes, are two faces of the same experience, opposite ways of rendering sequence and doubleness. De Man's distinctions are illuminating for our understanding of the fusions in "I felt a Funeral in my Brain," for the poem exhibits a double sense of its own experience and of the form in which that experience is to be rendered. With no terms of its own, it is through its very disembodiment, its self-reflexive disassociation, that the experience wields the power it does. If it could be made palpable and objectified, it might be known and hence mastered. Thus the allegory of the funeral attempts to exteriorize and give a temporal structure to what is in fact interior and simultaneous. Because we see the stages of the funeral (stages that correspond to steps that will complete the repressive instinct) we cannot help but view repression in terms of death. Thus the funeral imagery, replete with mourners, coffin, and service, seems both to distract from the poem's subject of repression and to insist on the severity of its consequences. But it is in the tension between the two modes of knowing and of representation, between an allegorical structure and an ironic one, that the poem's interest lies. For structure and sequence fall away in the ironic judgment of the poem's last line, which suggests, if implicitly, that action (exteriority) and knowledge (interiority) will always diverge. Even the attempt to reconstruct the experience and do it over with a different consequence leads, as it did the first time, to blankness. This divergence is further exemplified in the odd order of the poem's events: the funeral precedes death, at least the death of consciousness. Such inversion of normal sequence necessitates a figural reading of the poem and makes perfect sense within it, for Dickinson seems to be claiming we cannot "not know" in isolation and at will. What we choose not to know, what we submerge, like the buried root of a plant that sucks all water and life toward its source, pulls us down with a vengeance toward it.

If "'Twas like a Maelstrom with a notch" suggests that agony may be a metaphor for death, and "I felt a Funeral in my Brain" that death is a metaphor for repressed agony, the problem of fusion becomes even more complex in the following poem, where it is truly impossible to tell whether death is a figure or the thing itself. In "'Tis so appalling it

exhilarates," as in other poems discussed in chapter 1 in which naming
is an indirect venture, this poem begins with an elusive "it":

> 'Tis so appalling—it exhilarates—
> So over Horror, it half Captivates—
> The Soul stares after it, secure—
> A Sepulchre, fears frost, no more—
>
> To scan a Ghost, is faint—
> But grappling, conquers it—
> How easy, Torment, now—
> Suspense kept sawing so—
>
> The Truth, is Bald, and Cold—
> But that will hold—
> If any are not sure—
> We show them—prayer—
> But we, who know,
> Stop hoping, now—
>
> Looking at Death, is Dying—
> Just let go the Breath—
> And not the pillow at your Cheek
> So Slumbereth
>
> Others, Can wrestle—
> Your's, is done—
> And so of Wo, bleak dreaded—come,
> It sets the Fright at liberty—
> And Terror's free—
> Gay, Ghastly, Holiday!   (P 281)

While the subject remains unspecified, its identity seems almost not to
matter, for that obscurity is overpowered in significance by the initial
formulation which suggests a relationship between extremity and exhila-
ration, dread and release, excruciation and ease. The necessary arena for
the free-play of terror is guaranteed by the absolute finality of the feared
thing, and whether the finality is one of actual death or whether it is of
a truth so "Bald" and "Cold—" as to precipitate the death of illusion is
irrelevant. For to conceive of death seems to be to suffer its consequences, even if only in the imagination. "Looking at Death, is Dying—,"
or as Shakespeare wrote analogously in Sonnet 64 of the "ruin" implicit

in the very "rumination" of loss: "This thought is as a death which cannot choose / But weep to have that which it fears to lose." In both instances the mind is liberated from hope and from the attendant anxiety about achieving its object. Since the task of Dickinson's poem is to distinguish between process and conclusion, intimation and knowledge, the dread of terror and its safe arrival, it rests its case on the implicit assertion that you cannot top or bottom a superlative. The content of the superlative thus matters very little; what must be appreciated is the consequence of mastering it.

In the poems discussed thus far in which Dickinson effects a fusion between death as figure and death as fact, the status of death—both called into question by the confusion between figure and fact and simultaneously dismissed by our inability to resolve it—is relegated to a secondary position, and what we are concerned with is a speaker's mastery of a condition that she understands no more than we do. In "'Twas like a Maelstrom with a notch" the anticipatory state preceding death so partakes of death's characteristics that even on this side of death the speaker is not safe from them; in "I felt a Funeral in my Brain" the death of meaning blots consciousness out, brings a death to the mind so total that the body responds by losing cognizance of itself. In "'Tis so appalling it exhilarates" any ultimate horror has the severity of death; that there is no distinction between the two seems to be precisely the lesson of the poem. In brief, all of these poems exemplify a duality that is both conscious of itself and dismissive of consciousness.

How such fusions of meaning occur is the explicit subject of the following poem in which Dickinson examines the very process whereby the synthesis we have been discussing comes into being:

> There's a certain Slant of light,
> Winter Afternoons—
> That oppresses, like the Heft
> Of Cathedral Tunes—
>
> Heavenly Hurt, it gives us—
> We can find no scar,
> But internal difference,
> Where the Meanings, are—
>
> None may teach it—Any—
> 'Tis the Seal Despair—

> An imperial affliction
> Sent us of the Air—
>
> When it comes, the Landscape listens—
> Shadows—hold their breath—
> When it goes, 'tis like the Distance
> On the look of Death—   (P 258)

How does "light" come into relation with "Despair—" and "Despair—"
into relation with "Death—"? What are the generative fusions of the
poem and why is the grammar of its concluding lines itself so confusing?
We note that light is a "Seal" or sign of despair and we remember that
Dickinson was much too conscientious a reader of the Bible and particularly of the Book of Revelation not to have intended "the Seal
Despair—" to point to an experience that was, if a secular experience can
be so, both visionary and apocalyptic. In the Bible, however, while the
self is "not worthy to open the scroll and break the seals" that will reveal
divine agency, in the speaker's world meaning must be deduced within
the privacy of a solitary consciousness. Thus "None may teach it [to]
any [one else]"; "None may teach it any[thing]" (it is not subject to
alteration); "None may teach it—[not] any[one]." But the "Meanings"
of the event are not self-generated; if this is a poem about the solipsistic
labor of experience, it is not about autism. To be credited as vision,
despair must also seek its connection to the generative source outside
itself. For light may seal despair in, make it internal and irrevocable,
but the irrevocability, by a line of association that runs just under the
poem's surface, prompts the larger thought of death.

   In fact, the poem is about correlatives, about how interior transformations that are both invisible and immune to alteration from the outside
world are at the same time generated by that world. The relationship
between the "Slant of light" in the landscape and the "Seal Despair—"
within may be clarified by an analogy to Erich Auerbach's distinction
between figure and its fulfillment,[5] for the "Slant of light" and the "Seal
Despair—" are not in this poem merely premonitions of death, but are,
in fact, kinds or *types* of death.[6] Indeed it could be asserted that in the
entire Dickinson canon, despair is often a *figura* for death, not as Auerbach uses the word to specify related historical events, but rather as he
indicates the word to denote an event that prefigures an ultimate occurrence and at the same time is already imbued with its essence. Figural
interpretation presupposes much greater equality between its terms

than either allegory or symbol for, in the former, the sign is a mere form and, in the latter, the symbol is always fused with what it represents and can actually replace it. While it is true that figural interpretation ordinarily applies to historical events rather than to natural events, and while the "Slant of light" and the "Seal Despair—" are indeed natural and psychological events not separated by much time, they have a causal or prefigurative relationship to each other that is closer to the relationship implicit in the figural structure than to that in the symbolic one. Certainly it would be incorrect to say that they are symbols. "Light" and "Seal," however, are in relation to "Death—" as a premise is to a conclusion. Auerbach, speaking of the relationship between two historical events implicit in the figural structure, writes, "Both . . . have something provisional and incomplete about them; they point to one another and both point to something in the future, something still to come, which will be the actual, real, and definitive event."[7] We may regard the "Slant of light" and the "Seal Despair—" as having just such a signatory relationship as that described above. For the light is indirect; it thus seeks a counterpart to help it deepen into meaning. The "definitive event" in the poem to which "light" and "Seal" point is, of course, "Death—." While we would expect the departure of the light to yield distance from the "look of Death—," instead the preposition "on" not only designates the space between the speaker and the light but also identifies that light as one cast by death, and in turn casting death on, or in the direction of, the speaker. The "Slant of light," recognized only at a distance—its meaning comprehended at the moment of its disappearance—is revelatory of "Death—", is "Death['s]—" prefiguration. Figure fuses with fact, interprets it, and what we initially called the confusion of the two now makes sense in the context of divination.

If the light is indeed one of death, then we have the answer to why and how it "oppresses" in the first stanza and to the earlier oblique comparison of it to "Cathedral Tunes—." What Dickinson achieves in the poem is truly remarkable, for she takes a traditional symbol and scours it so thoroughly of its traditional associations with life that before we get to the poem's conclusion the image leans in the direction of mystery, dread, and darkness. By the time we arrive at the final simile and at the direct association of light and death we are not so much surprised as relieved at the explicitness of the revelation. It is the indirect association of "light" and "Death—" (the "Slant" that pulls them together at first seemingly without purpose) that prompts "Despair—." We feel it indirectly, internally, obliquely. Were we to know it, it would be death. For Dickinson, death is the apocalyptic vision, the straightening of premonition into fact, figure into fulfillment.

The fusions I have been discussing either between literal reality and its metaphoric representation (where literal reality permanently assumes those metaphoric characteristics that seemed initially intended only to illuminate it) or between the more formal *figura* and its fulfillment (where events contain in a predictive relationship the essence as well as the form of each other) raise the question of whether we can ever know anything in its own terms, and suggest perhaps that knowledge is not, as we might have thought, absolute, but is rather always relational. If these fusions link the historical or natural world with the divine one, the analogue with the real thing, they are predicated on a structure of simultaneous correspondence rather than of linear progression. The truth that is "Bald, and Cold—" *is* death, it does not lead to it. The "certain Slant of light," although it prefigures death, also already contains its essence. The thing in other words is saturated in the terms of its own figuration. Given the synchrony of this relationship, we are not very far from those poems that strain to annihilate the boundaries of time itself and to treat death as if its very reality could be cast into the present tense, experienced, and somehow survived. The effort to know what cannot be known, to survive it, is thus carried one step further in those poems in which the speaker travels over the boundary from life to death to meet death on its own ground. Given the presumption of the quest, figural structure often gives way to allegory or at any rate to the acknowledgment of the inadequacy of simple analogue, for on the other side of death true knowledge can find no correspondences.

III

It was Heidegger who asserted that we perceive time only because we have to die. In chapter 1 we saw how for Dickinson, too, despair or living death associates itself with timelessness, "When everything that ticked— has stopped—." In the following poem, actual death turns analogy into metaphor, the dead person imaged as a stopped clock:

A Clock stopped—
Not the Mantel's—

Geneva's farthest skill
Cant put the puppet bowing—
That just now dangled still—

An awe came on the Trinket!
The Figures hunched, with pain—
Then quivered out of Decimals—
Into Degreeless Noon—

It will not stir for Doctor's—
This Pendulum of snow—
This Shopman importunes it—
While cool—concernless No—

Nods from the Gilded pointers—
Nods from the Seconds slim—
Decades of Arrogance between
The Dial life—
And Him—

(P 287)

The dead person's "Arrogance" inheres in his silence, his stoic resistance to the "importun[ing]" of those who would set him going again. Given the enormousness of his refusal, the task of vitalizing him is regarded as a mechanical feat that meets overwhelming failure. If life is a "Dial" measured by the degrees to which it can undergo transformation, death is inert, a "Pendulum of snow—." This, of course, is one way of figuring it—the riddle of the human being no longer alive and therefore unrecognizable as human. For the dead person is a "Trinket" and a "puppet," and comes closest to becoming a "Figure" only in its earlier proximity to the pain of temporality. If part of Dickinson's intention in the poem is to make us "guess what" or "guess who" the subject is, it is largely a consequence of her insistence on our participation in the mystery of death's temporal transcendence.

But despite Dickinson's depiction of the clock-person, life is not synonymous with time. For life endures, or fails to, in the face of time that is continually passing away. It is to rectify this discrepancy, to cure the difference between time and the life that is at odds with it, that Dickinson suggests a temporal transcendence more daring than that of death's. Thus in her proleptic utterances, the dead person becomes one with time either dramatically, as in the preceding poem of the stopped clock, or more subtly, by collapsing the boundaries between past, present, and future. Moreover, the speakers' failure to distinguish temporal categories, the predicated fusion *between* them, suggests an analogous fusion *with* them. In this second fusion internal or subjective time (that clock by which a self measures what is of importance to it) becomes one with external or objective time (which encompasses, disregards, and most usually opposes such private meanings). That external events rarely coincide with internal ones, that our inner thoughts have their own tempo and hence their own significance—can, for example, race at breakneck speed while the clock on the wall goes steadily as usual—are facts so obvious they barely require elaboration. Of the difference between internal and external time, Friedrich Kümmel has written: "If only internal time had reality, death would have no meaning and, conversely, where only external time ruled, life would come to an end."[8] But the fusion between the two in Dickinson's poems lies precisely in the fact that although the speaker *has* died, life has not come to an end. As a consequence, the dead person, having transcended time, can speak from beyond the grave. For the dead person who is like the Roman god Janus (the god of gates and transitions, who looks with one face into the past and the other into the future), speech seems to be a function of the expansion of the present to include past and future, as well as of the synthesis of subjective and objective time. Put succinctly, the speaker has passed the boundary of life while, at the same time, retaining all of the characteristic features of life: memory, feeling, expectation, and the ability to speak and tell stories of these.

Erwin Panofsky provides us with an interesting counterpart to this phenomenon in the visual arts. In his essay "Poussin and the Elegiac Tradition,"[9] Panofsky traces the transformation of the grammatically correct interpretation of the phrase *Et in Arcadia ego*, as it is represented in a painting by Guercino, to a misattribution of the phrase and a break in the medieval moralizing tradition, as it is represented in a painting by Poussin.[10] Both paintings show human figures confronting death. But in Guercino's work the shepherds depicted are startled by their confrontation with death and the shock of their encounter seems naturally, as well as grammatically, to attribute the words "Even in Arcadia, there am I" to the death's-head, that is, to death itself. In Poussin's painting, we see four figures standing in front of a tomb, no longer in dramatic discovery of death, and attending tranquilly to speech that it therefore makes more sense to attribute not to the tomb but to the dead person who is buried within it. Thus it suddenly seems right to mistranslate the accompanying Latin phrase as "I, too, lived in Arcadia," that is to ascribe its words to a dead Arcadian shepherd or shepherdess.[11] The misattribution of the Latin phrase prompted by Poussin's representation may do violence to Latin grammar but, Panofsky insists, it is in harmony with the new conception of the painting, which "projects the message of the Latin phrase from the present into the past—all the more forcibly as the behavior of the figures no longer expresses surprise and dismay but quiet, reminiscent meditation. . . . [With the] whole phrase projected into the past: what had been a menace has become a remembrance."[12]

The transformation from terror to meditation, memento mori to elegy that Panofsky describes between Guercino's representation and Poussin's can be seen equally between those poems of Dickinson's that come upon and stop short of death's boundary and those poems that transcend it. In addition, the capacity to remember death rather than to anticipate it, to make past an experience of death that can really only be future, seems to have a similar consequence in Poussin's painting and in Dickinson's poems: in both cases it bequeaths speech to the dead person. We shall turn first to Dickinson's proleptic utterances (looking initially at three poems that stop short of the boundary line and, in so doing, mark it), then back to Panofsky's essay when, with more grounding in the questions it raises, we may explore its insights further. In scrutinizing Dickinson's proleptic poems, I shall be primarily interested in the two phenomena I have sketched above: the fusion of subjective and objective time, and the power of speech beyond the grave.

i

In the following poem in which the speaker documents the experience of near-death, the depiction is surrealistic, punctuated by the gaps in thought that attest to the terror of fragmentary comprehension:

> That after Horror—that 'twas *us*—
> That passed the mouldering Pier—
> Just as the Granite Crumb let go—
> Our Savior, by a Hair—
>
> A second more, had dropped too deep
> For Fisherman to plumb—
> The very profile of the Thought

> Puts Recollection numb—
>
> The possibility—to pass
> Without a Moment's Bell—
> Into Conjecture's presence—
> Is like a Face of Steel—
> That suddenly looks into our's
> With a metallic grin—
> The Cordiality of Death—
> Who drills his Welcome in—   (P 286)

Indeed one might speculate that it is the speaker's lost grip on the land that makes *it* appear to suffer dissolution. The dream-like image of a "mouldering Pier—," eaten away partly by water, partly by the spectre of death, belongs to and marks the end of the earthly terrain. Before that spectre the earth itself is reduced to a "Granite Crumb." Since the first stanza represents a state of rapid transition and passage, it is fitting that what the speaker comprehend be partial and partially rendered. Thus although the first stanza's last line implies a subjunctive ("If we had dropped a hair further, we would have met our savior"), the assertion is truncated and elliptical in the extreme, utterance representing the split-second of a miss and its retrospective appreciation. But, in fact, the speaker is not able to penetrate the instant of near-annihilation. Scrutiny does not expand the experiential instant, cannot pry it apart for more substantial examination. The recollection, like the reality, will not open itself up. A "profile of the Thought" is the most that can be tolerated without the speaker's blacking out. In stanza two, as in the first stanza, we are conscious of how thin and inhospitable to knowledge the moment of transition appears even in memory. The speaker gains entry to the experience only by distorting it, by re-presenting it in terms blunt and crude enough to provide room for her exploration.

Only the concluding stanza accomplishes what the first two cannot. It acknowledges the reserve of the boundary line, that fact that it provides no warning or "Bell—" of the enormity of transformation it is facilitating. The stanza then freezes its own conception so that "Conjecture's presence—" (that which can only be present to us by conjecture, specifically death) hardens into static knowledge. In the last five lines of the poem all the earlier characteristics of the experience suddenly reverse themselves and what was evasive is now inevitable; what vague, now harrowingly delimited. The "Face of Steel—," the "metallic grin—," the "drill" of the "Welcome" close upon the speaker in the half-lewd gesture that, as we have seen, frequently connects death and sexuality in Dickinson's work, and nail her down. In the first two stanzas she had been suggesting that she could not know this experience if she tried; in the last stanza it is clear that she cannot help but know it. The passage completed, even if only conceptually, guarantees all the inevitability that attends any certain state. Only the shadow line separating life from death, which may be glimpsed and touched but not seen or inhabited, is a featureless no man's land free of specific characteristics. At the end of the poem the speaker is still tottering on the edge of the line dividing life from death, but the strength of the completed conception no longer admits of any resolve to turn back.

The attempt to glimpse death's visage while escaping its grip, to know its features from a distance, to straddle the line between ignorance and knowledge, is an abortive one in the preceding poem, and Dickinson acknowledges that fact. One cannot have knowledge and be protected from its consequences at the same time. The "possibility—to pass" over the line is "like a Face of Steel—" precisely because of how absolutely it seals off the route back.

If "That after Horror that 'twas *us*" represents an involuntary and sudden arrival at the line that separates life from death, the following two utterances suggest more considered attempts to anticipate such a juncture and, through anticipation, to forestall its consequences. In "I read my sentence steadily," the wit of the intellectual construction hastens to announce its nonchalance at the "sentence" of death, but the poem's cavalier railery and its matter-of-fact evenness of tone are belied by the profusion of pronouns and the schism within the self that they imply:

> I read my sentence—steadily—
> Reviewed it with my eyes,
> To see that I made no mistake
> In it's extremest clause—
> The Date, and manner, of the shame—
> And then the Pious Form
> That "God have mercy" on the Soul
> The Jury voted Him—
> I made my soul familiar—with her extremity—
> That at the last, it should not be a novel Agony—

> But she, and Death, acquainted—
> Meet tranquilly, as friends—
> Salute, and pass, without a Hint—
> And there, the Matter ends—   (P 412)

Charles Anderson's fine discussion of the poem as a dream-trial in which the mind discovers that the body has been condemned to death and, given no possibility of appeal, attempts to deal with the sentence by so fragmenting the self that it escapes realistic association with the condemned person[13] renders further elaborate comment redundant. But in the context of our discussion, we should note that the purpose of the "Review" is to domesticate "extremity—," to make it "familiar—" so that the line separating life from death is apprehended prior to the speaker's encounter with it. In fact, the nature of her acquaintance with death remains deliberately unspecified, and the result is an intimation of an unsettling partnership, more strange for going unacknowledged ("without a Hint—"). We might simplify the problem by saying that acquaintance without recognition is what the speaker desires and hence depicts: to meet death without recognizing it, to be spared recognition, to have the body dissolve (as the pun in the last line smartly indicates) without the soul's witness to the dissolution, so neatly to dispose of the "Matter" (the subject and the body) that pain is an extravagance cleverly evaded. If the flippancy of the formulation and all the legal wrangling deny that the "Agony" of ending cannot, by definition, but be "novel," Dickinson faced it squarely in a more sober utterance:

> Our journey had advanced—
> Our feet were almost come
> To that odd Fork in Being's Road—
> Eternity—by Term—
>
> Our pace took sudden awe—
> Our feet—reluctant—led—
> Before—were Cities—but Between—
> The Forest of the Dead—
>
> Retreat—was out of Hope—
> Behind—a Sealed Route—
> Eternity's White Flag—Before—
> And God—at every Gate—   (P 615)

In an earlier poem whose narration of a journey away from life recalls "Our journey had advanced," Dickinson had written:

> 'Twas the old—road—through pain—
> That unfrequented—one—
> With many a turn—and thorn—
> That stops—at Heaven—   (P 344)

But we note significant differences between the two narrations. For one thing, the traveler in the first poem, as later stanzas indicate, is not the speaker; for another, the journey's end is, finally, "too out of sight—" to apprehend; but most important, since the terminal point in "'Twas the old road" is heaven, the brink of the speaker's vision, the boundary point that prohibits further travel, remains just this side of death. Such a designation of boundary is, as we have seen, characteristic of the poems we have been examining. In "That after Horror that 'twas *us*," and even in poems whose subject is the relationship between figural and literal death ("I felt a Funeral in my Brain," and "'Twas like a Maelstrom with a notch"), the placement of boundary occurs at that moment prior to death—or, in the case of the former poem, prior to unconsciousness— which mediates between life and death. In "Our journey had advanced," however, as Geoffrey Hartman, Robert Weisbuch, and Harold Bloom have suggested,[14] an interesting displacement is effected: death, no longer the terminus of experience, becomes instead a mediating point, a middle ground from whose territory a speaker can gaze further, into the reaches of eternity. The poem's premise, in other words, might be explained as follows: if death is not conclusion, is in fact only a step, albeit a signifi- cant one, along the way then it can be depicted as known or, at any rate, subject to knowledge. For the psychological requirement of such poems seems to be not that death be depicted as unknowable, but rather that *some* terminal point be depicted as unknowable. Once one adds a new element to the customary sequence, a "beyond" to death, one extends and amplifies the phenomenologically inhabitable territory, and re- locates the crucial boundary point not at the moment of death, but rather after it.

In "Our journey had advanced," which almost asks to be read as a diagram subject to its own revision, our picture of the poem's geography alters with the speaker's own more sophisticated appreciation of it. The first stanza seems to imply a conventional terminal point to experience: one branch of the fork is "Being" itself, the other branch is "Eternity—"

or death; "Eternity—" is an implied consequence of death, with an effective fusion between the two.[15] However, this way of depicting it is apprehended as mistaken close-up. "Sudden awe—" is a consequence of the speaker's recognition that death and "Eternity—" are not the same; the fork cannot be directly traversed, and the mediating point that separates "Being" from "Eternity—" has dimension and territory of its own. Indeed, as depicted, there is an implied vastness to "The Forest of the Dead—." What had seemed like a "Between—," a point that barely needed mention, has become a formidable space in its own right. Given such a recognition, the territory must now be mapped in new terms. The fork that, in stanza one, involved a simple and single split and that implicitly suggested options, in the concluding stanza straightens and narrows to preclude choice ("Retreat—was out of Hope—") and also to suggest that the road traversed is one-way ("Behind—a Sealed Route—"). What had been represented as a "Fork" is now more accurately depicted as a chronological progression: "Before—" (previous to this) "were Cities—," but they are past. "Between—" (the boundary point swelled to new dimension by the housing of its inhabitants) is "The Forest of the Dead—." Death, in other words, is present. And "Eternity's White Flag—Before—" (ahead) is future.

The two opposite connotations of "Before—" (meaning "prior to" and "in front of") within so brief a space afford a mimetic parody of the poem's pattern of intersecting "identities" that, upon scrutiny, turn out to be different, as "Eternity—" is, for example, different from death, although in stanza one they are perceived implicitly as the same. What appears single or unitary in meaning and identity ("Eternity—" and death) is double; what double (the two-pronged fork of "Being" and "Eternity—") is at least triple, as the designations of "Cities—," "Forest," and "White Flag " illustrate. For "Eternity—" is not "Term[inus] —," or at least not as the speaker initially thought, but rather lies before her. If, as we saw in the previous chapter, in "Behind Me—dips Eternity—/Before Me—Immortality—," the speaker is, rather simply, the "Term between—" the two, in this more complicated geography, "at the boundary" or "Before—" designates "on both sides of." For in "Our journey had advanced," the boundary line can be re-placed or dis-placed in direct proportion to the speaker's recognition that ending itself, neither stable nor certain, remains subject to perpetual re-definition. In a letter to the Norcross sisters, Dickinson had confessed: "I cannot tell how Eternity seems." Then gesturing toward her own evasiveness: "It sweeps around me like a sea" (L 785).

In "Our journey had advanced," the representations of boundary correct each other as vision sharpens into revelation and revelation, at the poem's conclusion, fades into blankness. The point at which the multiple conceptions of boundary intersect and the fact of the intersection is of significance, for the poem concludes by obliterating the very distinctions it has been at such pains to establish. White, that color enigmatic for interpretation in all of Dickinson's poems, is here a manifest emblem of inscrutability, a symbol purified of specific content. It signals the existence of eternity, marks it, and just as insistently seals it from view. If "Eternity's White Flag—" is the sign of meaning that cannot be divined at a distance, the poem's concluding line points to the agent of that meaning. But unlike the carefully charted areas of "Being," death and "Eternity—," "God—at every Gate—," or ubiquitous presence, obscures distinction and insists on showing up the intersection of meanings about which I spoke earlier. The poem concludes with a suffusion of whiteness and vigilance, both of which overpower and imply the merging of the separate states previously articulated. The speaker's apprehension of "Eternity—" and of God's presiding presence over everything has not so much its own meaning as an effect of obliterating discrete meanings. Swallowed up in the enormousness of colorlessness and divine presence, the terminus of meaning and distinction intersects with the end of their necessity.

ii

"That after Horror that 'twas *us*," "I read my sentence steadily," and "Our journey had advanced" allow us to linger in death's presence without actually going beyond it. Unlike the poems that fuse the literal and the figural and unlike those that effect temporal fusions between life and death, these utterances are halted from fusion by the very prohibition to knowledge that experience implies. The following two poems defy such prohibitions. While the temporal fusion between life and death is more apparently dramatic than any we have encountered so far, its result seems to throw death into a form that shrugs off comprehension or correspondence. Death, in these poems, though assumed and, in one instance, personified, is not fused or confused with anything; it is most distinctly itself, and in both of the poems I shall examine its purpose seems to be the implicit chastisement of the speaker for the boldness of the poems' very premise. Make the future present though she will, death's meaning still lingers beyond it. A speaker may put herself in a carriage with death and hand him the reins, but for all the intimacy this implies, the journey's end remains a mystery.

The crossing point between life and death is seen from a new perspective when a dead person reflects on the past-tense occurrence of the moment of her dying and, in so doing, reconstructs it as if it were present. Dying here is not projected or imagined. It is rather recollected:

> I heard a Fly buzz—when I died—
> The Stillness in the Room
> Was like the Stillness in the Air—
> Between the Heaves of Storm—
>
> The Eyes around—had wrung them dry—
> And Breaths were gathering firm
> For that last Onset—when the King
> Be witnessed—in the Room—
>
> I willed my Keepsakes—Signed away
> What portion of me be
> Assignable—and then it was
> There interposed a Fly—
>
> With Blue—uncertain stumbling Buzz—
> Between the light—and me—
> And then the Windows failed—and then
> I could not see to see—   (P 465)

We must imagine the speaker looking back on an experience in which her expectations of death were foiled by its reality. The poem begins with the speaker's perception of the fly, not yet a central awareness both because of the way in which the fly manifests itself (as sound) and because of the degree to which it manifests itself (as a triviality). As a consequence of the speaker's belief in the magnitude of the event and the propriety with which it should be enacted, the fly seems merely indecorous, as yet a marginal disturbance, attracting her attention the way in which something we have not yet invested with meaning does. In a poem very much concerned with the question of vision, it is perhaps strange that the dominant concern in stanza one should be auditory. But upon reflection it makes sense, for the speaker is hearing a droning in the background before the source of the noise comes into view. The poem describes the way in which things come into view, slowly.

What is striking in the second stanza is the speaker's lack of involvement in the little drama that is being played out. She is acutely conscious that there will be a struggle with death, but she imagines it is the people around her who will undergo it. Her detachment and tranquillity seem appropriate if we imagine them to come in the aftermath of pain, a subject that is absent in the poem and whose absence helps to place the experience at the moment before death. At such a moment, the speaker's concern is focused on others, for being the center of attention with all eyes upon her, she is at leisure to return the stare. Her concern with her audience continues in the third stanza and prompts the tone of officiousness there. Wanting to set things straight, the speaker wishes to add the finishing touches to her life, to conclude it the way one would a business deal. The desire to structure and control experience is not, however, carried out in total blindness, for she is clearly cognizant of those "Keepsakes—" not hers to give. Even at this point her conception of dying may be a preconception but it is not one founded on total ignorance.

The speaker has been imagining herself as a queen about to leave her people, conscious of the majesty of the occasion, presiding over it. She expects to witness death as majestic, too, or so one infers from the way in which she speaks of him in stanza two. The staginess of the conception, however, has little to do with what Charles Anderson calls "an ironic reversal of the conventional attitudes of [Dickinson's] time and place toward the significance of the moment of death."[16] If it did, the poem would arbitrate between the social meanings and personal ones. But the conflict between preconception and perception takes place inside. Or rather preconception gives way only to darkness. For at the conclusion of the third stanza the fly "interpose[s]," coming between the speaker and the onlookers, between her predictive fantasy of the event and its reality, between life and death. The fact that the fly obscures the former allows the speaker to see the latter. Perspective suddenly shifts to the right thing: from the ritual of dying to the fact of death. It is, of course, the fly who obliterates the speaker's false notions of death, for it is with his coming that she realizes that she is the witness and he the king, that the ceremony is a "stumbling" one. It is from a perspective schooled by the fly that she writes.

As several previous discussions of the poem have acknowledged,[17] the final stanza begins with a complicated synesthesia: "With Blue—uncertain stumbling Buzz—." The adjective "stumbling" (used customarily to describe only an action) here also describes a sound, and the adverb "uncertain" the quality of that sound. The fusion would not be so interesting if its effect were not to evoke that moment in perception when it is about to fail. As in a high fever, noises are amplified, the light in the room takes on strange hues, one effect seems indistinguishable from another. Although there is a more naturalistic explanation for the word "stumbling" (to describe the way in which flies go in and out of our hearing), the poem is so predicated on the phenomenon of displacement and projection (of the speaker's feelings onto the onlookers, of the final blindness onto the "Windows," of the fact of perception onto the experience of death) that the image here suggests another dramatic displacement—the fusion of the fly's death with her own. Thus flies when they are about to die move as if poisoned, sometimes hurl themselves against a ceiling, pause, then rise to circle again, then drop. At this moment the changes the speaker is undergoing are fused with their agent: her experience becomes one with the fly's. It is her observance of that fly, being mesmerized by it (in a quite literal sense now, since death is quite literal), that causes her mind to fumble at the world and lose grip of it. The final two lines "And then the Windows failed—and then / I could not see to see—" are brilliant in their underlining of the poem's central premise; namely that death is survived by perception, for in these lines we are told that there are two senses of vision, one of which remains to see and document the speaker's own blindness ("and then / I could not see to see— "). The poem thus penetrates to the invisible imagination which strengthens in response to the loss of visible sight.

I mentioned earlier that the poem presumes a shift of perspective, an enlightened change from the preconception of death to its perception. In order to assume that the speaker is educated by her experience, we must assume the fact of it: we must credit the death as a real one. But the fiction required by the poem renders it logically baffling. For although the poem seems to proceed in a linear fashion toward an end, its entire premise is based on the lack of finality of that end, the speaker who survives death to tell her story of it. We are hence left wondering: How does the poem imagine an ending? If it does not, what replaces a sense of an ending? How does it conceive of the relationship between past, present, and future? To address these questions adequately, we need to look at some theories of time against which the poem's own singular conception may more sharply be visible.

In *Cosmos and History*, Mircea Eliade writes of the primitive desire to make past and present coexist. What supersedes time is a life structured by the repetition of archetypal acts, structured, that is, by "categories and not . . . events. . . . although [the life] takes place in time, [it] does not bear the burden of time, does not record time's irreversibility; in other words, completely ignores what is especially characteristic and decisive in a consciousness of time. Like the mystic, like the religious man in general, the primitive lives in a continual present."[18] In the primitive world that Eliade describes historical acts still occur, but their meaning is metahistorical. Events bear an associative or analogical relationship to each other.[19] The replacement of analogues by unique events, events that guarantee a new present at every moment and, in so doing, render the past irretrievably past, is contingent upon the acknowledgment that experience has a terminal point.

One might, in fact, say it is the garden of Eden that teaches us it is impossible to conceive of a past purified by the attendant conception of its loss. For to understand the meaning of permanence is already to have surrendered the fact of it.[20] If we imagine the Fall to be that moment when man first perceives past and future as forever exiled from the present, lying always outside of it, the new conception destroys the illusion of events as repeating themselves, moving reversibly or in a cyclical direction. Indeed the very premise of Christianity and its providential history depends upon such an eschatology,[21] for while the Old Testament promises a divine judgment that will take place within history, the New Testament promises a judgment that will end it.

The impulse to see patterns in history is very close to the interpretation of events as patterned by ritual repetition or analogue, and in this respect history is a comparable fiction, that which provides significance to what would otherwise be mere chronicity. But the difference between ritual event and historical event lies in the latter's consciousness of the conclusion to all events. In *Christ and Time*, Oscar Cullmann distinguishes between *chronos*, or passing time, and *kairos*, "a point of time that has a special place in the execution of God's plan of salvation,"[22] that is, a crucial moment in the drama of eschatology, one that gains significance by its relation to the end. If a shift from the ritual organization of experience to its temporal organization necessitates the acknowledgment of time, many of whose moments are empty of significance, the fiction of history is a means of preserving and systematizing *kairos*, of attending to critical events of the past by regarding them as events of crisis. Imaginative fictions, less constrained because they are not under compulsion to be even selectively true, similarly rescue the world from a random succession of moments; in the world of the imagination the subject matter is always the interruption of daily events by the extraordinary. But *kairos* must come to terms with the facts of chronicity, with the ordinary generation of moments, and this inevitably involves the compunction to understand the very relationship between past, present, and future that ritual repudiates. Augustine spoke of the three temporal senses as "the present of things past, the present of things present, and the present of things future."[23] Attending to his mental synthesis of the three as he recited a psalm, he arrived at the following description:

> I am about to recite a psalm that I know. Before I begin, my expectation extends over the entire psalm. Once I have begun, my memory extends over as much of it as I shall separate off and assign to the past. The life of this action of mine is distended into memory by reason of the part I have spoken and into forethought by reason of the part I am about to speak. But attention is actually present and that which was to be is borne along by it so as to become past. The more this is done and done again, so much the more is memory lengthened by a shortening of expectation, until the entire expectation is exhausted. When this is done the whole action is completed and passes into memory. What takes place in the whole psalm takes place also in each of its parts and in each of its syllables. The same thing holds for a longer action, of which perhaps the psalm is a small part. The same thing holds for a man's entire life, the parts of which are all the man's actions. The same thing holds throughout the whole age of the sons of men, the parts of which are the lives of all men.[24]

Contrary to Augustine's attempt to distinguish between the three temporal senses, the intention of much modern poetry and fiction lies precisely in the effort to fuse past and present, meaningful event and trivia. Thus the distinction between mere chronicity and crucial event, which the historical fiction tried so hard to establish, has been effectively annihilated.[25] As Robbe-Grillet writes in *For a New Novel*, "In the modern narrative, time seems to be cut off from its temporality. It no longer passes. It no longer completes anything. . . . Here space destroys time, and time sabotages space. Description makes no headway, contradicts itself, turns in circles. Moment denies continuity."[26] We may say that the representation has gone full circle: from the primitive denial of

time and the "pastness" of experience, to the creation of a historical fiction in which experience is obsessed with the fact that it must end—and,
in which, therefore, the present is in constant need of understanding its
relationship to the past that generated it and to the future in which it
will conclude—and, finally, as some critics would have it,[27] the return in
modern literature to the representation of experience as timeless and
mythic. But what if these ostensibly alternate ways of representing
experience are, in fact, not alternate at all, but must be seen as mutually
exclusive possibilities that therefore, as with the dialectical voices discussed in chapter 2, always appear in contradictory relationship to each
other? For to stop the succession of moments is, nonetheless, to have
their inevitable passing firmly, even desperately, in mind.

If we date our perception of radical boundaries that forever seal us
from worlds we forever long to inhabit with the Fall, then we cannot see
the denial of temporal and spatial features of experience as a return to
mythic or ritual primitivism since that route is unalterably sealed, but
must ask what in its own right does such denial mean? With this question
we find ourselves back at the specific questions raised in connection with
Dickinson's "I heard a Fly buzz when I died," but now with a context in
which to consider them, for there the poem denies the very eschatological fact that its meaning depends upon.

I mentioned earlier that one consequence of the absence of a fixed
boundary line between life and death is the fusion of subjective and
objective time. In "I heard a Fly buzz," in other words, we have no
sense of subjective or interior time as substantially different from objective or exterior time. Perhaps this is always the case in the lyric, for the
lyric—unlike the novel, whose task it is to legislate the conflict between
social and personal reality—presents interior reality as if there were no
other with which it must regretfully contend. Hence the sense of leisure
about speech (even passionate speech) in the lyric. Marvell's lover (pro-
tests to the contrary) can woo his lady for as long as he likes; the borders
of the poem withstand any external interruption and, as long as the
reader's eyes are on the page, effectively banish it. Sir Walter Ralegh
"give[s] the world the lie" with more fervored documentation than we
can sustain in comparable moods of skepticism. Dylan Thomas's recollection of childhood in "Fern Hill" walls out for the duration of the
poem the very adult world he claims he cannot be free of. Even Milton's
dream of his dead wife, "my late espoused saint," disappears only when
he violates recollection by seeking to prove its existence in reality: "But

O as to embrace me she inclined/I waked, she fled, and day brought back my night." The poem, like Milton's vision, sustains its integrity for as long as one does not puncture it with the outside world. For the poem, like the vision, shrinks from mediation. Before the attempt at mediation with the social world, the poem ruptures, breaks off; it will not come into relation with, be on the same plane as, the social world. While this could, of course, be said of any imaginative fiction—talk to a character in a novel and he will not answer—no imaginative fiction is as resistant to the interruption of its interior speech as the lyric. For the lyric, unlike the drama or the novel, does not have to contend with authorial description, explanatory asides, or any other manipulative intrusion of its space.[28] Nor need it weather the periodic interruptions guaranteed by act, scene, or chapter divisions. Most important, however, it must attend to no more than one (its own) speaking voice. This fact makes the self in the lyric unitary, and gives it the illusion of alone holding sway over the universe, there being, for all practical purposes, no one else, nothing else, to inhabit it.

As a consequence of the banishing of the social world, the network of lines that comprise the pressures of social or objective time are equally consigned to temporary obscurity. The consignment makes room for the poem by allowing it to hang, as it were, in front of social time much the way a painting hangs in front of a wall. While this covering procedure is, as I have been suggesting, a customary occurrence in all lyrics, it becomes noteworthy when a poem explicitly denies an aspect of social or objective fact that we know, on other terms, to be undeniable. The assertion that one can come back from the dead to tell one's story of it so clearly counters the possible that our attention is focused on the effective annihilation of reality; for in this case, the fiction not only "covers" reality, it also insists that reality does not exist. This may make "I heard a Fly buzz" appear to possess the characteristics Robbe-Grillet attributes to modern literature: the embrace of timeless, mythic reality, the externality and hence congruence of thought and event, all effective activity manifest on one plane. But appearance is, in this case, illusion. For the lyric which seems to evade social reality must at some point acknowledge its attachment to the social world which, however denied by the illusion of the lyric's freedom, must nonetheless be assured by its desire for intelligibility. At what point do illusion and reality intersect and how does illusion manage to camouflage the intersection with sufficient art to deny it? For since the relationship I have been describing is a covert one, it follows that in every fiction there will be a crucial tension between the fact of such a relationship and the lyric's efforts to deny, disguise, or transform it.

In order to maintain its status as fiction the lyric must assert its deviance from the strictures of reality and, at the same time, assert the unreliability of the adherence to the impossible. Thus not only tension but contradiction itself is at the heart of the lyric's power over us—the sort of contradiction avoided in the poems discussed in chapter 1 and exploded in those discussed in chapter 2. The contradiction is less visible but nonetheless there in poems like Herbert's "The Collar" in which the rebellion against God's service is relinquished at the moment the lyric touches the surface of reality and finds its fantasy of rebellious freedom replaced by the proper alliance of choice and service. We view contradiction in Frost's "After Applepicking" where the poem slips in and out of dream with such rapidity that the middle of the dream-state effectively precedes its genesis, and the moment prior to the beginning of the dream coincides with the dream's completion. We view contradiction in Stevens's "The Snow Man" in which the ordinary connotations of "cold" receive redefinition, and what instinct would call impoverishment, art claims as the superior appreciation of unadorned reality. We view it in Hopkins's "Carrion Comfort" where the knot of the speaker's feelings generates their own opposite impulses. And even in non-ironic lyrics, as for example, Thomas Nashe's "A Litany in Time of Plague," we view it in the intersection of contrary meters—the plague's swiftness of passage and the prayer "I am sick, I must die./Lord have mercy on us," with which the poem attempts to slow time's pulse.

The contradiction between social and private time is the lyric's generating impulse, for the self who would keep its own time, who would live in a world of perpetual *kairos* where events are significant because of the power one has to transform them, must acknowledge the less malleable dictates of the outside world, its scrupulous if simple-minded adherence to *chronos*. In "I heard a Fly buzz when I died," the collision between the two senses of time occurs at the poem's ending, and is just as resolutely uncommented upon by it. For the demands set by the fictional world of *kairos*, and by the equally clamoring world of *chronos*, make no concessions to each other. The most that can be hoped for is the discovery of the coincidence of the two, their temporary appearance at the same moment and along the same temporal plane. Hence in "I heard a Fly buzz," the moment of perception coincides with the moment of

death at the poem's ending and, in so doing, effects a temporary rap-
prochement between the two. The conflict that it has been the poem's
function to *manifest* here comes to an end. But we might more properly
conclude not that the conflict has reached resolution, since by definition
there is no resolution, but rather that it has momentarily played itself
out. Indeed it is the genius of the poem to collapse the distinction
between subjective and objective time, to assert that an eternity of
consciousness and a finite consciousness painfully subject to instant
termination at the mere caprice of an insensate world are time schemes
compatible, even complementary. Thus two notions logically exclusive—
that death is the end of life, specifically conceived of as loss of consciousness, and that perception is the end of life (consciousness continued,
even heightened)—are in the poem stalwartly presented as if they were
the same thing.

The relationship between perception (or consciousness) as terminus
and death as terminus thus comes to be the implicit subject of the poem.
The illusion that perception as finality replaces the finality of death so
seems to prompt an exchange of the ordinary characteristics of each that
perception assumes many of death's properties: secrecy, private apprehension, and closure. As a consequence of the intersection of perception
and death, the boldness of the poem's flaunting of border is softened
since its progression from the fact of death to the recollection of dying
and back again to the moment of death leaves the reader at a conventional moment. It is as if the poem had moved along the same ground
twice, but each time in an opposite direction: once from death back to
life and, the second time, from life to death. Death, so often conceived
by Dickinson as a journey, is here retraveled and hence presumed to be
understood. In the previous chapter I suggested that the meaning of an
experience could not be ascertained until its conclusion; hence the
"Loaded Gun . . . /Without—the power to die—" (P 754) eludes interpretation. In these poems, too, completion is meaning now no longer
from the point of view of the fragmentary life, but rather from the
point of view of the life in touch with its own totality. If this is magical, Dickinson seems to assert that only from such magic can meaning be made. Like Eliade's description of the replacement of experience
as event with experience as category, dying is here categorical rather
than conclusive. That assumption is examined more explicitly in
what is perhaps Dickinson's most complex utterance on the subject
of death:

Because I could not stop for Death—
He kindly stopped for me—
The Carriage held but just Ourselves—
And Immortality.

We slowly drove—He knew no haste
And I had put away
My labor and my leisure too,
For His Civility—

We passed the School, where Children strove
At Recess—in the Ring—
We passed the Fields of Gazing Grain—
We passed the Setting Sun—

Or rather—He passed Us—
The Dews drew quivering and chill—
For only Gossamer, my Gown—
My Tippet—only Tulle—

We paused before a House that seemed
A Swelling of the Ground—
The Roof was scarcely visible—
The Cornice—in the Ground—

Since then—'tis Centuries—and yet
Feels shorter than the Day
I first surmised the Horses' Heads
Were toward Eternity—   (P 712)

Yvor Winters has spoken of the poem's subject as "the daily realization of the imminence of death—it is a poem of departure from life, an
intensely conscious leave-taking."[29] But in its final claim to actually
experience death, Winters has found it fraudulent. There is, of course,
a way out of or around the dilemma of posthumous speech and that is
to suppose that the entire ride with death is, as the last stanza indicates,
a "surmise," and "'tis Centuries—," a colloquial hyperbole. But we
ought not insist that the poem's interpretation pivot on the importance
of this word. For we ignore its own struggle with extraordinary claims
if we insist too quickly on its adherence to traditional limits.

In one respect, the speaker's assertions that she "could not stop for
Death—" must be taken as the romantic protest of a self not yet disabused

of the fantasy that her whims, however capricious, will withstand the larger temporal demands of the external world. Thus the first line, like any idiosyncratic representation of the world, must come to grips with the tyranny of more general meanings, not the least of which can be read in the inviolable stand of the universe, every bit as willful as the isolate self. But initially the world seems to cater to the self's needs; since the speaker does not have time (one implication of "could not stop") for death, she is deferred to by the world ("He kindly stopped for me—"). In another respect, we must see the first line not only as willful (had not time for) but also as the admission of a disabling fact (could not). The second line responds to the doubleness of conception. What, in other words, in one context is deference, in another is coercion, and since the poem balances tonally between these extremes it is important to note the dexterity with which they are compacted in the first two lines.

There is, of course, further sense in which death stops for the speaker, and that is in the fusion I alluded to earlier between interior and exterior senses of time, so that the consequence of the meeting in the carriage is the death of otherness. The poem presumes to rid death of its otherness, to familiarize it, literally to adopt its perspective and in so doing to effect a synthesis between self and other, internal time and the faster, more relentless beat of the world. Using more traditional terms to describe the union, Allen Tate speaks of the poem's "subtly interfused erotic motive, which the idea of death has presented to most romantic poets, love being a symbol interchangeable with death."[30] It is true that the poem is charged with eroticism whose end or aim is union, perhaps as we conventionally know it, a synthesis of self and other for the explicit purpose of the transformation of other or, if that proves impossible, for the loss of self. Death's heralding phenomenon, the loss of self, would be almost welcomed if self at this point could be magically fused with other. The young boy in Whitman's "Out of the Cradle Endlessly Rocking," learning the lessons of sexuality and the lessons of death as one, would readily have understood Dickinson's conception of death as a courtly lover who, growing less genteel, ravishes life. The child in Whitman's poem, it will be remembered, listening to the aria sung by a he- and a she-bird, understands love's "reverberations" at the same moment he intuits "the unknown want, the destiny of me." Meaning, when he can verbalize it, shapes itself as the knowledge of death:

Whereto . . . the sea,

Delaying not, hurrying not,
Whisper'd me through the night, and very plainly before daybreak,
Lisp'd to me the low and delicious word death,
And again death, death, death, death,
Hissing melodious, neither like the bird not like my arous'd
   child's heart
But edging near as privately for me, rustling at my feet,
Creeping thence steadily up to my ears and laving me softly all over,
Death, death, death, death, death.
. . . .
The word of the sweetest song and all songs,
The strong and delicious word which, creeping to my feet,
(Or like some old crone rocking the cradle, swathed in sweet garments,
   bending aside,)
The sea whisper'd me.

If death is more openly seductive in Whitman's poem, this is in keeping with the difference in temperament between the two poets. It should be noted that for both poets, however, death is essence of the universe as well as its end, and the self is wooed and won by this otherness that appears to define the totality of experience.

Indeed the trinity of death, self, immortality, however ironic a parody of the holy paradigm, at least promises a conventional fulfillment of the idea that the body's end coincides with the soul's everlasting life. But, as in "Our journey had advanced," death so frequently conceptualized as identical with eternity here suffers a radical displacement from it. While both poems suggest a discrepancy between eternity and death, the former poem hedges on the question of where the speaker stands with respect to that discrepancy, at its conclusion seeming to locate her safely in front of or "before" death. "Because I could not stop for Death," on the other hand, pushes revision one step further, daring to leave the speaker stranded in the moment of death.

Along these revisionary lines, the ride to death that we might have supposed to take place through territory unknown, we discover in stanza three to reveal commonplace sights but now fused with spectacle. The path out of the world is also apparently the one through it and in the compression of the three images ("the School, where Children strove," "the Fields of Gazing Grain—," "the Setting Sun—") we are introduced to a new kind of visual shorthand. Perhaps what is extraordinary here is the elasticity of reference, how imposingly on the figural scale the images can weigh while, at the same time, never abandoning any of their quite literal specificity. Hence the sight of the children is a circumscribed one by virtue of the specificity of their placement "At Recess—in the Ring—" and, at the same time, the picture takes on the shadings of allegory. This referential flexibility or fusion of literal and figural meanings is potential in the suggestive connotations of the verb "strove," which is a metaphor in the context of the playground (that is, in its literal context) and a mere descriptive verb in the context of the implied larger world (that is, in its figural context). The "Fields of Gazing Grain—" also suggest a literal picture, but one that leans in the direction of emblem; thus the epithet "Gazing" has perhaps been anthropomorphized from the one-directional leaning of grain in the wind, the object of its gazing the speaker herself. The "Children" mark the presence of the world along one stage of the speaker's journey, the "Gazing Grain—" marks the passing of the world (its harkening after the speaker as she rides away from it), and the "Setting Sun—" marks its past.[31] For at least as the third stanza conceives of it, the journey toward eternity is a series of successive and, in the case of the grain, displaced visions giving way finally to blankness.

But just as after the first two stanzas, we are again rescued in the fourth from any settled conception of this journey. As we were initially not to think of the journey taking place out of the world (and hence with the children we are brought back to it), the end of the third stanza having again moved us to the world's edge, we are redeemed from falling over it by the speaker's correction: "Or rather—He passed Us—." It is the defining movement of the poem to deliver us just over the boundary line between life and death and then to recall us. Thus while the poem gives the illusion of a one-directional movement, albeit a halting one, we discover upon closer scrutiny that the movements are multiple and, as in "I heard a Fly buzz when I died," constitutive of flux, back and forth over the boundary from life to death. Despite the correction, "Or rather—He passed Us—," the next lines register a response that would be entirely appropriate to the speaker's passing of the sun. "The Dews drew" round the speaker, her earthly clothes not only inadequate, but actually falling away in deference to the sensation of "chill—" that displaces them as she passes the boundary of the earth. Thus, on the one hand, "chill—" is a mere physiological response to the setting of the sun at night, on the other, it is a metaphor for the earlier assertion that the earth and earthly goods are being exchanged for something else. Implications in the poem, like the more explicit assertions, are contradictory and reflexive, circling back to underline the very premises they seem a moment ago to have denied. Given such ambiguity, we are constantly in a quandary about how to place the journey that, at any one point, undermines the very certainty of conception it has previously established. Something of the same ambiguity, and for similar reasons, is revealed in George Herbert's "Redemption":

> Having been tenant long to a rich Lord,
> Not thriving, I resolved to be bold,
> And make a suit unto him, to afford
> A new small-rented lease, and cancell th' old.
> In heaven at his manour I him sought:
> They told me there, that he was lately gone
> About some land, which he had dearly bought
> Long since on earth, to take possession.
> I straight return'd, and knowing his great birth,
> Sought him accordingly in great resorts;
> In cities, theaters, gardens, parks and courts:
> At length I heard a ragged noise and mirth
> Of theeves and murderers: there I him espied,
> Who straight, *Your suit is granted*, said and died.

More boldly perhaps and with an acutely dramatic sense of its own contradictions, "Redemption" fuses past and present; earth and heaven; the feudal lord with his earthly mansion and the heavenly Lord with His divine estate; the lease of a new house and the lease afforded by the new dispensation; the speaker as individual man making a petition to God and as all mankind for whose collective sake Christ sacrificed His life. These fusions are complemented by a series of effective displacements each of which depends upon the disregard of conventional boundary. Thus, for example, the speaker travels to heaven (without dying) where he expects to find Christ (whose existence he could not possibly know about prior to the occurrence in the last line) and finding Him absent (on earth for the explicit purpose of granting the petition the speaker has not yet made to Him) the speaker returns to earth (mistakenly imagining that wealth houses divinity) only to be distracted by the "ragged noise and mirth" of the crucifixion itself and the simultaneity of Christ's death and man's redemption. The intent of such fusions and boundary-crossings or, at any rate, their *primary* effect, is two-fold: first, to cast the problem of man's salvation in inescapably personal terms that bring him into direct and literal relationship with Christ so that he finds himself both the explicit cause of the sacrifice and its only beneficiary; and second, to depict both the petition and its granting as unalterably present tense. No longer relegated to historical fact, in the timeless world of need and its fulfillment, the moment is charged with the history-making event of man's redemption, which converts past into an ineluctable present, and insists that meaning win its way free from generalization.

While Dickinson's representation of the ride with death is less histrionic, it is as insistent in our coming to terms with the personalization of the event and of its perpetual reenactment in the present. For the grave that is "paused before" in the fifth stanza, with the tombstone lying flat against the ground ("scarcely visible—"), is seen from the outside and then (by the transformation of spatial considerations into temporal ones) is passed by or through: "Since then— 'tis Centuries—." The poem's concluding stanza both fulfills the traditional Christian notion that while the endurance of death is essential for the reaching of eternity, the two are not identical, and by splitting death and eternity with the space of "Centuries—," challenges that traditional notion. The poem that has thus far played havoc with our efforts to fix its journey in any conventional time or space, on this side of death or the other, concludes with an announcement about the origins of its speech, now explicitly equivocal: "'tis Centuries—and yet/Feels shorter than the Day." What in "There's a certain Slant of light" had been a clear relationship between figure and its fulfillment (a sense of perceptive enlightenment accruing from the movement of one to the other) is in this poem manifestly baffling. For one might observe that for all the apparent movement here, there are no real progressions in the poem at all. If the correction "We passed the Setting Sun—/ Or rather— He passed Us—" may be construed as a confirmation of the slowness of the drive alluded to earlier in the poem, the last stanza seems to insist that the carriage is standing still, moving if at all, as we say, in place. For the predominant sense of this journey is not simply its endlessness; it is also the curious back and forth sweep of its images conveying, as they do, the perpetual return to what has been perpetually taken leave of.

Angus Fletcher, speaking in terms applicable to "Because I could not stop for Death," documents the characteristics of allegorical journeys as surrealistic in imagery (as for example, the "Gazing Grain—"), paratactic in rhythm or structure (as indeed we can hear in the acknowledged form of movement: "We passed . . . We passed . . . We passed . . . Or rather— He passed Us . . . We Paused . . ."), and almost always incomplete: "It is logically quite natural for the extension to be infinite, since by definition there is no such thing as the whole of any analogy; all analogies are incomplete, and incompletable, and allegory simply records this analogical relation in a dramatic or narrative form."[32]

But while the poem has some of the characteristics of allegory, it nonetheless seems to defy such easy classification. Thus the utterance is not quite allegory because it is not strongly iconographic (its figures do not have a one-to-one correspondence with a representational base), and at the same time, these figures are sufficiently rigid to preclude the freeing up of associations that is characteristic of the symbol. We recall Coleridge's distinction between a symbolic and an allegorical structure. A symbol presupposes a unity with its object. It denies the separateness between subject and object by creating a synecdochic relationship between itself and the totality of what it represents; like the relationship between figure and thing figured discussed in the first part of this chapter, it is always part of that totality. Allegory, on the other hand, is a sign that refers to a specific meaning from which it continually remains detached. Through its abstract embodiment, the allegorical form makes the distance between itself and its original meaning clearly manifest. It accentuates the absolute cleavage between subject and object. Since the speaker in "Because I could not stop for Death" balances between the boast of knowledge and the confession of ignorance, between a oneness with death and an inescapable difference from it, we may regard the poem as a partial allegory. The inability to know eternity, the failure to be at one with it, is, we might say, what the allegory of "Because I could not stop for Death" makes manifest. The ride with death, though it espouses to reveal a future that is past, in fact casts both past and future in the indeterminate present of the last stanza. Unable to arrive at a fixed conception, it must rest on the bravado (and it implicitly knows this) of its initial claim. Thus death is not really civilized; the boundary between otherness and self, life and death, is crossed, but only in presumption, and we might regard this fact as the real confession of disappointment in the poem's last stanza.

Ahab, in *Moby Dick*, whom Daniel Hoffman has characterized as having "The most allegorical mind of any character in American fiction"[33] because of his willful insistence on reducing protean experience to his monomaniacal meaning for it, wished to strike through the "pasteboard mask" of appearances to reality. Ishmael, no less mesmerized by the mask, albeit attributing a different name to it, spoke of that image which man is drawn to in rivers and fountains as "the ungraspable phantom of life." Treat that "phantom" as symbol, however, and the self, rapt in the contemplation of its own reflection, falls toward it in fusion and, like Narcissus, drowns. *Moby Dick* may in fact be viewed as a struggle between allegorical modes of perceiving the world and symbolic ones. The extremity of either choice is black magic—the egotistical projection of the self, or the resolute withholding of it. In *American Renaissance*, F. O. Matthiessen's suggestive discussion of the symbolic and allegorical biases of Melville and Hawthorne seems, at times, to intend a definition of the pervasive dialectic of nineteenth-century America,[34] for in the one case man attempts to transform the world by reshaping it, in the other, he "deals with fixities."[35] Paul de Man, too, imagines the dialectical pull between symbolizing structures and allegorizing ones to define Romanticism and also to characterize its moral overtones, for the belief in organic totality is a delusive myth. Elaborating on the distinction between allegory and symbol in the specific terms of the temporal difference that separates the self from that with which it desires to fuse, de Man calls to mind the dilemma of Dickinson's speaker in "Because I could not stop for Death": "Whereas the symbol postulates the possibility of an identity or identification, allegory designates primarily a distance in relation to its own origin, and, renouncing the nostalgia and the desire to coincide, it establishes its language in the void of this temporal distance. In so doing, it prevents the self from an illusory identification with the non-self, which is now fully, though painfully, recognized as a non-self."[36] The self is not the thing it aspires to know. Nor can its representation of reality dissolve the distinction between the two.

I dwell on such issues because they provide a context for that curious shift from the assertion of knowledge in "Because I could not stop for Death—" to the confession of its failure, from the intimation that the ride to death defies the phenomenal characteristics of the world, to the admission that it does not. This pendulum that swings back and forth across the boundary separating life from death, time from timelessness, becomes the dialectic in which the self comes to terms with its impulse for fusion and identic relationship, and with the loss attendant upon the realization that such fusion is truly illusory. The self coming to terms with the fact of its mortality from which no fusion with death can rescue it cannot complete or make good on the certain knowledge that the poem's first stanza implicitly promised. The effort to make all events associative ones, or "repetitive," in the sense of identic (to recall Eliade's description of the primitive organization of experience) is to deny the most painful boundary between self and other that the world makes manifest, to cheat the world of its otherness and hence, of necessity, the self of its defining integrity.

Yet art does attempt such a cheat: it will make its voice heard, will *have* a voice where no voice can really be, and this willful fact brings us back, as I promised, to Panofsky's essay on how the phrase *Et in Arcadia ego*, once attributed to a death's-head, grew with Poussin's painting of the scene to be attributed to a dead person himself; how, concomitantly, what was once a matter of terror became merely an occasion for meditative speculation on the fact of death. In Guercino's painting of the death's-head the fact of terror and the unknown quality of death are wedded to each other. For it is clear that the skull which represents death is a mere emblem of it, a sign that conceals its meaning. Similarly, in those poems discussed in the first half of this chapter, death's appearance is incomplete and unknown, a "boiling Wheel" or a "Maelstrom, with a notch," and hence prompts terror. The soul is "secure" only in the presence of "A Sepulchre" for, in the terms of "There's a certain Slant of light," figural reality loses its indirection or "Slant" only when it straightens into the fulfillment of death. In lieu of that fulfillment, these poems collapse the distinction between subject and object, figure and thing figured, as if collapse into, or fusion with, the object in question might substitute for knowledge. In the proleptic utterances, however ("I heard a Fly buzz when I died" and "Because I could not stop for Death"), which speak as if from beyond the grave, the turmoil of the earlier poems has been smoothed into tranquillity, for in the beginning of "Because I could not stop for Death," as in Poussin's painting, death is no otherness and it does not create otherness by its occurrence; the dead person still assumes mortal shape and still possesses voice sufficient to speak. That terror should disappear as a consequence of knowledge gained about the thing feared is not especially surprising. But what if the nostalgia implicit in both Poussin's painting and Dickinson's poem is occasioned not simply by the loss of life, but also by the loss of self, its translation into a mere emblem of survival, no longer recognizable in human terms?

Dickinson's intuition that she must preserve an otherness in order to preserve a self abruptly distorts the seeming unity of personae in the carriage. The acknowledgment of time ("'tis Centuries—and yet/Feels shorter than the Day") is equally an acknowledgment that the desired and, for a time, achieved fusion between subjective and objective time will not hold. The speaker can finesse the illusion of such unity, but the last stanza points up all the problems with which it must come to terms. The experience of death still leaves eternity an unknown; the journey cannot be completed conceptually, is in need of an end that is not, and will never be, conceptually forthcoming. For allegory must come to terms with the conceptual inadequacy of its desire, with the real zero beyond which invention cannot go. Despite the fact that the allegoric impulse is contrary to the mimetic one—would rather perfect the world than represent it—it must nonetheless fall back on the same storehouse of images. Thus the transformation from the death's-head to the dead man who has words and, in Dickinson's poems, from the terror before death to the imaginative construction of speech after it, civilizes death in the only way we apparently know how. But such "civility" is an illusion. Death without the death of speech, death without the cessation of time—in a land of unlikeness, a true Arcadia, this is no place we know.

Where does the ride with Death and Immortality take place? And is it possible to say with any certainty how long—centuries or a day—it lasts? I suggested earlier that lyric time, although at some points coincidental with actual time, hangs in front of it observing only those properties of actuality that it chooses. Perhaps it would be more accurate to say not that the lyric defies the temporal-spatial axis but that it has its own referential axis, neither clearly future (though an utterance often implies its own continous action) nor clearly past (though it often seems past because its own action is predicated on itself as on a history). "'Tis so appalling—it exhilarates—/So over Horror, it half Captivates—/The Soul stares after it, secure—." "Stares," we might say, timelessly or for all time. Similarly, the "certain Slant of light,/Winter Afternoons—/" "oppresses" with a present-tense verb of sufficient heft to secure both past and future under its aegis. "Slow tramp the Centuries,/And the Cycles wheel!" When and where are irrelevant questions. Even the past-tense "Because I could not stop for Death" brings us up short against the present of its disturbing conclusion. The speaker in the throes of the movement that pulls her forward seems to turn for a moment toward us and, in so doing, to stop the carriage's action allowing us to place it. And while "I heard a Fly buzz when I died" is narrated wholly in the past, it is no less adamant in its illusion that the incidents it relates are present. One might hazard the generalization that although Dickinson's poems on death assume the past tense with characteristic regularity precisely so that the death the speaker claims to have survived will be credited as a fait accompli, nonetheless, the very task of the entire poem is to re-present it.

George Wright, in "The Lyric Present: Simple Present Verbs in English Poems," offers conclusions to an important statistical study he has compiled on verb forms in the lyric.[37] As the title of his essay implies, Wright documents the fact that the tense most characteristic of, and most frequently used in, the lyric is the simple present tense. But this present seems to contain a multiplicity of temporal features that we ordinarily think of as mutually exclusive. It is past-like as well as indicative of future. It locates action temporally, but not in time as we know it. Although timeless, this present tense implies duration. The distance cast by "the look of Death—" remains. Giving way to nothing else, it is what we return to every time we reread the poem. And, Wright suggests, the lyric not only implies temporal permanence and permanent temporal elusiveness, but a corresponding spatial dislocation as well, as its contradictions preserve the structure of the ambiguities that element it. A poem especially evasive about its spatial location is Yeats's "Among School Children," for if we ask where "Labour is blossoming or dancing," we are answered, but mysteriously:

> Labour is blossoming or dancing where
> The body is not bruised to pleasure soul,
> Nor beauty born out of its own despair,
> Nor blear-eyed wisdom out of midnight oil.

A present that houses the past as well as the future and that, moreover, evades spatial location and fixture is very close to the creation of a temporal myth built betweeen past and future, real and imagined time, this world and some other. Keats's "Do I wake or sleep" poses a question about his state in the aftermath of the vision, but answer it either way and the vision still remains fixed, even in the permanence of its fleeting. The present tense is so characteristic of the lyric that Wright terms it "the lyric tense," and he adds that its assertion of presence may be the poem's dominant symbolic gesture—an idea we shall examine in the next chapter—as it transfixes reality so that reality remains caught precisely at the moment of its passing: "The lyric tense detail is almost always felt as symbolic, and as with Yeats's swans that drift or his birds that reel, the tense often appears at the most climactic moment, the moment at which some symbolic transformation, some metamorphosis takes place. . . . On such occasions the device of lyric tense seems not merely to frame but almost to *be* the metaphor."[38]

Such metaphors inhere not simply in the slowing of action but also in the attribution of pivotal meaning to it, as if the poet assumed that, were action visible, the relational ties between subject and object might sharpen to clarity. These relations, the ones between subject and object, as well as between one temporal category and another, are, as I have been suggesting, compressed in the lyric or collapsed by it in what sometimes seems to be a mimetic gesture of the perceptual syntheses characteristic of thinking itself. Thus the poems are projective in nature, enacting the very displacements of experience. In them perception refuses to be riveted to one spot, shifts, as in "Our journey had advanced," to relocate itself in accordance with the progressive lessons of experience. The displacements we have seen (from the "Failed" windows in "I heard a Fly buzz when I died" to the "Gazing Grain—" in "Because I could not stop for Death") remind us how thoroughly the world remains saturated in our perceptual terms for it, how seductive syntheses and fusion are when we are overtaken by the starkness of the world's own terms. The color white, purged of meaning (which so haunts Dickinson's work, as we remember it haunts Melville's), is perhaps the way the world looks when we represent it accurately, but at such moments it is also bleached to nothing. The problem, of course, is how to give it coloration, to see it, as we say, in its own terms, for the very conception that something *has* its own terms is itself an anthropomorphic one. If the lyric shrinks from mediation with the outside world, it seeks no less to preserve the integrity of its own temporal fusions, for to mediate between them, to establish discrete barriers between past, present, and future is to distort the very synchrony of its knowledge. In Augustine's terms "the present of things past, the present of things present, and the present of things future" all have in common the shared moment of their acknowledgment.

Contradiction between social and personal time is, as I implied previously, the lyric's generating impulse, and Dickinson's proleptic utterances, by exaggerating these contradictions, draw our attention to them. The greatest contradiction lies in the lyric's fixity of its own present. This mythologizing of the lyric present, the insistence that present and, by implication, presence can achieve permanence is perhaps accounted for by the tenacious hold the past has on the present, by its dexterity in casting itself up as if it still were. Hence the fusion between past and present is often so axiomatic as to escape attention, though in the next chapter we shall see that loss discovers its origin when space comes to intervene between the two. The present, here, then, seems permanent partly by virtue of how thoroughly it confuses itself with its own history, on the one hand, and its destiny, on the other. Unable to separate itself from what it has been and from what it desires to be, the present in Dickinson's poems (as if by association) projects even more daring fusions between the time before death and that after it. A passage from Beckett's *Malloy* which Wright calls our attention to indicates how natural such fusions are: "When I try and think riding I lose my balance and fall. I speak in the present tense, it is so easy to speak in the present tense, when speaking of the past. It is the mythological present, don't mind it."[39] The present may be described as that moment in which all past moments (potentially) coincide with consciousness, just as the future only exists insofar as it can be conceived of or conjured by a consciousness that is present. The present is thus that fulcral moment that not only arbitrates between past and future but that also embodies them. For of themselves, both past and future may be conceived of as having subject without locution, spirit without body, the evasiveness of pure air. "Everything we say/of the past," wrote Wallace Stevens, "is description without place." Indeed, the same is true of our words for the future. Only the present has a sure space of its own.

In the poems discussed in the first two chapters, death is eschewed, because it details the end of the self; here it is desired, but minus its consequences. Thus permanence (and hence an endless present) is attributed to death, and longed for in the form of fusion with it. Fusions are actively sought and achieved in the poems discussed in the first part of this chapter. In such poems, a state fuses with the terms of its own figuration, as death fuses with the image of light. In the proleptic utterances, however, where the fusion is sought perhaps even more strenuously because the stakes are higher, the gain of temporal fusion seems to necessitate the sacrifice of union between subject and object. The premise of these poems may be that temporal collapse will blur the distinction between subject and object, death and self, will make them one; the poems discover, however, that to preserve identity time and space must intervene. For the pain that binds the self to its own boundaries also defines it. What is restrictive in one context is definitional in another. Thus the poem may subject the world to reconstruction, but only one feature at a time. Temporal fusions *or* the fusion between subject and object— either may be ventured but not, apparently, at the same time. For knock down all the walls of the house at once and the structure crumbles to ruin.

Dickinson once wrote of "An Omen in the Bone/Of Death's tremendous nearness—" (P 532). Perhaps she took the omen for prophecy and with characteristic impatience pushed it toward a fulfillment she herself could appreciate. For her lyrics, as I have been suggesting, attempt to cross boundaries, to blur distinctions between life and death, time and timelessness, figure and its fulfillment, or, to put it more accurately, to wear a passage between them—which is the poem—and, in so doing, to seek refuge in a presence whose permanence will withstand temporal change. They thus go in search of the very mythical time that Wright tells us is characteristic of most lyric poems. For the idiosyncratic fusions Dickinson's lyrics make explicit, most lyrics imply. They record an event that, in Wright's words, "has happened—is happening—happens."[40] In the mythological present the self goes forth bravely into places it does not and cannot know, dreaming the very landscapes to which it will forever be denied real access. It seeks symbolic correspondences and stumbles upon differences. It desires to break loose into timelessness and feels instead the weightless net of temporal ensnarement. It would give anything to become an otherness, but it must settle for itself. So it learns how to celebrate that self, even the confusions of its own contradictory impulses. In the process, and shaking itself free from all that would disembody it, the self finds a present, a being, and a voice. These the lyric memorializes.

The Mourning That Is Language

And now it was a name I sought, in my memory, the name of the only town it had been given me to know. . . . And this name that I sought, I felt sure that it began with a B or with a P, but in spite of this clue, or perhaps because of its falsity, the other letters continued to escape me. . . . And even my sense of identity was wrapped in a namelessness often hard to penetrate. . . . Yes, even then, when already all was fading, waves and particles, there could be no things but nameless things, no names but thingless names.

    —Samuel Beckett

The mirror is a contrivance for seeing things not visible directly by the eye, such as one's own face, and the object seen is called a virtual image because its position in touch-Space is that from which the rays of light would come if the real luminous point were there.

    —Samuel Alexander

"'IT IS FINISHED' can never be said of us" (L 555), Dickinson wrote, and her poems on death, as if to insist on the literal interpretation of such a reading of experience, push the point. For while the most profound estrangement is that precipitated by death, in Dickinson's poems death is not loss for the dying person but is rather reunion. So, at least, is the poems' premise: life must be sacrificed, selfhood go by the way, all defining characteristics dismissed, but the recompense for these exactions is the end of the solitary self, the loss of the boundary between self and object, not because they are dead to each other but rather because

136

they are fused with each other. Perhaps the fantasy accounts for why Dickinson's speakers practice dying with frequency. In so doing they court not death but rather union; indeed, as I have commented before, many of Dickinson's formulations on death are explicitly sexual. She had written: "Death is the supple Suitor/That wins at last—" (P 1445). The world, then, is not destroyed for the self as a consequence of death but is rather reconstructed, and there are poems in which speakers implicitly imagine death as the phenomenon that makes relatedness possible.[1] Hence a dying speaker becomes one with the death's-head that at that moment is also the personification of otherness. The union of subject and object requires death because it requires the cessation of time, just as it requires the collapse or transformation of spatial distinction. For the death world is a purely symbolic one in which the body is exchanged for meaning; or, to put it differently, it is a world in which meaning is not hindered by limitations of any sort, and relatedness not defined by, or as a consequence of, identic separation. If only the end could not be, or could be survived beyond, there might yet be hope for the abolition of the more intractable boundary, the one that separates selves.

The immortality myth[2] implicit in the poems on death that we have examined in the previous chapter is not especially unique. In the words of another, older text, when St. Paul in the Letter to Romans (7:24) asks "Who shall deliver me from the body of this death?" the terms of deliverance seem also to be the loss of the body if that loss could be followed by a higher union. It is in the service of union that the displacements in Dickinson's poems unfold: the "failed Windows," the "Gazing Grain—,"—all the projective fusions discussed in the last chapter are symptoms or manifestations of the desire to be one with the object of one's longing. Thus displacement itself must be regarded as a phenomenon devised to counter those boundaries that impose the intolerable distinction, and Romanticism, so obsessed with the point at which relationship becomes fusion because it cannot help it (or because it does not wish to help it), must recognize its desires, pushed to the extreme, in that longing for death which will deliver it to coincidence.

The dead speakers in Dickinson's poems resist transformation; they stubbornly remain their mortal selves. Death is a phenomenon subject to the speaker's reconstruction; either she cannot imagine it at all ("and then/I could not see to see—" [P 465]) or she must imagine it as other than it is. Thus in the hierarchy of Dickinson's formulations, loss comes after death. She herself stated this matter-of-factly when she wrote:

"Death—is but one—and comes but once—/And only nails the eyes—" (P 561). And, again, addressing herself to comparative terms: "Parting is one of the exactions of a Mortal Life. It is bleak—like Dying, but occurs more times" (L 399). The preceding calculations imply subtlety rather than an evasive metaphysics, the ability to discriminate certain refinements: "Suspense—is Hostiler than Death—" (P 705), for in Dickinson's cosmology loss is the most irreparable phenomenon and confers the greatest transfiguration.

Since loss and pain connote a greater finality for Dickinson than death does, we must look to her treatment of them to see how she comprehends ending when it cannot be refuted. In part 2 of this chapter we shall explore the perimeters of Dickinson's understanding of loss as it exists within the self and between persons. Here we shall be concerned with how pain replaces the lost presence and comes, in fact, to represent it. We shall also look at the way in which temporality, the driving force behind such a substitution, puts space at the center of being. In part 3 we shall be concerned with those Dickinson poems that show the self to duplicate external loss by its own negation of feeling, especially the feeling of pain, and we shall compare the way in which the resulting space harks back to a lost presence much as a poem harks back to its external reference. The relationship between space and presence, as between poem and reference, may be defined as one of alterity. In part 4 we shall turn to poems in which loss, no longer located within the confines of the self, exists rather in the natural and phenomenal world, becoming, therefore, part of the landscape, and we shall consider how this landscape presents itself as the ultimate alterity whose status replaces that of death. Throughout the chapter we shall be looking at language's attempts to word space back together, and in part 5 we will turn explicitly to the relationship between loss and language.

II

Time, as Dickinson had written in terms almost as blunt, is misery: "The Months have ends—the Years—a knot—/No Power can untie/To stretch a little further/A Skein of Misery—" (P 423). While the skein may be stretched, it may not be broken; like the skin (that word that it seems only vaguely to displace), the skein is continuous. The very fact of its protraction points up the source of the speaker's misery: the inability of a life to be derailed from its own course, to have more than one

course, or to travel it in anything but solitude.[3] Duration accentuates solitude, for multiply the points of a life in time, either backward toward the past or forward toward the future, and the line of
duration becomes proof of the inevitability of solitude, admitting
as it does of the intersection of lives at an astoundingly small number
of points. Narratives chart intersections, and we might conceive of them
as attempting to prove, by the way they fill up their own spaces with the
plurality of intersections and pluralistic significances, that moments of
solitude are the exception rather than the rule. In fact one of the social
functions narratives perform is to assure us that intersections occur, as
they frequently do not in real life, and turn into points of real coincidence and meaning. If coincidence is seen as occasional, as Dickinson
suggests, then sequence and duration example its infrequency. The
moment after coincidence is the moment of loss. Imagine a time in
which time stands still, however, and loss becomes a meaningless concept
because difference is itself meaningless. In the resulting fantasy, stasis
confers either union or, as in the case of the following poem, unconsciousness of any alternative to its absence. For pare all of temporality
to a single moment and awareness of the shadows that fall from one's
heels as one walks, distinguishing the self from its own image and that
image from the difference of the ground, dwindles to nothing:

> There is a Zone whose even Years
> No Solstice interrupts—
> Whose Sun constructs perpetual Noon
> Whose perfect Seasons wait—
>
> Whose Summer set in Summer, till
> The Centuries of June
> And Centuries of August cease
> And Consciousness—is Noon.   (P 1056)

Stasis is an image so difficult to sustain that it pivots on the verge of
a passage the very existence of which the poem's premise has denied.
Summer will last forever, but that is presumably only "till . . . August
cease." The poem is, as it suggests, a "construct[ion]," and with the
last line it brings together into one space the problem of temporality and
consciousness of it that we began, in the last chapter, to examine. At
the point of their intersection, is consciousness a state that is extinguished
in the trance of undifferentiation (like the mind that reaches bottom and

has "Finished knowing—") or does it, as the poem seems to suggest, blaze into clarity and distinction? Finally, insofar as difference, however it defines itself and between whatever terms, is a permanent fact of our experience—that fact which necessitates cognition, language, and symbolizing structures themselves—we must ask how this poem and Dickinson's poems in general attempt to cure imperfections so central that they come, in the end, to constitute definitions of existence.

Jacques Derrida has spoken of what he calls "differance," using the word to call attention to its two related meanings: first, to name that which is deferred, delayed, distanced by *time* as it separates entities and, secondly, to name the intervening *space* that removes entities from each other, making them differ from, be not identical to, each other. The relationships between the two features, between deferral and difference, delay and nonidentity, are clarified in the following passage whose subject is signification but could as well be the relationship between any two terms:

> Differance is what makes the movement of signification possible only if each element that is said to be "present," appearing on the stage of presence, is related to something other than itself but retains the mark of a past element and already lets itself be hollowed out by the mark of its relation to a future element. This trace relates no less to what is called the future than to what is called the past, and it constitutes what is called the present by this very relation to what it is not, to what it absolutely is not; that is, not even to a past or future considered as a modified present. In order for it to be, an interval must separate it from what it is not; but the interval that constitutes it in the present must also, and by the same token, divide the present in itself, thus dividing, along with the present, everything that can be conceived on its basis, that is, every being—in particular . . . the substance or subject. Constituting itself, dynamically dividing itself, this interval is what could be called *spacing*; time's becoming-spatial or space's becoming-temporal (*temporalizing*).[4]

"Differance" seems intolerable, as loss is intolerable, and identity therefore craves not merely to prove itself in oblique connection to its past and future or to otherness, but to be that past and future, to become the otherness. Where union is impossible, identity resists the discovery of otherness as if otherness were a contagion or a death. Derrida writes: "Everywhere, the dominance of beings is solicited by differance—in the sense that *sollicitare* means, in old Latin, to shake all over, to make the whole tremble."[5] Perhaps what motivates terror is, as I suggested in my earlier discussion of "My Life had stood a Loaded Gun," that otherness is regarded as the power to kill. If what is not the self will overcome it, then to recognize "differance" is mortal danger. Or perhaps the recognition of otherness necessitates an acknowledgment of boundary too painful because of its attendant configuration of loss. One solution to the dilemma is to experience loss as if it were an extension of one's own identity—a clever strategy for dismantling terror by regarding the images that fill the mind, however removed in actuality, as part of the totality of the self that conceives of them. In the following poem loss is the feature in which the speaker recognizes herself, the mirror where it all becomes clear:

> Like Eyes that looked on Wastes—
> Incredulous of Ought
> But Blank—and steady Wilderness—
> Diversified by Night—
>
> Just Infinites of Nought—
> As far as it could see—
> So looked the face I looked upon—
> So looked itself—on Me—
>
> I offered it no Help—
> Because the Cause was Mine—
> The Misery a Compact
> As hopeless—as divine—
>
> Neither—would be absolved—
> Neither would be a Queen
> Without the Other—Therefore—
> We perish—tho' We reign—   (P 458)

In the self-reflexive parody of completion, pain is identity. For "So looked itself—on Me—" is both a response that mirrors the speaker's original stare and, at the same time, a projective impulse, with "looked itself" as a hostile verb: "It made me look like it, confused my image with its own." Not a parenthetical or appositive pronoun that restates the subject, "itself—," in the idiomatic context of these lines, is a reflexive *object* of a suddenly transitive form of the verb "look." To look oneself "upon—" another is, moreover, a rewriting of "to look on" that underscores the inevitable result: the other will have the image thrust upon it as a reflection that usurps its own image. But for all of the reflection (with the intended double meaning of that word) the speaker's relationship to the image remains unclear. Language in the last two stanzas is especially ambiguous and paradoxical, and the source of the ambiguity evolves out of a possessive pronoun. Absence cannot be "Help[ed]" "Because the Cause was Mine—" is a diagnosis that implies, contrary to the earlier line ("So looked itself—on Me—"), that it is the speaker who has projected absence onto the image and then identified herself with it. Perhaps what is absent is the self; the cause of absence is self-projection, and "Misery" is its consequence. "Hopeless—" because impossible, "divine—" in pathetic mimicry of God's manifestation in absence, the speaker's insistence on the "Compact," on contingent identities that will not recognize boundaries, is disintegration in the end: "We perish—tho' We reign—." For all of its self-reflective terms, the poem seems strangely without a subject. Although it tries to reify absence and hold on to it as personified identity, the final result is vacancy.

Usually Dickinson took a decidedly different view of the matter, knowing that "Absence disembodies—" (P 860). Insisting on the internality of pain, she remarked, "Gethsemane—/Is but a Province —in the Being's Centre—" (P 553). The attempt of the latter formulations is to acknowledge the invisibility of loss, and they identify their pain rather than themselves in the discrepancy between the visible form of the lost thing and the trace of its presence still retained by the mind.

"Praise it—'tis dead—" (P 1384), Dickinson wrote bitterly, and the dash separating the command and the explanation are, in this case, a meaningful testament to the space that puts itself between negation and our words for it. Perhaps, though, in the context of how many of Dickinson's poems do praise what is lost or dead, we must take another look at the command and wonder seriously whether she might somewhere have believed that praise led to resurrection. For if we regard memory as a kind of resurrection, a keeping there of what is really absent, then praise functions as a stalling technique, an effort to tease the finality of departure away, to coax presence back to life, to keep it, if nowhere else, in articulated consciousness. Against the negation of loss she sets her poems. To infuse them with power, to make them "work," requires certain adjustment. Pain, for example, must be regarded as a residue or trace of presence, loss itself seen as a standing-instead-of; to hold on to it is to retain the thread whose end leads to the missing object.

Thus we find in Dickinson's poetry that odd embrace of seemingly paradoxical statements elevating the moment of loss to supremacy. She spoke, for example, of a "sumptuous Destitution–/Without a Name–" (P 1382), and if we are to understand the terminology in anything but the simplest manner, we must ask how, in her lexicon, loss became an experience so hospitable to its own contradiction. Much of the power of paradoxical lines is a direct consequence of how unabashedly they accommodate opposite meanings, utterance bodying forth the condensations of experience. Distilling, condensing, rarifying–paradox is alchemist's art, and its volatile transformations are especially notable in a work quite different from Dickinson's, that unique document from the Renaissance, Sir Walter Ralegh's *Ocean to Cynthia*, which calls attention to its own histrionic shifts of feeling. There, after extravaganzas of praise for the queen interrupted by venomous passages of recrimination, the speaker stumbles upon the commonplace grief of his own experience: "She is gone, she is lost, she is found, she is ever fair." But what is sequential in recognition for Ralegh is simultaneous for Dickinson, who speaks of "A perfect–paralyzing Bliss–/Contented as Despair–" (P 756). The adjectives modify crosswise as well as in the linear manner that their placement suggests, so that "perfect–" describes not only the "Bliss–" but also paralysis and, reaching into the next line, associates itself with "Content[ment]." Similarly, "paralyzing" implicates "Despair–" as well as "Bliss–," and the experience resonates with the simultaneity of the multiple crossings. "Bliss–" paralyzes by stunning both in its first, positive sense of striking immobile out of wonderment, transfixing, and in its second, negative sense of shocking into stasis, riveting the speaker to the source of her attraction, rendering her unable to move on or elsewhere. "Bliss–" is "Contented" in the obvious sense of satisfied or appeased and, by a path that requires the crossing of the adjective so that it most directly applies to the comparative term, "Despair–," too, is "Contented," quiescent and passive. The ultimate "Content[ment]," given this linguistic index, is death. Thus we read synchronically of a "perfect–" "Bliss–"/"Despair–," a "paralyzing" "Bliss–"/"Content[ment]," and, finally, of "Contented" "Bliss–" as it intersects with the "Content[ment]" of "Despair–." The latter crossing brings "Bliss–" and "Despair–" into direct relationship, which of course has been the line's intention all the time.

Dickinson could be more explicit about the way in which recollection taps the source of life and annihilation at once:

> Rehearsal to Ourselves
> Of a Withdrawn Delight—
> Affords a Bliss like Murder—
> Omnipotent—Acute—
>
> We will not drop the Dirk—
> Because We love the Wound
> The Dirk Commemorate—Itself
> Remind Us that we died.   (P 379)

The "Bliss like Murder—" is the impassioned side of the "Bliss—" that is "Contented as Despair—." Clean-cut as absence, memory is murder because of its perpetual killing-off in the mind of presence. Memory defines its space (hollowing out of conception the exact shape of the something missing) and simultaneously fills it with its own representation. Memory implies a double negation, for loss must be (be acknowledged) before it can be done away with, and it is from the paradoxical reaches of the phenomenon itself that Dickinson's lexical structures borrow their power. The last two lines of the previous poem play upon their own ambiguous grammar so that, on the one hand, we read "We love the Wound/The Dirk Commemorate—Itself/Remind Us that we died" and, on the other, we read "The Dirk Commemorate—Itself/[and] Remind Us that we died." In the latter, "the Wound" is not only associated with "Withdrawn Delight—," as the first reading suggests, but also more globally with the murdered person who becomes literally equivalent to the source of her own loss.[6] Thus "Itself" is not a reflexive referring to "The Dirk" or to "Commemorat[ion]," but is rather a reflexive referring to the speaker who has bowed to the "Omnipoten[ce]" and omnipresence of loss by assuming its exact shape.

The paradox of loss is one Dickinson appreciated explicitly when she wrote: "It is the Past's supreme italic/Makes the Present mean—" (P 1498). Conferring both meaning (sense) and reduction, grief becomes at once power and paralysis. Dickinson put it succinctly: "To feed upon the Retrograde—/Enfeebles—the Advance—" (P 904). The self-regarding and sometimes self-contradictory formulations (along with the ones that are more explicitly paradoxical)[7] have been remarked upon by most of Dickinson's critics as if they were a reflection of her idiosyncratic

interpretation of experience. But memory is always both acknowledged
loss of presence and its articulated representation. Dickinson's formulations are not unique because they invent the structure but rather because
they name it. And indeed, as chapter 1 suggests, true naming is a phenomenon as complex as it is dialectical. The relationship between presence and representation, however, *is* unique in Dickinson's corpus.

In the balance of her poems, presence must be defined in two senses:
first, as an immediate and literal being there (the opposite of absence);
second (in seeming extension of the "voice" I spoke of in chapter 2),
as being unmediated by event or language, pure essence, and therefore
pure revealed totality. It is easy enough to see how immediate being
becomes confused with an impossible totality of being, the lost object
confused with a perfection that never was, and in Dickinson's poems this
confusion is directly responsible for the representational gesture, as if
the speakers somehow imagined that to get the lost object back, to
repossess it, is to recover that wholeness of which they will be an undifferentiated part. Thus although I shall initially be speaking of presence
in its most restricted, literal sense, it should not be forgotten how
thoroughly the two senses remain fused in Dickinson's characteristic
use of the word. The comparative terms in which presence and its
representation are adumbrated are almost always assigned temporal
value, the moment or instance standing for presence, the century or
decade for representation. Reading a friend's letter, she remarks: "It had
like Bliss—the minute length" (L 628), and she frequently talks about
"The Moments of Dominion/That happen on the Soul/And leave it with
a Discontent/Too exquisite—to tell—" (P 627). Such moments must
compensate for their brevity by the way in which they inscribe themselves indelibly on consciousness. Inscription thus becomes temporal
transcendence: "Transporting must the moment be—/Brewed from
decades of Agony!" (P 207). For if presence is literally momentary, its
aftermath is endured in the "Centuries of Nerve—" (P 561) that register
loss.

This is cataclysmic language, and if with the preceding lines one has a
greater tendency to fragment her words in the repeating, to quote out of
context, it is partly dictated by the way in which the temporal designations of presence and absence subordinate their contexts or leap out of
them altogether. For in Dickinson's equations the signs for past and
present ("moment" and "century") or for presence and loss (signs
that are themselves reduced to mere shorthand notation for the categories

they imply, reduced, to invoke Derrida's word, to a mere trace) fragment the logical world, including the logical system of language. Although the temporal signs of presence and loss are often connected by coherent narrative structures that offer to situate them in a context, they frequently throw off their contexts in much the way that an object in an electrical field threatens to destroy anything in its immediate vicinity—we recall the jolting disruptions of "I got so I could take his name."

Loss wreaks havoc on contexts because the story or narrative breaks away under the violence of the terms that element it, but the rupture of context is different in kind from those we observed previously. In these poems disorder is not a consequence of the absence of diachronic progression, as it was in the poems discussed in chapter 1, where the names for an experience existed outside of a history or genesis. Nor is it a consequence of a seemingly logical structure that appears to tell a story that, upon closer scrutiny, is disrupted by a contradictory voice, as we saw with the poems discussed in chapter 2. Nor is disruption the pendulum swing of temporal advance and retreat, the back and forth over the boundary line from life to death, that we observed in chapter 3. Disruption in the poems exists despite narrative coherence and diachronic structure. Like loss itself, though not, I suspect, in conscious parody of it, the temporal signs of presence and absence concentrate or condense their meanings as if in opposition to the lexical frameworks from which they receive both ostensible structure and meaning. Thus the condensations enact the very severative charge that their meanings denote, as if not only their content but also their form broke away from the rational, the discursive, the connected. The break—and it is a break well documented by the pervasive and habitual citing of particular epithets outside of their total contexts—is a metaphor for the separation that loss implies and for its subsequent construction of a double structure for experience in which the lost object continues to bear the weight of its meaning outside of the context that would explain it. The effect of such nodes or concentrations of meaning is that we perceive a given narrative at two levels: first, as it proceeds discursively from beginning to end to tell a coherent story, a story usually circumstanced by loss; and second, as the story's vital meaning is abbreviated in a moment of rupture or at a moment of synaptic connection ("Moments of Dominion," "Centuries of Nerve—"). The traces or condensations of meaning both exist in time and rise above it in the perpetual stalling of momentary significance that lasts, as the first two stanzas of the following poem eloquently put it, sometimes as long as an eternity:

> Because that you are going
> And never coming back
> And I, however absolute
> May overlook your Track—
>
> Because that Death is final,
> However first it be
> This instant be suspended
> Above Mortality—   (P 1260)

As in many of Dickinson's poems (see, for example, "There is a Zone whose even Years"), the partially rendered subjunctive verb argues reality around and becomes, in the end, in the uncontradicted state of its "be[ing]," dictate as well as expression of desire. Raised not only above time but above human life as well, the concentration of meaning is literally "suspended" above the mundane temporal connection and "suspended" as well synchronically or vertically, infused in the cells of the event itself. Given their dynamic opposition to the ordinary, it is not difficult to see why the concentrations of meaning except themselves from their context, for any connection seems trivial to the extent that it has been categorically prohibited with the object of true longing. Thus the condensations tolerate syntactic connection the way they tolerate temporality itself by making clear that the object of primary connection is missing.

The narratives in which the traces of meaning subsume their own history, though controlled by sequence, progression, and adamant linear structure, nonetheless give the illusion of having at their center a snag or rip or even a large rent and sometimes of what the French call a *béance*— a yawning or gaping, a quintessential openness that is marked by the temporal phrases I have been pointing to, as a patch is a marking, and, at the same time, designated by those patches as a permanent imperfection, a hole so radical that it can never be mended.[8] Dickinson spoke tersely on the subject when she wrote:

> To fill a Gap
> Insert the Thing that caused it—
> Block it up

With Other—and 'twill yawn the more—
You cannot solder an Abyss
With Air.   (P 546)

Jay Leyda, writing of Dickinson's poems, called them poems of the "omitted center,"[9] and while by center he meant "biographical circumstance," we may nonetheless transpose the term for our own purpose since it conveys the sense of a complete structure whose central space is haunted by absence. The holes in the structure of experience existing in spite of the linear connections that would thread them back together are revealed not, as discussed in chapter 1, as a consequence of missing features in the narrative, but precisely in the temporal nodes of meaning, those traces whose mere existence stands for (and therefore stands in the absence of) that which, were it present, would invalidate the very need for utterance.

In the following poem, meaning yields to the more dominant sense of space left in its midst, as if space were a clearing, a doing away with the detail that life and its interpretation require:

> The Auctioneer of Parting
> His "Going, going, gone"
> Shouts even from the Crucifix,
> And brings his Hammer down—
> He only sells the Wilderness,
> The prices of Despair
> Range from a single human Heart
> To Two—not any more—   (P 1612)

The poem is manifestly difficult to figure and the conceit seems more like an animated abstraction, a cartoon representation of what absence might look like. The "Auctioneer," the "Crucifix," the "Wilderness," and "Despair," do not together add up to much of a story. For while the first few lines suggest that what is being sold is gone-ness, that what is knocked down from the cross is death,[10] the last few lines insist that absence is not done away with but is rather purchased. In the negative transaction, "Despair" is the remainder or, to alter my metaphor, it is that middle term which stands between the speaker and the human heart she purchases by accepting the terms of its loss. We can read the beginning in this light: "The Auctioneer of Parting" is the strict God who exacts the sacrifice of presence, even the sacrifice of His son, and who shells out in its place the trace of what was, the "Despair" with which memory encodes itself, from which it recreates its past and daydreams its future. But whatever the anxieties of the story's coherence, they are quickly dismissed by the poem's central rhetorical strategy, its dramatization of the small tear that rips into a "Wilderness of Size" (P 856). Shocked by the brazenness of absence made visible, that oxymoron on which the poem's first two lines hinge, we do not much care about the way in which the story concludes, since our attention remains riveted on the process of loss, its "'Going, going, gone.'" While the poem is less coherent than most of Dickinson's utterances in which the trace or condensation of meaning dominates the narrative by poking holes in it, it ably demonstrates the way in which designation can become distraction so that for the reader, too, loss is a meaning that subsumes everything, a transparency there is no way to see around.

Sometimes in this poetry so filled with loss that a recent study of it has evocatively titled itself *The Landscape of Absence*,[11] the implosions of meaning are as dense and knotted as loss itself:

> More Life—went out—when He went
> Than Ordinary Breath—
> Lit with a finer Phosphor—
> Requiring in the Quench—
>
> A Power of Renowned Cold,
> The Climate of the Grave
> A Temperature just adequate
> So Anthracite, to live—
>
> For some—an Ampler Zero—
> A Frost more needle keen
> Is necessary, to reduce
> The Ethiop within.
>
> Others—extinguish easier—
> A Gnat's minutest Fan
> Sufficient to obliterate
> A Tract of Citizen—
>
> Whose Peat life—amply vivid—
> Ignores the solemn News
> That Popocatapel exists—
> Or Etna's Scarlets, Choose—   (P 422)

R. P. Blackmur's comments on the solecism of the poem notwithstanding,[12] the very condensations at which he aims his criticisms dramatize the range and repertoire of extinction as it cuts man down to size. Extinction equals not exactly zero, but zero minus measureless degrees. To speak impressionistically for a moment, we might say that the poem chills its readers with the dry ice of its words, verbally shaping the plenitude of thanatotic possibility, urging that we note the degree of terminal cold as one registered by individual difference. The two images in stanza one, ostensibly unrelated, complete each other by pictorial association. The going out of "Ordinary Breath—," that passive image of a body left in the lurch, deflated of breath, changes in the third line to a dynamic vision of the breath that snuffs out light, as in the blowing out of a candle. The two images, so far synecdoches for death, turn to explicit statement in stanza two, where the hearsay evidence of "Renowned Cold" is immediately complemented by terse, flat statement testifying in terms that are meant to grate with the severity of their verdict to the bare minimum ("A Temperature just adequate") necessary to sustain life. "Anthracite" is a coal containing little volatile matter. To live "So Anthracite" is to live in the hard black world of utter abandonment where life "gone out" is the curse of deprivation without death. However, as the last three stanzas propose comparative terms for the degrees around zero (actually, Dickinson's register of negation is more interestingly vertical than horizontal, implying that negation has relative depth/intensity as well as relative degree), the poem's subject suddenly shifts from the boundary line between life and death where it has been situated to speculation about what pushes one over the line.

In that wonderful condensation of tropical heat, passion, and life itself, Dickinson seizes on a metaphor ("The Ethiop within") that anticipates what, a century later, will be Wallace Stevens's epithet for the source of life, "Major Man," of whom he says almost, it seems, in intentional echo, "The hot of him is purest in the heart." "To reduce/The Ethiop within," we learn from the next stanza, is to kill it, for life (despite the earlier insistence to the contrary) seems not to be relative but rather an absolute state the dimunition of which means death. Those "who extinguish easier—," so delicate they cannot withstand the fanning of a "Gnat's" wings (which presumably produces lethal cold), do not, contrary to the initial image of the candle, expire gently. Rather they explode. For although the last stanza ostensibly defines this expiration in opposition to the potential eruption of Popocatapel and Etna, it is the similarity of the three forces (the "Peat life—amply vivid—," which, by virtue of the prominence given to it as the poem's ending, lingers in the finality of our impression. However diminished life looks from the out-side, then, it is "The Ethiop within," or what remains in its wake, that gives the volcano-person life sufficiently charged to explode. Thus the "Tract of Citizen—" (designation gnomic as what it is describing: place without distinguishable person, person without seeming life) whose "Peat" could vault upward in true volcanic color, shows us spiritlessness provoked into violence after all. Such an end is not passive, but rather threatens to blow its subject to bits in tenacious contrast to the earlier idea about the calmness of death, and also in contrast to the compara-tively tame threat of either Etna or Popocatapel,[13] whose force remains governed by our knowledge that it exists. Indeed the final implied con-trast between opposites, between the candle blown out in the first stanza and the life blown to bits in the last one, between a single flame and a volcanic fire, is a measure of the amplitude of negation, its index when we see it in its full range.

Such concentration on absence as annihilation testifies to the fact that Dickinson is, if nothing else, and in terms more crudely insistent, our greatest rhetorician of loss. "I would eat evanescence slowly," she wrote in 1866 to Mrs. Holland (L 318), and truly loss seems to have been a daily fare of her existence, something to be savored and in the savoring known. The poems interest us, however, if they do, not as biographical spectacle but rather as shared testament to an old story we all know. Freud spoke of this story as one of the first, the one in which the self discovers its boundaries as partly defined by the exclusion of that which it desires. In the beginning the self imagines that what exists in the mind must be. But "to be" is a mere infinitive, subject to multiple conjuga-tions. The first subtlety the child learns is predicated on absence; as a consequence of it he must distinguish between his image of an object and its form in reality, and frequently the two do not coincide. Thus the very discovery of otherness is a "re-discovery," answering as it must to the original image in the mind without which no recognition could be: "The first and immediate aim of the process of testing reality is not to discover an object in real perception corresponding to what is imagined, but to *re-discover* such an object, to convince oneself that it is still there." Given the prototype of otherness as self, no wonder the self longs to convert the former, to put fusion to the task of its obliteration. Freud continues: "An essential precondition for . . . testing reality is that objects shall have been lost which formerly afforded real satisfaction."[14] That the predicate of being should be absence, that on which it is founded, that on which it founders, seems like an even more confounding proposition when, as in the more recent works of Jacques Lacan, not the object but rather the subject is seen in terms of the gap that constitutes it. According to Lacan, man's acknowledged center is nothing less than an otherness, an absence that inhabits him as if he were its home. "The unconscious," Lacan writes, following Freud closely, "is the discourse of the Other";[15] it is that language whose meaning we do not know, the page that is a blank, the censored chapter.[16] Lacan speaks of man's "radical ex-centricity,"[17] his standing outside himself, for although man is certain in positing the existence of a self, he is not certain of possessing it. Lacan's vision of a displaced subject that resists the very consciousness that claims to know it is, of course, modeled on the Freudian topography in which the unconscious conceals its meanings and where the claims of immediate consciousness to have knowledge of the whole are themselves no guarantee of truth; indeed quite the contrary, for in the Freudian universe consciousness is what displaces, stands instead of, the true subject. Paul Ricoeur regards the displacement in terms of the discrepancy it posits between being and our cognition of it: "Psychoanalysis drives a wedge between the apodicticity of the absolute positing of existence and the adequation of the judgment bearing on the *being-such*. I am, but what am I who am? That is what I no longer know. In other words, reflection has lost the assurance of consciousness. *What* I am is just as problematical as *that* I am is apodictic."[18] If man is an otherness even to himself, an unknown from which he is distanced and by which he is more than partially defined, then the loss of an object— the world's otherness—is a secondary loss, only a mirror for the more immediate estrangement inside.

But the language of distance and difference is not categorically a psychological or a philosophical one. Much of theology is concerned with the relationship between negation and absence, a concern that steels itself in the belief that the two need not be seen as equivalent, but rather as those simultaneous states that can withstand each other. Paul Tillich writes, "A revelation is final if it has the power to negate itself without losing itself."[19] Negation without loss is what Dickinson recorded in "The farthest Thunder that I heard"; it is what memory records any time it records anything at all, paying homage to the subtractive laws of reality at the same time that it preserves the trace that withstands the departure of its object. Negation without loss is one of the fundamental tenets of Christianity, which would perhaps express the notion differently in the more conventional terms of sacrifice. For sacrifice "begotten by God," as we are told in the Old Testament, enacts this very dialectic of presence and absence—the loss of the desired object and its subsequent reinstatement, the relinquishing of a part for the promise of a regained whole, Abraham's hope that God might be bargained with. "Renunciation—," we recall Dickinson's saying, "is a piercing Virtue—" (P 745), more piercing still when it must acknowledge that it will not be repaid with the replacement of the relinquished object. If we imagine sacrifice to be negation without loss, a trading of absence for presence, of self for other, then we see that sacrifice is the quintessential gamble, the last hope of an impossible repossession. David Bakan, whose observations on pain we looked at briefly in chapter 1, makes the point with clarity:

> A confounding of self and other is present from the beginning in sacrifice. One gives up what one loves—"giving up" being ambiguously intransitive and transitive. On the one hand, sacrifice is transitive, entailing the killing of someone else. On the other hand, sacrifice is intransitive, entailing surrender of an important part of one's self for the "redemption" of the remainder. It is exactly the same mechanism that I identified in the discussion of pain, where a part of the body becomes "it" in preparation for its sacrifice. . . . [20] If the act of sacrifice is, as I have indicated, an act of self-injury, it is equally an act of audacity. To kill is always to pre-empt the natural death of any organism, which is inevitable in any circumstances. It puts death under the control of the will, giving the illusion that otherwise there is immortality. Christianity is based on the recognition of the audacity associated with sacrifice. It makes the major sacrificial act of history one of God himself.[21]

Sacrifice is thus that redemptive act which God entreats man to imitate but without the same immortal consequences.

In "Murke's Collected Silences," Heinrich Böll tells of a sound technician who records silences on tape (silences spliced from the space between words or from their erasures). The story dramatizes one form of negation without loss, for Murke's erasures body themselves forth reminding us that in the beginning, before the word, there was nothing. If we think of how much of the world is composed of similar spaces—

spaces to be crossed as an ocean is crossed (Dickinson called death "the Hyphen of the Sea—" [P 1454]), spaces to be navigated as movement is a navigation from one place to another, spaces in consciousness (the pure blanks to which we give ourselves every night in sleep), spaces in thought where connection stops short—we know this is a list with an infinite series, that to leave off naming absence is not to complete it, is itself a space in the continuum that seems to stretch forever. In the traditional Christian terms we have been alluding to, Dickinson regarded God as such a space: "They say that God is everywhere, and yet we always think of Him as something of a recluse" (L 551), and more coyly of her family: "They are religious—except me—and address an Eclipse, every morning—whom they call their 'Father'" (L 261). Sacrifice is the consequence of an assessment of spaces, a contribution to the continuum in the hopes that an offering will leave the rest of the self intact. This is the illusion of immortality, as Bakan calls it, transposed to a present reward. It is Abraham's lesson imitated, the self banking on the hope that the willing of sacrifice will obviate its necessity.

In a life that sometimes seems defined by one's relationship to the spaces ("Emerging from an Abyss, and reentering it—that is Life, is it not, Dear?" [L 1024]), sacrifice is the strong-arming of one's desires, bending them to the shape of a more imperious will. The volitional muscle sometimes asserts its strength in outright renunciation; more often, as we have seen, it exercises its power by the reading of value/virtue in the enforced loss, a value that is tantamount, at least by comparison, as the following poem suggests, to immortality:

> Must be a Wo—
> A loss or so—
> To bend the eye
> Best Beauty's way—
>
> But—once aslant
> It notes Delight
> As difficult
> As Stalactite—
>
> A Common Bliss
> Were had for less—
> The price—is
> Even as the Grace—

> Our lord—thought no
> Extravagance
> To pay—a Cross—   (P 571)

The custody of the eyes, the willing of them away from the object of their desire, the training of sight upward both toward "Stalactite—" and in its image, is "difficult" as the formation of that hard beautiful substance, much of whose beauty is a direct consequence of its arduous evolution. Neither common, simple, nor immediate, "Best Beauty" is the absolute "Extravagance," the giving up of all. In another poem, the directive to "Deal with the soul/As with Algebra!" (P 269) is stoicism at its most uncompromising, an imperative to treat mortal losses and gains as if they were trivial exponentials, powers raised to negligible degree. When she couldn't do it, when she felt herself caged in the human flesh, Dickinson resorted to a new ultimatum:

> If your Nerve, deny you—
> Go above your Nerve—
> He can lean against the Grave,
> If he fear to swerve—
>
> That's a steady posture—
> Never any bend
> Held of those Brass arms—
> Best Giant made—
>
> If your Soul seesaw—
> Lift the Flesh door—
> The Poltroon wants Oxygen—
> Nothing more—   (P 292)

The speaker here summons a disregard for the very "Nerve," which in the poems we examined earlier was seen to be loss's best register of pain. If feeling at all is the equivalent of feeling negation ("If your Nerve, deny you—"), the best way to repudiate negation is to transcend it, "Go above your Nerve—," is to appeal to a numbness imitative of death, one we will examine more closely in the next section of this chapter.

When the rarified atmosphere "above [the] Nerve—" is aspired to and, however briefly, attained before the speaker retreats from the extremity of the imitated death-trance, the attainments constitute installments on the purchase of immortality. The problem with such a premise, and Dickinson knew it as well as Bakan, is that sacrifice, to paraphrase the latter, may give one longevity but it never yields immortality. That there is no immortality is a state of affairs we accede to with comfortable sophistication, a loss we have most of us agreed upon. But there are losses that strike us harder because they go against the grain of more immediate desire. I remarked earlier that the trace of presence—its condensation or reduction to essence—was present in the very temporal manifestations of loss as a node of representative meaning. My assertion implies a correspondence between an object that is removed and the lingering trace (whether that trace be manifest in a word, a memory, or a mere sign) that re-places it, and this in turn implies that if we cannot recover the lost presence, it is nonetheless there, at a remove, distanced by time and space, to be recovered. Derrida, using Freud's terms with more persuasive coherence than Lacan although toward the same end, tells us differently:

> If the diverted presentation continues to be somehow definitively and irreducibly withheld, this is not because a particular present remains hidden or absent, but because differance holds us in a relation with what exceeds (though we necessarily fail to recognize this) the alternative of presence or absence. A certain alterity—Freud gives it a metaphysical name, the unconscious—is definitively taken away from every process of presentation in which we would demand for it to be shown forth in person. In this context and under this heading, the unconscious is not, as we know, a hidden, virtual, and potential self-presence. It is differed—which no doubt means that it is woven out of differences, but also that it sends out, that it delegates, representatives or proxies; but there is no chance that the mandating subject "exists" somewhere, that it is present or is "itself," and still less chance that it will become conscious. . . . With the alterity of the "unconscious," we have to deal not with the horizons of modified presents—past or future—but with a "past" that has never been nor will ever be present, whose "future" will never be produced or reproduced in the form of presence. The concept of trace is therefore incommensurate with that of retention, that of the becoming-past of what had been present. The trace cannot be conceived—nor, therefore, can differance—on the basis of either the present or the presence of the present.[22]

If all that we know of presence is its trace, and that trace too is an absence, a sign that designates presence by differing from it, and if it cannot be recovered because it nowhere exists—hanging somewhere in the midst of that *béance* I spoke of earlier—then presence is only a metaphysical fiction, an impossible other, a true alterity. These are not, to be sure, Dickinson's terms. She said it with less philosophical fuss, but the knowledge is hers, and the complexity of its designation is implicit. Negation without loss is what she seemed to hope language would be, a testament to loss which if it could not replace presence must at least stand as witness to that fact. In an utterance palpably anguished by its framing thought, she wrote: "'No' is the wildest word we consign to Language" (L 562). Given her linguistic range on the subject of loss, we have some idea of what she meant by the superlative, and perhaps language would turn out to be the greatest negation. There will be more to say on this subject but before proceeding with it, we must look first at that group of poems which attempt to duplicate the spaces in the world by creating corresponding spaces in feeling.

III

"The natural world may be conceived of as a system of concentric circles, and we now and then detect in nature slight dislocations which apprise us that this surface on which we now stand is not fixed, but sliding." So Emerson wrote in "Circles," an essay that Dickinson, speaking as she did repeatedly of "Circumference," surely read.[23] Her own configurations were spatial rather than centered, with loss, as we have noted, the space at the center of which lies existence. When Dickinson felt the "slight dislocations" of which Emerson spoke, she became a mere "Speck upon a Ball—" who "Went out upon Circumference—/Beyond the Dip of Bell—" (P 378). Concentric circles falling out of alignment with the world, her poems designate a space less circumscribed than the one Emerson knew. And the "sliding" he describes (Dickinson echoes the word: "I touched the Universe—/And back it slid—and I alone—/A Speck upon a Ball—") in Dickinson's depiction is the world folding itself in measured retreat away from the speaker. Sometimes the self sustains the rupture, like Donne's image of a circling compass, holds on to its connection with the lost object, the trace "harken[ing] after" what has been lost. Then presence is, as we have seen, a rare essence spanning the distance, a "gold to airy thinness beat."

As often however, rupture is pain. But pain in Dickinson's poems is not always a feeling; it is sometimes presented in a spatial configuration, a blacking and blanking out. We have looked briefly, in chapter 1, at the way in which pain is the line drawn around a speaker's experience, separating her from vision, thought, and, above all, from the framing utterance. "Blow has followed blow, till the wondering terror of the Mind clutches what is left, helpless of an accent—" (L 792), Dickinson writes to Mrs. Holland after the death of her mother in 1882. Pain is the space where words would be, the hole torn out of language. Sometimes, in its self-consuming totality, it is amnesia:

> There is a pain—so utter—
> It swallows substance up—
> Then covers the Abyss with Trance—
> So Memory can step
> Around—across—upon it—
> As one within a Swoon—
> Goes safely—where an open eye—
> Would drop Him—Bone by Bone.   (P 599)

The anesthetizing of the senses, the transformation from sensate body to senseless thing, is clearly an emergency measure, and we are so alerted from the poem's first line where the radical alteration of categories, adverb becoming adjective with the last two letters in "utterly" sliced off, is the beginning of the process that hacks away at consciousness to leave a bare nothing. Or perhaps "utter—" is simply an adjectival abbreviation for "uttermost." Unmindful any longer of its cause, pain is first of all a marshaling of forces against language that would need to know historical particularities in order to name them; it is a substitution of "utter—Trance—," for "utterance." "Substance," which specifies the genesis, history, and cause of pain, but only the way an abstraction specifies, steers clear of pain's subject (even while alluding to it), and this is no accident since we see the subject only from a distance, as it is disappearing. The subject is a brief parenthesis between two parts of the separated verb that successfully keeps it in line by flanking it. "Safe Despair it is that raves—/Agony is frugal" (P 1243), Dickinson had written, distinguishing between an explosion of despair outward, toward the world that caused it, and its inward collapse. Raving is "Safe," a hurling of expostulations against a world from which the self still hopes justice. In the dreadful economy of "a pain—so utter—" the self has forgotten the world, falling back instead upon its own person which it devours, hollowing experience to the shape of an "Abyss." But the "Abyss" of self-recrimination, the self tearing at itself in lieu of the abandoned world, is still not a real absence; feeling pulses across the space that pain has taken over and it can be ministered to only with anodyne as severe as "Trance—." We note that the poem charts a progression of departures from feeling, and its first step (that of the unhinging of pain from its situational context) has been accomplished. The second step is more directly concerned with the detachment of consciousness from feeling in the "Trance—" that accomplishes the latter's repression. Repression here, unlike what we have seen in "I felt a Funeral in my Brain," does not precipitate a fall to unconsciousness but is rather the anesthetic that prevents it. "Delirium— diverts the Wretch" (P 708) by putting a hard finish on pain, making its surface so protectively adamant that "Memory" can track across it without touching what is underneath. This is image made palpable as a floor to be walked on; it is, in fact, just that: partitioning the self from the excess of its excruciation, the plank is both floor and ceiling, providing a passageway for consciousness that is, at the same time, lid to the more chaotic strains below.

The final analogy, following "Memory['s]" ventures grown progressively more audacious as it moves "Around—across—upon it—," suggests that sight would not only be recognition but also spatial cavern. As Dickinson has phrased it, however, with the middle step of recognition left out or translated immediately into its consequences, "an open eye—" equals descent, the sensation of falling and falling apart simulated in the imagined sadism of the last line: "Bone by Bone." For the speaker who makes herself into an unrecognizable object or a "Him—" (a numbing technique we have witnessed before in "I read my sentence steadily"), either alternative, sight or "Swoon—," is tantamount to death, death by disintegration or death by analogy to "Swoon—." In either case the self is translated from life into other, foreign terms. As Dickinson wrote: "A Doubt if it be Us/Assists the staggering Mind" (P 859). The embrace of "Trance—," while catering to one aspect of the self made docile by belief in it as a remedy, is no match for that more canny representative of personhood, the self who engineered the remedy in the first place and who, as the last line of the previous poem makes clear, appreciates the necessity of its own drastic measures. In that central image of the human timepiece, Dickinson had admitted: "Behind the most unconscious clock /What skilful Pointers move—" (P 1054). Given such a complex notion, unconsciousness is not so much a floor as it is a one-way mirror laid horizontally across the self, transparent from the bottom up but sealing off vision to the person in a state of ordinary presence looking down on it.

The self divided into spaces—spaces of clear perception, spaces closed from view—recalls Starobinski's remarks cited in the last chapter about the connection between depth and interiority. In Dickinson's poems pain is a widener and deepener of spaces. Existing not only in the self's interior, even the world is projected as a space that must be filled: "At leisure is the Soul/That gets a Staggering Blow—/The Width of Life—before it spreads/Without a thing to do—" (P 618). Graphed as a huge "Width" or as smaller spaces broken by areas of undistinguished matter, life is an avoidance, a stepping around, of absences: "I stepped from Plank to Plank/A slow and cautious way/The Stars about my Head I felt/About my Feet the Sea" (P 875). When unconsciousness or repression fail, what is left in their wake is not the descent that the speaker in the poem discussed earlier feared, but rather the skewing of ordered categories, the collapse of all distinction between the "Plank[s]" and what separates them, between interior and exterior. Then spaces are no longer seen and feared but are rather inhabited and experienced characteristically as overwhelming size, the flooding of the self's boundaries that will no longer contain it:

> A nearness to Tremendousness—
> An Agony procures—
> Affliction ranges Boundlessness—
> Vicinity to Laws
>
> Contentment's quiet Suburb—
> Affliction cannot stay
> In Acres—Its Location
> Is Illocality—   (P 963)

As in "There is a pain so utter," we see the ways in which pain taxes language, creating nouns out of adjectives, words out of syllabic addition, sentences out of hyperbole. Indeed the grammar of pain is, as Dickinson's own so frequently tends to be, a parsing of conventional agreement that reassigns linguistic value or invents it when necessary. Invention involves a poking around in the corners of language, an attempt to find there words for the crevasses that drive designations apart and in which certain experiences sit as if in need of dictional rescue. Dickinson's linguistic ventures, understood in this light, are not so much hyperbole as a wrestling with established categories in the hope that the new words introduced by force into the language might make themselves heard. Because the experiences that want words lie outside of conventional designation, they must claim their space, if at all, in territory proximate to the norms of language that apparently wish to crowd them out. The creating of new words is an attempt to reintroduce presence into reality, to close up gaps in the referential scheme, and though the words fail to accomplish this, they are nonetheless balm to the very pain whose expression is their task. For "Agony," like its articulation, lies "Vicinity to Laws." Neither "stay[ed]" by nor able to "stay" in civilized territory ("Contentment's quiet Suburb—"), "Agony" classifies "Boundlessness—" and passes through its area ("ranges" it in both senses of the word), defined by its very proximate relationship to the known that it is not. Pain, however, can be hyperbole with a vengeance, and to protect herself the speaker must keep distance from the feelings that would subsume her. The *"nearness* to Tremendousness—" (a subtly voiced recognition that "Tremendousness—" must not envelop the self if the self is to give it voice) positions the speaker outside of conventional linguistic territory and outside, too, of the feeling that threatens to define experience by becoming equivalent to it. "Vicinity" to both civilized location and the wilds of "Agony," the speaker occupies the space between the two in which words are legislated in reference to the laws of both.

While the speaker in the previous poem avoids being overwhelmed, there were instances when pain was a gathering of unruly forces that no reason had power to subdue. "The Parting I tried to smuggle resulted in quite a Mob at last!" (L 359), Dickinson writes of such an attack. She had more to say about this and she expressed her defeat characteristically in the breakdown of temporal sense, the inability to remember the past that once was and the future that will succeed:

> Pain—has an Element of Blank—
> It cannot recollect
> When it begun—or if there were
> A time when it was not—
>
> It has no Future—but itself—
> It's Infinite contain
> It's Past—enlightened to perceive

New Periods—of Pain.   (P 650)

Wholly self-referential, the present is all. Again, characteristically, the grammatical malapropism immediately signals that utterance has taken on the task of redefinition. To be "Blank—," as to be dead, is a condition, an uncompromised state of being. "*Element* of Blank—" would seem like a contradiction in terms were it not the mediating qualifier that eased so extreme a definition into the established lexical structure. For as we learn from the rest of the utterance, "Blank—," though an "Element," is the only one. Thus whatever concessions the initial qualifier makes to established convention are unequivocally withdrawn by the terms of the poem's conclusion. "Blank—" is the renunciation of temporal category, the lapse of memory that makes the present the be-all and end-all, the defunct imagination that cannot be required to think beyond what is. Projecting itself in all directions, it is the stone thrown in the water around which the circles widen, the movement that can never get beyond its own initial impulse. Hence future *is* past, repeats it as if it were infinite regress. But the poem tells us about no future we know; the standard vocabulary of familiar temporal designation merely points in the direction of that which it is at a loss to specify. Outside of the temporal framework, suspended from it, the future is a repetition of past where repetition is heavy with the weight of its own recurrence. Repetition is both the same thing and something more. This "addition" makes repetition a transcendent experience, altering it even in the re-enactment ("enlighten[ing]" it). Dickinson's designation for that repetition which differs is "New Periods—of Pain," a category of experience that fuses past and future into the unavoidable novelty of the present. The last line is also a play on the sense of "Period—" as end, here duration and absolute finalty being hideously interchangeable.

The present may subsume its own temporal progressions, but the consequence is to yield no connection as we know it. Pain is the space in which the present detaches itself from connection, a "Period—" to everything but itself:

> Great Streets of silence led away
> To Neighborhoods of Pause—
> Here was no Notice—no Dissent
> No Universe—no Laws—
>
> By Clocks, 'twas Morning, and for Night

> The Bells at Distance called—
> But Epoch had no basis here
> For Period exhaled.   (P 1159)

In the convergence of "Morning" and "Night," the two brought together
not by the speaker's intimation of the passage of time but rather of its
past ("Night" perceived simultaneously with "Morning"), the speaker is
at a standstill, a self-confessed dead-end. The detachment of existence
from recognizable landscape, cosmos, and law is the post-mortem of
temporality; its death is literalized in the poem's concluding line, "For
Period exhaled." The space of the negation is filled with inoperative
temporal vestiges: the "Clocks" that fail to tell time so that their hours
differ appreciably from each other, "Epoch" expelled from the storehouse of relevant concepts, the personification of time that has drawn its
last breath. The landscape is one of wreckage, a field strewn with broken,
out-of-date, or dismantled timepieces, and the poem insists that while
time no longer passes, it also fails to pass from the speaker, does not
leave her be, but rather goads her with the shell of its own disembodied
workings. Dickinson's transformation of temporal succession (time
accumulating horizontally) into a temporal garbage heap (time accumulating vertically) is illuminated by a long-sighted glance ahead to Samuel
Beckett's *The Unnamable* in which the unspecified voice, like Dickinson's
speaker, is interred under the weight of dead time:

> The question may be asked, off the record, why time doesn't pass,
> doesn't pass from you, why it piles up all about you, instant on in-
> stant, on all sides, deeper and deeper, thicker and thicker, your time,
> others' time, the time of the ancient dead and the dead yet unborn,
> why it buries you grain by grain neither dead nor alive, with no mem-
> ory of anything, no hope of anything, no knowledge of anything, no
> history, and no prospects.[34]

Dead time buries like snow and seemingly, as the stream of negations
at the passage's conclusion implies, with its silence. In Dickinson's
temporal graveyard, too, the "silence" at the poem's beginning is the
cessation of the clock's tick-tock, the space (or "Pause—") between the
two that lengthens into an infinity. Yet despite the explicit assertion that
time is dead and despite the fact that the utterance is past tense, a recollection voiced from the beyonds of God knows where, the illusion it
casts as palpably as the shadow of our original timepiece, the sun, is of

time's presence and present. As in the following poem in which the mind's schism, the halving of a whole that cannot be put back together again, precipitates the spillage of temporal sequence, the grammatical past tense gets canceled out by consequences so pervasive that they insist on being read as present or present progressive:

> I felt a Cleaving in my Mind—
> As if my Brain had split—
> I tried to match it—Seam by Seam—
> But could not make them fit.
>
> The thought behind, I strove to join
> Unto the thought before—
> But Sequence ravelled out of Sound
> Like Balls—upon a Floor.   (P 937)

The rupture of temporality depicted as if beginning, middle, and end of "Sequence" were a circumstantial rather than integral order, an arrangement that cannot be gleaned out of context, suggests so much distrust of any temporal scheme (including the one out of which the poem is narrated) that we translate its own past into a present or continuous action. Indeed the unraveling of "Sequence" is a disaster as inaudible ("out of Sound") as "Balls—" of yarn, which cannot be heard and therefore cannot be reconstructed. The poem's grammatical past tense, in this light, is wishful thinking, a fiction.

   In a recent article on Dickinson, David Porter writes, "The crucial affair for [Dickinson] . . . is living after things happen. It is a preoccupation with afterknowledge, with living in the aftermath."[25] Similarly stressing the importance of the past in Dickinson's poetry, Georges Poulet observes, "Nothing is graver . . . than the apparition, in the closest succession, of . . . two moments, in one of which everything is given, and in the other everything taken away."[26] Though both Poulet and Porter are right to notice the importance of the past in the poems I discussed in the previous section, in the utterances on pain that we are currently examining, where the past exists, it is articulated, as we have seen, as if it were present. To modify one of Porter's formulations, the alternatives in Dickinson's poems are not "past or void" but rather "void or present," for in the poems on pain, at any rate, the past seeps backward into the crevasses of the moment when it was first present, and it is precisely at this point that utterance meets up with recollection. In the previous chapter we considered the phenomenon of present tense in the lyric; Porter and Poulet, placing significant emphasis on the aftermath of Dickinson's poems, offer us an occasion to examine briefly the way in which lyrics often allude to prior events, are as if predicated on prior events, and as such may be thought of not so much as past but as referential in nature.

In his discussion of the rise of the early Greek lyric, Bruno Snell notes the frequency with which "again" becomes a stereotyped formula of opening lines.[27] The invocation of an earlier event may also be seen in initial lines of the English lyric. We recall "Lycidas": "Yet once more, O ye Laurels, and once more/Ye Myrtles brown . . . I come to pluck your Berries harsh and crude." Here the poetic garlands are summoned as they have been before, but now for a specific task: to pay elegiac tribute to Edward King. "Once more the storm is howling, and half-hid/Under this cradle-hood and cover-lid/My child sleeps on," begins Yeats's "A Prayer for My Daughter," and since it is the speaker's impassioned belief that he must save his daughter from the anarchical disorder that has maddened his own life, utterance is appropriately grounded in the terror of natural repetition. "Winter again and it is snowing," the man estranged from his child in Snodgrass's *Heart's Needle* observes, marking the seasonal return that amounts to difference: "Although you are still three,/You are already growing/Strange to me." We might in fact hazard the generalization that poems which call attention to themselves as a repetition with a difference are often elegiac in nature, and the purpose of the "again" is not to chart sameness but rather disparity, to distinguish the unique event recorded by the poem from its too easy resemblance. By alluding to a past, elegies can also summon the genesis of their own mourning as, for example, Whitman's elegy for Lincoln does: "When lilacs last in the dooryard bloom'd, . . . I mourn'd, and yet shall mourn with ever-returning spring." Sometimes poems are seeming repudiations of a past event, a way of transforming it, as we see in Carew's dismissal of questions that, in reality, weaves them into the fabric of a love poem: "Ask me no more where Jove bestows,/When June is past, the fading rose;/For in your beauty's orient deep,/These flowers, as in their causes, sleep." Or they may point not so much to a past event as to a history of pastness: "Whan that Aprille with his shoures soote/The droghte of March hath perced to the roote." "When" clauses are indicative of past events that, once introduced into the world, have the potential to reoccur. For example, in the Shakespeare sonnet that begins,

"When my love swears that she is made of truth/I do believe her, though I know she lies," the state of lying is an instance of a continuous past (albeit one that may be temporarily suspended), and it comes very close in its effect to actions that are worded as if they were continuously present: "The woods decay, the woods decay and fall,/The vapors weep their burthen to the ground,/Man comes and tills the field and lies beneath,/And after many a summer dies the swan." So laments Tennyson's Tithonus, that unhappy mortal who has been cursed with immortality and who speaks, as he lives, in a perpetual present. In Tennyson's lines past is rendered as if it were prediction, prophecy so fused with history that it is hard to tell them apart.

But as my examples should have begun to clarify, whether a poem is actually cast in past tense has little to do with how it appears. In Blake's "Poison Tree," notwithstanding the insistent stance of the initial past-tense verbs, the speaker remains so envenomed that his recapitulation of murder is a reenactment of it, a doing it over, as the sudden verb change in the last line makes clear: "In the morning glad I see/My foe outstretch'd beneath the tree." The point to be stressed is that even if not explicitly past tense, almost all lyrics are referential in nature and what they refer to is a reality outside of the poem, but one that is summoned as its backdrop. "Had we but World enough, and Time,/This coyness, Lady, were no crime." "Coyness," to which Marvell's poem musters a rebuke, lies outside of the present that invokes it. Thus if poems are not themselves finished actions, they nonetheless allude to them, and these allusions constitute the predicate of utterance, its stable ground. Past-tense verbs are more frequently a marker of a given utterance's referential value (of what, in the world, it is concerned with) than of its temporal cast. Because all utterances are referential, they will also have some relation to an alterity, a state that precedes them, precipitates them, and that they are not. It is this state of otherness, this alterity, that the lyric strives to convert.

The previous remarks offer a perspective for Porter's and Poulet's observations about "aftermath" in Dickinson's poems. "Aftermath," we might say, is the lyric's point of reference, that from which it seeks to depart. "Aftermath" may even be a poem's grammatical tense, but that does not necessarily coincide with what we could call its manifestational tense, with how it appears to present itself.[28] John Lynen on the subject of Dickinson's tenses gets them right when he notes their tendency to be both present and eternal, present tense stretching backwards and forwards in time as if it were all. The resulting double and seemingly contradictory movement has the effect of keeping the present static. Lynen writes, "[In Dickinson's poems] we see realization rather than change, the discovery of what is there rather than the advent of something new, a clarification of consciousness rather than a transition from one state of mind to another."[29] Thus actions may be said neither to begin nor end but rather always to remain in progress. The present's continuousness is particularly horrifying when, as we recall, its subject is that of pain's "Element of Blank—," and with the last observation we are back where we left off, at the temporal junkyard documented by the poems in which time is an endless reminder of its own stasis.

Once Dickinson attempted to chart the stages of pain as if in an effort to break the spell of its present hold by getting it to admit of both past and future. But each stage of the process seems to offer only a more resolute fixity, translating temporal process into a mere index for loss, stasis, and finally death:

> After great pain, a formal feeling comes—
> The Nerves sit ceremonious, like Tombs—
> The stiff Heart questions was it He, that bore,
> And Yesterday, or Centuries before?
>
> The Feet, mechanical, go round —
> Of Ground, or Air, or Ought—
> A Wooden way
> Regardless grown,
> A Quartz contentment, like a stone—
>
> This is the Hour of Lead—
> Remembered, if outlived,
> As Freezing persons, recollect the Snow—
> First—Chill—then Stupor—then the letting go—   (P 341)

"Great pain" is the predicate on which the sentence of fixity lies, the prior experience against which feeling hardens in intransigent difference. The relationship between the adjective in "formal feeling," the adverb in "The Nerves sit ceremonious," and the simile, "like Tombs—" is a relationship of progressive clarity; the connections get made in the underground touching of the roots of each of these words; the "formal feeling," "ceremonious," is a feeling of death. And as if in parody of the initial image, in the next line the "Heart" too is a "stiff," unable to connect self to incident or to date.

Like the "Element of Blank—," like the "Trance—" that covers pain, and like the "nearness to Tremendousness—/An Agony procures—," the "formal feeling" is an abdication of presence, a fact that explains why the question the speaker puts to herself is framed by incredulity and designates the subject as someone else, a "He, that bore," why the time that precedes the present becomes mere undifferentiated space, "Yesterday, or Centuries before?" But unlike "Blank—," "Trance—," and "a nearness to Tremendousness—," the "formal feeling" is an anatomy of pain's aftermath from a distance, a self standing outside of the otherness that possesses it. Thus we are told of the parts of the body as if they were someone else's or no one's: "The Heart . . . the Nerves . . . the Feet . . ."; thus we are shown actions, how the body looks, what it does, rather than feelings. Thus the speaker arrives at a definition ("This is the Hour of Lead—") divorced from the experience because encompassing it. Thus the concluding simile departs from the present as if in analogy there were some further, final escape.

But although the initial images follow upon each other like a death, the second stanza makes clear that death is only an analogy for the body that has lost its spirit, for the vacancy of will. Given its absence, all action is repetition of movement without meaning, and as if to emphasize the attendant vacuousness, the lines repeat each other: "The Feet" "go round—" in circles, "Wooden," "Regardless grown," until the stanza's final line boldly flaunts its own redundancy. "A Quartz contentment" is "like a stone—" because quartz *is* a stone. However, perhaps Dickinson means us to see two images here, the transparent crystal and the grey stone to which it clouds, in a synesthesia that would equate the darkening of color with a formal hardening. As in "perfect—paralyzing Bliss—/ Contented as Despair—," contentment here is the ultimate quiet, the stasis that resembles death. "Wood," "stone," "Lead—"—the images to this point have been ones of progressive hardening. The image with which the poem concludes, however, is more complex because of its susceptibility to transformation, its capacity to exist as ice, snow, and finally as the melting that reduces these crystals to water. The poem's last line is an undoing of the spell of stasis. Because it is not another, different expression of hardness but implies a definite progression away from it by retracing the steps that comprise its history, we know that the "letting go—" is not a letting go of life, is not death, but is rather the more colloquial "letting go" of feeling, an unleashing of the ability to experience it again. To connect the stages of the analogy to the stages of the poem: "Chill—" precedes the poem, "Stupor—" preoccupies it, and "the letting go—" exists on the far side of its ending. The process whereby blankness has been called into existence, given palpable form, dimension, character, and movement enables the poem to specify what the previous poems on pain merely note. Dickinson's poems mostly take place "After great pain," in the space between "Chill—" and "Stupor—." "Life [is] so very sweet at the Crisp," she wrote longingly, "what must it be unfrozen!" (L 472). But the conversion of the body into stone was not lasting. She was not, as she sometimes seemed to declare herself, numb from the neck down.[30] Pain was the shot that inflicted temporary paralysis, a remedy that worked until the poems took over. Then she could spell out the words she swore consciousness refused her, "letting [the feeling] go—" into them where from a distance she could look.

We saw earlier how, in Derrida's terms, pain is a trace of lost presence, the record of its having been. Thus Dickinson's speakers "learn the Transport by the Pain—," sometimes seeming to harbor the belief that "Pain—" is "the Transport" it stands for. Pain is with us as a presence because pain stands for (in place of) presence. But pain, as we have seen in the last few pages, is also the past after which, from which, comes the "formal feeling" that is the poem. If we were to arrange the three terms in a sequence (present/ce, pain, and poem) they would, each one, hark back to a past that eluded all efforts to retain it. For the first temporal principle is one of alterity, the present differing from the past and the future from the present. We then have some idea of why Dickinson claimed in her meeting with Higginson not to have learned how to tell time until she was fifteen. For to tell time is to tell difference, to note the failure of resemblance ever to be the same as that from which it differs. Dickinson's poems on pain are an attempt to blank time out and to create, in its place, a space where the temporal apparatus of daily life has been as if disconnected. For presence is past, and even what follows presence (what Poulet calls the moment after loss) lies behind us. In the sequence of diminishing returns, what has been is, by definition, missing. What remains is a true blank, the genuine space at the thought of which despair "raves—," and around which words gather in the mourning that is language.

To know that the point of reference is a lost point is to feel Emerson's sliding on the surface of the earth, the space running by and around one. A consequence of temporality, the partitions between past, present, and future are the inevitable fissures that work their way like cracks through the totality of our existence. To acknowledge space meant to acknowledge not only incompletion but also the supremacy of beginnings over ends, to see that in fiction beginnings lead to ends, to true resolutions, not in imitation of life but in its stubborn contradiction. "Most of our Moments," Dickinson wrote knowingly, "are Moments of Preface—" (L 641). What follows them is not conclusion but rather the interruption of space. When the space threatened a "Width" she could not tolerate, she imposed the "Blank—" that annihilated temporality. For the "formal feeling" of numbness and the "formal feeling" that prompted words were related strategies. As she wrote in the well-known letters to Higginson: "I had a terror—since September—I could tell to none—and so I sing, as the Boy does by the Burying Ground—because I am afraid—" (L 261). And more directly: "My dying Tutor told me that he would like to live till I had been a poet, but Death was much of Mob as I could master—then—And when far afterward—a sudden light on Orchards, or a new fashion in the wind troubled my attention—I felt a palsy, here—the Verses just relieve—" (L 265).

Once, and in the terms Bakan suggested earlier, she attempted to bargain with loss: she would give up everything to be spared the sacrifice of the dreaded particularity:

> The Missing All—prevented Me
> From missing minor Things.
> If nothing larger than a World's
> Departure from a Hinge—
> Or Sun's extinction, be observed—
> 'Twas not so large that I
> Could lift my Forehead from my work
> For Curiosity.   (P 985)

Here for one of the few times in Dickinson's work we are shown the lost source rather than simply its consequences. Indeed one might say that if the observations in "A nearness to Tremendousness," "There is a pain so utter," "Pain has an Element of Blank," "I felt a Cleaving in my Mind," and "Great Streets of silence led away" are views from within the fissured consciousness, and "After great pain a formal feeling comes" is a view *of* it, the speech in "The Missing All prevented Me" offers us a more global vision. J. V. Cunningham remarks of the poem: "Only loss of salvation justifies such hyperbole."[31] But is it hyperbole or statement of fact? The detachment with which the speaker in the conclusion contemplates the "Sun's" black-out and the world's coming apart at the seams does appear as if it has been preceded by a forfeit so monumental as to render any later particularity trivial, although all things include minor things without naming them. If the "Missing All—" is a loss of salvation, a blank spot where hope would be, it seems in the poem's terms a universal loss. The "Departure" from connection whose first crack of space shows itself in a cosmic slippage is not the speaker's lone plight, but reverberates from "the slight dislocations which apprise us that this surface on which we now stand is not fixed, but sliding." Perhaps that is why Dickinson can tolerate it long enough to record it. Pain, as the philosophers tell us, is private. It can be known by only one person, and can at most be acknowledged by another. "The prices of Despair/Range from a single human Heart/To Two—" (P 1612), though in the absence of the second person, a given speaker can only answer for herself. But the distinctive feature of "The Missing All prevented Me" is its impersonality, the largesse with which departure characterizes not only psychological reality but also physical and natural fact. No longer a reading of the universe based on solipsistic experience, no longer the impressionistic "Blank—," that drug taken to knock out the speaker's real sense of loss; instead this is loss acutely seen and objectively rendered. Not lifting her head, not needing to lift her head, the speaker sees it anyway, has seen it before all around her, a loss that no longer needs to be projected outside of the self as in "Like Eyes that looked on Wastes," but that is at last recognized as the true face of the natural world, what Dickinson had elsewhere called "the Distance/On the look of Death—."

IV

We have observed in the previous section that Dickinson often treats the past as if it were a presence and, in so doing, solicits our disregard for a poem's literal grammatical tense in favor of a symbolic temporal order whose latent intention is to rid itself of time altogether. Thus all principles of succession are converted into ones of simultaneity. "Sequence ravell[ing] out of Sound" results in the "Blank—" or space to which consciousness reverts once it has freed itself from the necessary adding up of its losses. The return of conception to pure space (both domain and domain of absence), space that has been liberated from temporal arbitrations, recalls Henri Bergson's crucial assertion that succession itself—the ability to fix moments of time and to treat them as if they were additive—would be impossible without the dimension of an undifferentiated space against which we arrange the symbolic representation of moments or sensations as if they were as discrete, palpable, and subject to computation as actual objects: "No doubt it is possible . . . to conceive the successive moments of time independently of space; but when we add to the present moment those which have preceded it, as is the case when we are adding up units, we are not dealing with these moments themselves, since they have vanished for ever, but with the lasting traces which they seem to have left in space on their passage through it."[32]

Time thus understood as the medium in which we differentiate internal states of feeling by making them additive is nothing but space miscalled, and internal states of feeling which, in reality, lack all physical dimension that would allow them to be differentiated as actual objects, become subject to numerical operation only by making symbols of them—exempting them from the flow of feeling, sensation, and cognition that is, in its true complexity and as we actually experience it, indivisible. For internal states permeate each other and are characterized by simultaneity rather than by succession; even when one precedes another, the relationship between the two is colored by the interdependence that comprises any whole state of consciousness. To stop the process of consciousness by attempting to measure its stages is not only to suggest that its moments are separable and therefore subject to discrimination, but also that a past moment continues to exist even when it is no longer, since only if it exists can it be compared to the present moment from which it is shown to differ.

Thus temporality must have illusion at its heart, and must be prompted by the desire to transform the "trace" of presence (Bergson's use of the word, it should be pointed out, is the same as Derrida's) into the lost presence itself, to retain in the insistence of the symbolic gesture that which no longer is. The playground for the illusion is a spatial one for, as Bergson writes, "Space is what enables us to distinguish a number of identical and simultaneous sensations from one another; it is thus a principle of differentiation other than that of qualitative differentiation."[33] In the fourth dimension of space which we call time,[34] we translate psychic reality into its physical counterpart, the literal flow of thought and feeling into symbolic structures, and the translation that both distorts the true self and sacrifices it to coherence exists in the service of the social reality of language:

> Consciousness, goaded by an insatiable desire to separate, substitutes the symbol for the reality, or perceives the reality only through the symbol. As the self thus refracted, and thereby broken to pieces, is much better adapted to the requirements of social life in general and language in particular, consciousness prefers it, and gradually loses sight of the fundamental self.[35] . . . We instinctively tend to solidify our impressions in order to express them in language. Hence we confuse the feeling itself, which is in a perpetual state of becoming, with its permanent external object, and especially with the word which expresses this object. In the same way as the fleeting duration of our ego is fixed by its projection in homogeneous space, our constantly changing impressions, wrapping themselves round the external object which is their cause, take on its definite outlines and its immobility.[36]

To represent consciousness as it really is, is to represent it as a simultaneity rather than as a succession. Only projected into space, however, as symbolic structure can consciousness be given sufficient edges to ease it into the dimensions of language or, more to the point, into the confines of an individual word. Thus the transformation of simultaneity into succession, of an intensive state of affairs into an extensive reality that, no longer fluid, has beginning, middle, and end as well as determinate points along the way, is a social gesture, the exchange of reality for symbol, of essence for object, of fluid process for fixed utterance. Since the casting of process into language delimits and defines, it represents the gain of an order to experience, but order, of necessity, replaces the experience. Thus loss of essence is the gain of an imaginary spatial dimension (quite distinct from the real spatial dimension in which palpable objects exist), and this substitution lies at the heart of our conception of time.

Dickinson's attempt to do away with time, an attempt that, as we have seen, sabotages some of her poems and structures others, may be construed as the expression of the desire to retrieve the lost presence by relinquishing those temporal demarcations that threaten to replace it. So she is constantly dismantling temporal categories and watching them collapse into a present that is eternal, as if in an effort to get back to a conception of space unsullied by temporal projection. But the effort has at its heart the mistaken belief that language and presence may co-exist; it refuses to acknowledge one is the replacement for the other, standing in lieu of that which it cannot represent and *have* at the same time. Possession and the positing of the desired object in words are absolutely antithetical endeavors; however the return to a world devoid of temporal designation is no paradise but only double jeopardy, the loss of presence and of the language (whose coherence is sacrificed along with that of temporality) that replaces it. Language, then, is loss's consequence. Loss gives birth to language in the strenuous aftermath of its own labor of grief at the price exacted by social existence. But loss is not simply the result of social process, of becoming a symbolizing creature; if it were we might all refuse representational coherence. It is also, independently, the first principle of the phenomenal world. Thus what in one context amounts to the symbolic construction of a space that can accommodate temporality, the spreading out of internal states of consciousness against a background so that they may be measured, is, in another context, the literal or natural space in which the trees grow and change, in which light comes and goes in the cyclical repetitions we name day and night, in which neither brass nor stone nor boundless sea lasts forever. It is on the recognition of the latter, more original space, space that is no longer consequence but that is rather cause, that the insights of the following poems devolve.

Having neither determinable origin nor explicable end, the existence of the unnamed substance in the following lines is sheer middle, the spaces on either side of the pheomenon that would explain it blocked from human scrutiny:

> It sifts from Leaden Sieves—
> It powders all the Wood.
> It fills with Alabaster Wool
> The Wrinkles of the Road—
>
> It makes an Even Face
> Of Mountain, and of Plain—
> Unbroken Forehead from the East
> Unto the East again—
>
> It reaches to the Fence—

It wraps it Rail by Rail
Till it is lost in Fleeces—
It deals Celestial Vail

To Stump, and Stack—and Stem—
A Summer's empty Room—
Acres of Joints, where Harvests were,
Recordless, but for them—

It Ruffles Wrists of Posts
As Ankles of a Queen—
Then stills its Artisans—like Ghosts—
Denying they have been—   (P 311)

The poem may recall, by way of partial model, George Herbert's "Prayer I," with the elaborate displacement of subject by accumulating metaphors funneled down, not quite into definition or noun, but into pronoun, a "something understood." For as in "Prayer I," Dickinson avoids any naming but the absented referentiality, the mere pointing at an otherness, of "It." In its blanketing sameness, snow blanks out naming—that specification which depends upon the showing forth of particularity. Indeed the transforming metaphors through which we recognize the covered objects, rescuing them from the obscurity of snow and uniform language alike, stand in lieu of the old names, which lie buried too deeply to permit identification.

Snow blots out the differentiation that landscapes the world, making "Mountain" and "Plain—" "Even," and hence unknown. It also cancels out the vestiges of seasonal difference marked for remembrance by "Acres of Joints, where Harvests were,/Recordless, but for them—." The consequence is emptiness unable to recall that it ever had an alternative, the phenomenal world so subject to cancellation that it absorbs its own annihilation with deference. While there is no manifest violence in the picture, snow nonetheless gentles distinction out of existence.

This would be a pastoral scene were it not for the opening and closing insinuations of an artistry akin to black magic. The uncertainty of natural cause or origin is pain pure and simple, itself a space existing where a picture should be. "The Supernatural is only the Natural disclosed," (L 278) Dickinson wrote, as if to say that what spooks us is not the thing itself but rather the sudden light in which we see its familiar context. Like the "Lightning on a Landscape" (P 974) in the poem discussed in chapter 1, and its exacting connection between "Flash—," "Click—," "Suddenness," and the unspoken "Calamity—" of death, the disclosures may be likened to the naming of knowledge already possessed but as yet unconscious of itself. Experience ready for a name, stumbling upon designation as it would upon its own conclusion involves, in fact, a magical attribution of meaning, the metamorphosis of what seemed blank into a space now charged with significance. The real illusion does not inhere in the transformation but rather in the deceptive leap from nothing to meaning, for the natural world, versed in such leaps, presents as fait accompli processes that cannot be witnessed. Thus the precise intention of many of Dickinson's poems on nature seems to be to return to an important space and to fill in the missing events. "Nature is a Haunted House—but Art—a House that tries to be haunted" (L 459A), Dickinson wrote cryptically. In the following poem goaded by a true presence of music that concludes almost before it is ever heard, the world of nature prods the poem. Haunted by music's absence, the borders of the poem fortify themselves, hoping that the space inside them will be canceled by spelling out exactly how it came into being:

> At Half past Three, a single Bird
> Unto a silent Sky
> Propounded but a single term
> Of cautious melody.
>
> At Half past Four, Experiment
> Had subjugated test
> And lo, Her silver Principle
> Supplanted all the rest.
>
> At Half past Seven, Element
> Nor Implement, be seen—
> And Place was where the Presence was
> Circumference between.   (P 1084)

Much of the poem seems to concern itself with the way in which elements compete with each other so that "melody" supplants silence and, in the last stanza, silence resumes its prior domain. For all the quasi-scientific vocabulary ("Experiment," "Principle," "Element"), the poem is largely pictorial, showing us the relationships between background and foreground and the way in which space alters with temporal perspective. The last two lines record a substitution that lies at the heart of

Dickinson's poems on the natural world: "Place was where the Presence was." This replacement of presence by space reveals the world, like a child's magic slate, to displace shapes, colors, indeed all formal elements, and return to an original blank. Though the disappearing act seems to be introduced by the temporal allusions that preface each stanza ("At Half past Three . . . At Half past Four . . . At Half past Seven"), seems, in other words, progressive, in fact the stanzas act more like flashcards on each of which one segment of the whole story is told complete (of the bird and its single voice against the silence, of the dominance of music, of the dominance of silence). The flashcards or still-lifes, to bring my metaphor back into the proper realm, are significant for the way in which they suggest the absence of any trace left from a previous moment/picture. Relegated not so much to the past as to that "Element of Blank—" about which Dickinson knew so much, a finished event leaves not memory but nothing, "Circumference between." As if this were a world of spatial scarcity in which two events could not coexist without one collapsing either into the other or into nothing, Dickinson's poem implies that in the fight for the finite space of being, something must be sacrificed. Although the battle over space is not the explicit subject of the poem, it is enacted by every stanza and commented upon by the last one. Much of what serves to isolate moments of a single event and to sever them from each other is that their departure is not a gradual giving way but an abrupt disappearance. As she wrote at the end of another poem on the barely witnessed chorus of birds:

> By Six, the Flood had done—
> No Tumult there had been
> Of Dressing, or Departure—
> And yet the Band was gone—
>
> The Sun engrossed the East—
> The Day controlled the World—
> The Miracle that introduced
> Forgotten, as fulfilled.   (P 783)

There is no way to comprehend such goneness for, unaccompanied by temporal progression or sequence, departure seems like annihilation itself.

The grammar of the last line, which could be read several ways ("Forgotten, as [if] fulfilled," "Forgotten [in the moment of being] fulfilled," or last, and, I think, most likely, "[as] Forgotten, as [it is] fulfilled"), stresses the absolute separation between the adequacy of fulfillment and the adjacency of consciousness. In the first stanza of the same poem, meaning itself lies adjacent to the speaker in all the surrounding areas out of which the present breaks in its inexhaustible attempt to differentiate itself:

> The Birds begun at Four o'clock—
> Their period for Dawn—
> A Music numerous as space—
> But neighboring as Noon—

The strange preterite with which the stanza begins shakes action loose of its certain context. The unorthodox tense has some of the force of "having begun," and the grammatical expectations prompted by the discrepancy between the main clause and the nonfinite verb form insist that we look ahead to the cessation of action even as its beginning is being invoked. "Music numerous as space—" is music that permeates space's individual and infinite points; but its presence, however plentiful, is an adjacency, is not where we are but is rather "neighboring" as the perfection the speaker here takes "Noon—" to be. Consciousness, we may speculate in passing, would *be* noon if only those proximate states could be brought back into alignment.

Music to hear, why hear'st thou music sadly? Music was not a random subject for Dickinson's concern with space and goneness. Turning her attention, as we will now turn ours, to poems that concern seasonal changes directly, she wrote: "These Behaviors of the Year hurt almost like Music—shifting when it ease us most" (L 381):

> A Light exists in Spring
> Not present on the Year
> At any other period—
> When March is scarcely here
>
> A Color stands abroad
> On Solitary Fields
> That Science cannot overtake
> But Human Nature feels.
>
> It waits upon the Lawn,
> It shows the furthest Tree

Upon the furthest Slope you know
It almost speaks to you.

Then as Horizons step
Or Noons report away
Without the Formula of sound
It passes and we stay—

A quality of loss
Affecting our Content
As Trade had suddenly encroached
Upon a Sacrament.   (P 812)

As in "There's a certain Slant of light," which is the predecessor to this poem, light is a mediation between natural and supernatural phenomena. Whereas in the earlier poem Dickinson indicated the mystery of light by its indirection or "Slant," here light is metamorphosed into its magic hue by the way in which it rides above the year ("on" it), an essence or extract of luminosity. The representation, isolating light from the objects it permeates in order to set it above them, throws into relief the spatial depth of the world being perceived. Indeed the texture of the landscape (the color that "stands abroad" . . . "waits upon the Lawn" . . . and "shows the furthest Tree") is a consequence of its spatial dimensions and of the way in which perception is apprehended by them.

Milton wrote a hymn to light, summoning it as coterminous with divinity: "Bright effluence of bright essence increate"; Hopkins spoke of light that "will flame out, like shining from shook foil"; and even Blake with his radically personalized theology knew that the darkness of suicide was the disastrous consequence of entertaining its necessity: "If the sun and moon should doubt/They'd immediately go out." Such meditations on light are visions about source, and they each have embedded in them a creation myth the playing out of which constitutes its discovery. This explains why light must be seen as separable from what it illuminates, for only through their detachment is beginning separated from being. Now Dickinson's poem does not suffer from being included in the previous observations, for the light that she fixes our attention on is cast in the bold generative effort to show the world made new as our perception can grasp it. But unlike the buoyancy of Milton's and of Hopkins's light, and unlike the animism of Blake's, the light in Dickinson's poem (even as early as the first three stanzas) specifies its distance

from the speaker who is its witness. Captivated by but unable to spell
out light's meaning, there is no rhapsodic praise here because there is
no understanding. Once again (as in "There's a certain Slant of light"
and "The Soul's distinct connection") we are shown a landscape struck
by a moment of *kairos*, its ordinary meanings razed to the ground, but
replaced by nothing; we see the form of revelation without a clue as to
its content. Tantalized by its proximate reach ("Upon the furthest Slope
you know/It almost speaks to you") the speaker strains after a oneness
with the light; to identify with it, to be one with it, to overtake it, would
be to undergo a transformation as severe as that survived by the landscape
under scrutiny. Bright effluence of bright essence increate. But the space
between Milton's Puritanism and Dickinson's is absolute: "It passes and
we stay—."

It is perhaps axiomatic in the very definition of a landscape that what
is specified therein be other than a human subject (and otherness would
of course also apply to the light that suffuses it), for only through the
estrangement of the subject from the landscape is the latter visible.
J. H. Van den Berg, attempting to document the historical transformation that culminated in the Romantic obsession with the self and its
severance from the outside world, speaks of Da Vinci's *Mona Lisa* as the
first figure to be estranged from the landscape and to point conspicuously, by the enigma of her smile, to a sealed inner self. The landscape
behind her is thus "the first landscape," the first depiction of the
natural world as a pure exterior. Van den Berg illuminates his provocative suggestion by allowing Rilke's remarks on the painting to tease it
out:

> This landscape is not the portrayal of an impression, it is not the
> judgment of a man on things at rest; it is nature coming into being,
> the world coming into existence, unknown to man as the jungle of
> an unknown island. It had been necessary to see the landscape in
> this way, far and strange, remote, without love, as something living
> a life within itself, if it ever had to be the means and the motive of
> an independent art; for it had to be far and completely unlike us—
> to be a redeeming likeliness of our fate. It had to be almost hostile
> in its exalted indifference, if, with its objects, it was to give a new
> meaning to our existence.[37]

The combination of estrangement and enchantment, the leaning toward otherness that bestows both meaning (insofar as it is apprehended)

and pain (insofar as it can never be perfectly apprehended), is the pivot on which all relations depend. Romanticism exploits the extremities of estrangement and enchantment or, to put it more accurately, it insists that the point at which the two meet is itself an extremity upon which significance takes a stand, a coordinate that hangs impalpably in space. The sole purpose of the "Light" in Dickinson's poem resides in its refusal to be personalized, to be accounted for or understood in anthropomorphic terms. If the possibility for redemption is predicated on difference ("it had to be far and completely unlike us—to be a redeeming likeliness of our fate"), space becomes the necessary mediation between the human subject and the indifferent landscape. Space is redemptive, however, only when there is yet some hope of compassing it. The hope in the poem is oddly enough the hope of language; if the "Formula of sound" could shape itself into meaning, language would bridge the otherness it does not transcend. But the "Light" cannot be argued into meaning; exterior to language, it remains dumb. Acutest at its vanishing point, only in the last stanza is "Light" expressed in comprehensive terms as the "Sacrament" the loss of which is earthly meaning. Here, as we noted earlier in "My Life had stood a Loaded Gun," experience is given a meaning (is given a word) only after it has concluded, only in the wake of its presence.

The "encroach[ment]" of "Trade" may be nothing more than the speaker's manifest effort to creep up on the "Light" and corner it in human terms, and her effort coincides with the "Light['s]" departure and, at one level, causes it. What is lost is presence—but presence as we have been currently discussing it: that phenomenon whose first principle is the alterity of otherness. What is lost is the landscape. Sacrificing it to her desire for the immediacy of meaning, the speaker violates the mediate space without which there is no world. The violation, of course, is inevitable, for enchantment with the remote landscape is predicated on the longing to near it. This "inclination toward exterior things,"[38] this living on longing as on a legacy, is the impulse toward otherness that is, at the same time, its extinction. Put out the light, and then put out the light—the attempt to make otherness over into one's own image, to foist upon it one's language, is its desecration, is its death. Loss is the something human that wants to paint the world in its own colors. Loss is longing in search of an object and, at least in this poem, it settles on the language that betrays it. For language can neither repair the space between the speaker and the light nor reproduce the light in comprehensible terms. Unable to express the difference it does not know how to convert, language confronts the despair of its own dead-end.

But if by definition the landscape is a difference, must it be inexpressible if it is to remain intact? The speech in the following poem suffers from bizarreness that is a consequence of the complexity of its charge: taxed with representing a difference it can barely comprehend, speech is flung out into the furthest reaches of its permissible space. There, on the edge of language, it stakes out its discoveries through the crabbed idiosyncratic markings that attest to foreign territory:

> Further in Summer than the Birds
> Pathetic from the Grass
> A minor Nation celebrates
> Its unobtrusive Mass.
>
> No Ordinance be seen
> So gradual the Grace
> A pensive Custom it becomes
> Enlarging Loneliness.
>
> Antiquest felt at Noon
> When August burning low
> Arise this spectral Canticle
> Repose to typify
>
> Remit as yet no Grace
> No Furrow on the Glow
> Yet a Druidic Difference
> Enhances Nature now   (P 1068)

The cryptogram on the minor key song of crickets celebrates summer's end and is really much closer in temperament not to Keats's "To Autumn," to which one might be tempted to compare it, but rather to his "Ode on Melancholy"; like the latter, the source of its pleasure is to brood on sorrow's mysteries. The poem depicts the celebration of a mass and, as if to insist that we hear the song in these terms, it is directly and indirectly invoked as a "Canticle" (the song sung at vespers), a "[G]radual" (the chant that dominates the Proper of the Mass), and as an "Ordinance" (the specific designation for a religious ceremony). If the dominance of liturgical nomination is one characteristic of the utterance, its seeming misappropriation of words is another. This is language that seems arbitrarily whimsical ("Further in Summer than the Birds"), and exasperatingly inexact in establishing references for its modifiers ("Pathetic from the Grass"). It is language whose superlatives are mere confabulated inventions ("Antiquest felt at Noon") and whose verbs are of indeterminate mood ("Arise this spectral Canticle"). It is language that is awkward and even abrasive ("Repose to typify"), language audibly strained almost to the breaking point.

Discounting ineptitude, such solecisms can only be produced by conception reaching to its own depths; in fact, the poem is very much concerned with the problem of inferring depth from a world whose visible dimensions deny it. The constructions noted above not only penetrate into unseen places as, for example, the first line does by its insistence on viewing the end of summer as its extremity or depth, they also anticipate the spaces to which the summer idyll will inevitably give way. Thus in the second line, the word "Pathetic" pries apart the halves of a construction and modifies several ways at once. Half adjective, half adverb, "Pathetic" mediates between speaker and landscape negotiating the space that the poem then inhabits. Dickinson wants to make the stages of perception visible as time-lapse photography, and the second stanza concludes with an outward movement that leads both to the furthest reach of the feeling tapped by this sight ("A pensive Custom it becomes/Enlarging Loneliness") and, in the next stanza, to the source of the extremity. For the center of the experience lies outside of it, in the outskirts of inference, and is liberated partly by a vertical movement downward, a sinking into essence ("August burning low"), and partly by a horizontal movement the median point of which is O, the "Noon" or no-time that "Noon" in these poems comes to signify. Like the light riding "on" the year in "A Light exists in Spring," August is also extract, a burning low to essence, and the essence belongs not simply to the landscape but also to the speaker. In such a state the soul can hear "Canticle" as "spectral" not only because its demarcations are ghostly but also because the absence posited in the last stanza is projectional in/of nature. Loss is a spectre, a displacement of presence that, as we have been saying, nonetheless retains its trace. Nothing in the last stanza has changed except conceptually, and conceptually everything has changed around the space that a lost stable reference implies. What is lost is again the landscape, this time not because the speaker has tried to convert it to her terms, but rather because she has noted the loss that inheres at the heart of its own.

The thought that lies too deep for tears is not here, as it was for Wordsworth, man's connection with the natural world as it survives its most devastating transformations, but rather the insight that transformation severs connection *before* it has actually occurred, in the contemplative reaches of the mind's compulsion to temporalize at all. For the structure of experience is not only a structure of incompletions but also a structure of differences. What is most completely itself will give way, will give itself away. The "Druidic Difference" is not the difference of seasonal change ("No Furrow on the Glow" of this heat), nor is it the difference of perceptible absence ("Remit as yet no Grace"). It is rather the recognition that otherness or difference is at the heart of visible presence; that what we see when we see what is there completely is always something else. The grief in the poem is prompted by its recognition of differences, of the vision that doubles when it is brought most sharply into focus. Like the medieval lady who stares into the mirror and sees not her own face but the skeleton rid of its earthly flesh, the vision of summer's zenith is a reading between the lines that blanks out earthly splendor in the nothing to which it will be reduced.

Man's fall out of alignment with nature, the lapsing of presence into difference and difference into death, is the proper subject of a whole tradition of mutability poems. When we think of the history of such poems and the poles toward which they tend to gravitate, we find, I think, two major tendencies illustrated, on the one hand, by the introspective tradition of George Herbert's "Church Monuments" in which flesh is seen as "but the glasse, which holds the dust/That measures all our time; which also shall/Be crumbled into dust," and, on the other, by Keats's great ode on nature's memento mori, the ripeness that is autumn. Or we see the fusion of the two seemingly disparate strategies (one of which looks inward in meditation at its own perspective death and the other of which casts a cold eye on the seasonal deaths to which it is witness) in poems like Shakespeare's Sonnet 73 or Hopkins's "Spring and Fall." To these alternatives of the meditative contemplation of one's own death or the meditation directed outward on the natural dyings of the season, day, hour, there are, of course, variations, but not as many as we might suppose. Even a poem as seemingly different as Herrick's banter about the urgency of marriage preparations in "To the Virgins to Make Much of Time" is really only a comic version of the first alternative.[39] Where, then, in the tradition do Dickinson's poems fit, for they are surely also mutability poems that attempt to chart in the outside world spaces

Dickinson also noticed within? From "At Half past Three a single Bird" and "It sifts from Leaden Sieves" we know enough to observe that Dickinson's perception of the natural world was frequently prohibitively naturalistic for, as with the poems on the birds, perception had to conjure presence from absence. Unlike Keats's "To Autumn" or Shakespeare's Sonnet 73, her poems, far from being enmeshed in the sensuous detail of their recollection, often start as if from a pure blank. If Dickinson's projections seem mechanical, the abrupt shifting from one still-life frame to another, it is partly because she is not recording the process of a disappearance but rather its fact. Thus some of the poems are characterized by the very absence of which they try to rid themselves.

In "A Light exists in Spring" and "Further in Summer than the Birds," description is, however, naturalistic. Yet despite the apparent resemblance between the latter two utterances and the tradition of mutability poems to which I have alluded, Dickinson's poems diverge from the tradition at a radical point: in her poems, not death but rather difference is the most intolerable manifestation of loss. Difference is the finality whose status replaces that of death: the difference between the speaker and the landscape in the one poem, and between the landscape and its own image in the other. Because discrepancy is located in conceptual space, its grief remains bound to the language in which the discovery of loss is made and made again each time words go in search of meaning's intimations. What in "A Light exists in Spring" cannot be specified or named, in "Further in Summer than the Birds" must be named only in absence. In the words of the first epigraph to this chapter, "There could be no things but nameless things, no names but thingless names." Such a state of affairs represents consciousness torn from the present either by the striving to subdue it through nomenclature or by the positing of nomenclature that embraces a reality larger than the visible and therefore different from it. In either case, language negates the very present to which it claims service, and it is to the complexity of this negation that we now turn.

V

I have been speaking of space both as a something absent and as a domain the fourth dimension of which is, in Bergson's terms, temporality itself, and it may now be useful to recall some of the points at which the two meanings intersect. We have seen the way in which presence in

Dickinson's poems is often reduced to the pain that stands for it (how pain is a condensation of presence, a reduction of its essence to a trace) and we have seen, further, the progression in the poems from presence to pain to blank. The "Element of Blank—" annihilates temporality, and it does so partially for the purpose of returning to a present uncompromised by temporal passage or, at any rate, not cognizant of it. Thus the pure space (space as absence as well as space as domain) to which consciousness is reduced mirrors the space that has replaced the lost object, mirrors loss itself. It is in the self's edging toward loss as toward an identity that we must suspect such mirroring as symptomatic of the illusion that the something missing can actually be reclaimed, that presence can be repossessed, will follow, from representation. For "Noon," Dickinson's metaphor for no-time, for temporal release, is also fixed or static time, and it is fixed specifically by language whose task it is to represent the lost object in the determinate space of its utterance and, by so doing, to repair it. But as I implied in the preliminary definition at the beginning of this chapter, the trace of presence, whether as pain or blank, does not correspond to a real presence existing in an adjacent space. Presence is pure memory or hallucination or dream—it is pure irreparable alterity, and because it is irreparably elsewhere, irreparably other, it can never be reclaimed.

We have looked briefly at the way in which the space between self and other defines alterity: it is what the self recognizes as other *within* itself in the form of an unconscious to which it can attest but not know; it is what the self rediscovers as other outside of its boundaries, a rediscovery predicated on images so archaic and primitive that they have been forgotten the way a beginning is forgotten. The space between the unconscious and its conscious signifiers is a barrier, on the one side language, on the other side presence; and it is dominated by the hope that language can indicate or intuit presence, can translate it out of its otherness. Similarly, though the space which mediates between self and other must be preserved in order to guarantee that the landscape, defined as an otherness, not be lost, it is nonetheless accompanied by the nostalgia for unmediated presence that could rid itself of language as of a need now relegated to the past of its own ancient history. Longing would like to stall temporality at the moment of its origins, and language in its service is a movement of perpetual return, a vain going in search of. Space exists, too, as the theological predicate of a distance that can never be traversed, that must experience presence through mediation. Finally, it exists in

the explicit realm of mimetic representation, for all poems, as I suggested earlier, are not so much past or present as they are referential in
tense, and what they refer to is no longer there.

The desperate lengths to which language can go to reaffirm its relationship with a life apart from representation is illustrated oppositely by
Wittgenstein and Derrida in the extremity of their claims made in the
name of language.[40] Perhaps the most crucial claim concerns the adequacy of representation to minister to the desire for presence. For
Wittgenstein (at least for the Wittgenstein of the *Investigations*) there is
finally no distinction between inner and outer, body and soul: the body
is the best picture of the human soul, and language is simply another one
of its gestures, showing forth the soul as if it were a transparency. Given
Wittgenstein's supposition, there is nothing that cannot be expressed,
and the dogmatism of the belief prompts us to suspect that it has hidden
roots in an unexpressed terror of the very privacy against which it pro-
claims. Oppositely, Derrida's assertion that no language has the primacy
of presence presupposes a space between presence and representation
that is as absolute as discourse can make it. Far from mirroring the soul,
representation is a shrinking from what in "The Motive For Metaphor,"
as if echoing Dickinson, Wallace Stevens called "The weight of primary
noon":

> The motive for metaphor, shrinking from
> The weight of primary noon,
> The A B C of being,
>
> The ruddy temper, the hammer
> Of red and blue, the hard sound—
> Steel against intimation—the sharp flash,
> The vital, arrogant, fatal, dominant X.

Words as manifestations of presence. Words as adjacencies to presence.
Words as ropes flung over impossible spaces, caught and held firmly at
the receiving end, their origin, by definition, unknown. Somewhere
between the desperateness of these hypotheses stand Dickinson's own
words on the subject.

The severance of letter from being, representation from presence,
signifier from signified, and its consequent and concomitant charge to
delegate begin, presence, and thing signified, by proxy, to the word, is
perhaps nowhere so explicit as in Dickinson's description of the personal

letter: "A Letter always feels to me like immortality because it is the mind alone without corporeal friend. Indebted in our talk to attitude and accent, there seems a spectral power in thought that walks alone—" (L 330). In the preceding passage we see the word raised above the consciousness whose task it is to express, or rather we see consciousness purified of the body that it inhabits, and we are given the unmistakable impression that not only can the word adequate consciousness, but that it is, in fact, superior to consciousness, having the power to rise above it as an essence. The desire for the word to supersede the body, to sanctify itself as definitive text no longer subject to the alteration, inexactitude, and temporality of speech seems to imagine a status for language exactly opposite to those proposed by both Wittgenstein and Derrida. Now letters, to which Dickinson's passage alludes, direct their speech within the context of established relationships and thus within the space that comes into play as a consequence of previously legislated territory. Poems, however, establish relationships, and while the space they inhabit must first be defined, definition strengthens itself on independence from a context that it then has a free hand in devising. Indeed we might speculate that the investment of language with independence, an investment we can assume in any poetry that communicates, is partly a consequence of the desire to sever language from all that smells of mortality, all that would contaminate it by its dwelling in a human realm. To give language a meaning and existence apart from life is to dream life into a being that is permanent, to cut desire from the necessity of its limitations, to shape desire into being in a space that can no longer be touched by being. The reification of the word, the breathing of life into it, and with life, design, and with design, designation apart from the desire that worded it, is predicated on the detachment of word from life not so that the word might create or mirror life (our usual conception of what mimetic art does) but rather that it might survive life. For the other side of language viewed as the loss of being is an immortality of the word that specifies being's death as its first, most urgent requirement.

That meaning can remain stable despite the absence of being; that meaning can remain stable only in the absence of being—these are radically different propositions, the second predicated on the despair of language ever to adequate presence without, at the same time, annihilating it. It is precisely with the dilemma of the relationship between word and presence, language and spirit, that Dickinson's most explicit statements on the subject contend. The metaphor she most frequently chooses is one of transubstantiation, the word back into flesh.

> A Word made Flesh is seldom
> And tremblingly partook
> Nor then perhaps reported
> But have I not mistook
> Each one of us has tasted
> With ecstasies of stealth
> The very food debated
> To our specific strength—
>
> A Word that breathes distinctly
> Has not the power to die
> Cohesive as the Spirit
> It may expire if He—
> "Made Flesh and dwelt among us"
> Could condescension be
> Like this consent of Language
> This loved Philology   (P 1651)

How is it that language requires strength? Or that it must work its power in the "stealth" of an inadmissible silence? Is it that strength must withstand the very incertitude of conversion on which its power is predicated, of presence into word, of word or logos into the transcendence of subject? Perhaps the real question is centered around the applicability of such a comparison, in the first place, between logos and godhead on the one hand and word and presence on the other. For the assurance that interrupts the beginning of the conditional statement ("It may expire if He—" by "'Made Flesh and dwelt among us'") will perhaps not hold true for the purely immanent logos of man. Again in the language of the Eucharist, Dickinson writes:

> He ate and drank the precious Words—
> His Spirit grew robust—
> He knew no more that he was poor,
> Nor that his frame was Dust—
> . . . .   (P 1587)

Words so empowered are themselves sacraments that transform. But the implicit celebration forfeits its gaiety in the following recognition that more often than not meaning is recondite:

> Your thoughts dont have words every day
> They come a single time
> Like signal esoteric sips
> Of the communion Wine
> Which while you taste so native seems
> So easy so to be
> You cannot comprehend its price
> Nor it's infrequency   (P 1452)

Sacramental language depends upon the sacrifice of presence, for the primacy of the word is the designation of presence now no longer experienced directly. The predicate of being guaranteed by the word ("So easy so to be") suffers a dissolution or displacement in the more ordinary circumstance of the loss of language where neither presence nor word is hypostatized; both cave in under the need that presses upon them. As a connection to experience once removed, being can be reinstated not through the return of presence (in the case of godhead that is no longer possible, in the case of our relation to each other, it was never possible) but rather through the *symbol* of presence, the word.

In a search instigated by longing, language is by definition a backtracking through the space left in the wake of presence, in the hopes that it might rediscover its source. I asserted earlier that presence is a memory or a hallucination or a dream, a pure alterity, and therefore nothing whose origin allows of rediscovery. It is a memory of a past before language and before the need for language, of that flickering beginning where fulfillment seemed, illusorily, to precede desire; it is the hallucination of a present in which language would founder forever on the admission of its own inadequacy; finally, it is the dream of a sympathetic future in which presence might resurrect itself on the cross of language's defeat. The desire for presence might even be expressed as the desire for consolation or cure, and it finds its disappointment in language to the precise degree that language fails as a remedy. For the discovery of meaning (if we take meaning now as synonymous with the sacramental word) is not necessarily the discovery of a meaning that consoles, and it is perhaps this abject fact that prompts the rejection of language as inadequate. Language does not fulfill the desire it can learn how to express. It connects saying with listening but it does not connect them through an identity; it does not overcome the separation it can be made to span. In its failure to dissolve differences between speaker and listener, in the positing of a space between them that is its habitation, language insists on the limitations of its mediacy. The sacrament of the Eucharist comes as close as possible to the thing itself, a symbol fully invested with the presence it represents. But even sacrament is predicated on the death of a presence; its meaning lies in its ability to overcome death not by the resurrection of presence, but rather by the fullness of the symbol that replaces it. I have been suggesting all along that desire for presence is at the heart of language almost as if what we desired through language were an extension of finite being. The impetus for meaning or for the extension of being sends language as far as it can go, and inevitably stops it short of the fulfillment of original desire. What stops desire is the limitation of its axis. What stops it is human limit. For presence must suffer a translation into language, a conversion that requires the replacement of one by the other as a source of hope.

Speaking of the conversion in an essay that proposes to show the way psychoanalysis is informed by semiology, Paul Ricoeur compares the dichotomy in Freudian thought between consciousness (an inadequate and incomplete sense of self/subject) and unconsciousness (a true sense of self/subject) to the linguistic dichotomy between mere undifferentiated signs with no meaning and a complex semantic system capable of positing a subject. The world of signs precedes that of semantic meaning just as the unconscious precedes the conscious. In both spheres the subject is a displaced one, in the one case by signs that threaten to be no more than formal differences, in the other case by the unconscious whose signs escape meaning until they have been interpreted. Only the semantic realm converts differences to references, as only language converts the unconscious to the conscious: "The semantic problem differs from the semiological problem precisely in that the sign, constituted by difference, is transferred to the universe by means of reference; and this counterpart that reference constitutes in relation to difference can legitimately be called representation."[41] But the conversion from difference to reference is predicated on the replacement of the unconscious by language, of presence by symbol. Because such a process seeks to convert desire into knowledge that may be critical of it, inchoate signs into comprehensive meanings, desire will resist the conversion, for it fears conversion means death, and it will do so by insisting that the proper claim to being is a first claim:

The anteriority, the archaism of desire, which justifies our speaking of an archaeology of the subject, forces us to subordinate consciousness, symbolic function, language, to the primary position of desire. . . . Freud, like Aristotle, like Spinoza and Leibniz, like Hegel, places the act of existing on the axis of desire. Before the subject consciously and willingly posits himself, he has already been posited in being at the instinctual level. That instinct is anterior to awareness and volition signifies the anteriority of the ontic level to the reflective level, *the priority of the* I am *to the* I think. What we said earlier in regard to the relation of instinct to awareness must now be said of the relation of instinct to language. The *I am* is more fundamental than the *I speak*. Philosophy must then get under way toward the *I speak* by starting from the positing of the *I am*; from the very heart of language.[42]

The transformations from a semiotic to a semantic sphere, from unconscious to conscious, desire to language, instinct to awareness, difference to reference, logos to godhead and back to logos again are those processes for which, in Dickinson's poetry, though perhaps not in these terms, the Eucharist may be said to stand as metaphor. In every one of the realms, transformation means the ceding of territory and, as this is the case, meaning is quickly identified with the loss and reduction that accompany it: the death of a false sense of self (which is, at the same time, a more gratifying sense of self) to a diminished unconscious power; of boundless desire to the language that assesses its limitations; of infinite possibility to specific designation; of ritual to the acknowledgment of its distance/difference from the event it reproduces. "It must be conceived without *nostalgia*,"[43] Derrida writes of a differance so central to being that "differance" might be thought of as its name, were being to have a name. But nostalgia or desire is the impetus for speech; in Ricoeur's words, desire is its axis. Desire is what fuels the inexhaustible search through words for the reference that will convert it from a nothing or an unknown to a name, and this impetus for naming is a far cry from that we noted in connection with the reductive definitional poems discussed in the first chapter. Desire posits a space where the name should be, and that name or symbol stands in relation to desire and to presence as a mirror to the real face it reflects. As the reflection in the mirror is not a real face, or is rather an image contingent upon the displacement of the face, so the symbol depends upon the displacement of the presence it articulates. The mirror is not the reality it reflects, as the symbol is not the presence it stands for. But without the mirror, as without the symbol, the thing itself can be felt but not seen, intuited but not known. The mirror is separable from the face it reflects, and what intervenes between the two is space, however illusorily we perceive space to exist behind the mirror or as part of it. Space is *between* the face and the mirror, and must stay between the two if the former is to be seen at all. Space is between desire and the symbol, presence and language, and must stay between the two as undifferentiated landscape.

"Oh, Vision of Language!" Dickinson wrote at the conclusion of a letter (L 782), and in seeming reference to nothing contextually surrounding it. This vision of language—fervently invoked, emphatically unspecified and, it seems, relied on as if it were salvation itself—was it a vision that existence might be worded into being, that language might be a vision of being, a mirror without which life failed at its own revelation? Certainly we can see in Dickinson's arduous struggle with words (a struggle that left its mark on her grammar, punctuation, and diction) the violence with which designation pulled itself out of the grips of insensate experience. Sometimes it could not win its way free, and in the following poem we see the pain of a space that will not let itself be worded:

> I found the words to every thought
> I ever had—but One—
> And that—defies me—
> As a Hand did try to chalk the Sun
>
> To Races—nurtured in the Dark—
> How would your own—begin?
> Can Blaze be shown in Cochineal—
> Or Noon—in Mazarin?   (P 581)

As one can imagine, there have been numerous attempts to supply words for this experience that stops short of them. Without contributing to the guessing game, we can observe that the adjacent meanings, the simile through which the speaker voices the inadequacy of language, posits an experience comprehended by the self but gainsaid to others, as utterance fails of a cohesive shape because of the privacy of its vision. Yet such is the usual case of despair erected on the solipsism of experience that cannot be exchanged through any known currency. The simile is concerned with the way in which language shadows the brilliance of true presence, and its concern is revealed in the familiar metaphor of noon which, as we have seen repeatedly, is a designation of consciousness that completes itself outside of temporality. Outside of temporality, or outside of the realm in which time and space diverge from each other, consciousness is a noon so dazzling that its rays make of the mirror a mere glare. So language sings light's praises by asserting its own inadequacy. So the thing itself, without representation, negates the world of imperfection from which representation arises. So language mourns the space it must faithfully record.

Language may be seen as most inadequate because it is a mediation. Neither be-all nor end-all, neither the "Hand" that tries "to chalk the Sun" nor the "Sun" itself, it is mere undistinguished middle. If we look back now to those poems discussed in chapter 1, we can perhaps see better why so many of them simplify the experiences they attempt to represent. Unwilling to establish a system of reference that acknowledges its connections to experience, meaning thins to the single dimension of a point along an undetermined line: it has no reference other than its desire for reference. Those poems shrink from the meaning that would center them between connections, as from a death. For meaning is a death involving, as I have said previously, the sacrifice of presence, desire, being itself. The relationship between meaning and mediacy, mediacy and death, may be illuminated by what may at first seem to be a digressive glance at Dietrich Bonhoeffer's reminder that in the Bible the tree of life is said to have stood "in the midst of the garden," in the middle of the earth: "It was in the middle—that is all that is said about it. . . . In the middle of the world which is at Adam's disposal and over which he has been given dominion is not Adam himself but the tree of divine life. . . . It is characteristic of man that his life is a constant circling around its middle, but that it never takes possession of it."[44] The tree of life which is the center of man's being is also the source of his limitation, and that limitation is not, as we might expect, exterior to the circle of his existence, but precisely its heart. Bonhoeffer continues:

> *Man's limit is in the middle of his existence*, not on the edge. The limit which we look for on the edge is the limit of his condition, of his technology, of his possibilities. The limit in the middle is the limit of his reality, of his true existence. In the knowledge of the limit on the edge there is constantly given the possibility of an inner boundlessness. In the knowledge of the limit in the middle all exis-

tence, man's being from every possible standpoint, is limited.[45]

To transgress the limit is to gain knowledge and death. Transgression displaces presence whether by knowledge or its designate language. True, Adam named the animals before the fall, but he had no real use for those names until after it. The desire for knowledge is, one might say, the desire for the possession of one's own center, the desire to know the presence around which existence circles; knowledge, in its turn, puts desire at the center of existence: death is the consequence exacted for this radical displacement, the price for the new center. The knowledge of good and evil, which is really, more fundamentally, the knowledge of difference, is predicated on the language that calls it into being. Man knows death through the primacy of language—the symbol of being's separation from itself. To live without language, without the mediacy of language, is to live without death, to exist still in the infancy of a time where the self feels no discrepancy between being and desire, moving around the very otherness that, as yet, it has no need to seek to overcome. With the displacement of the old center of existence comes the discovery of the *meaning* of limitation, comes the discovery of death. How thoroughly Dickinson associated meaning with death, art with the end of animus, may be seen in terms we have just noted in the following poem:

> Essential Oils—are wrung—
> The Attar from the Rose
> Be not expressed by Suns—alone—
> It is the gift of Screws—
>
> The General Rose—decay—
> But this—in Lady's Drawer
> Make Summer—When the Lady lie
> In Ceaseless Rosemary—   (P 675)

"Essential Oils—are wrung—." Whether the oils are perfume from the rose or speech from the lyric, to arrive at either essence, life must be pressed to the thinness of its own immemorial finish, must be condensed and, in the condensation, lost to the extract that will symbolize it. This is the tragic necessity that connects the two stanzas of Dickinson's poem, as it connects the mirror of language and the face which peers at the reversal suffered by its own reflection. For that "The General Rose—decay—" is cause as well as complement of the assertion "But this . . . Make Summer—," and the subjunctive tense of the last stanza urges us to recall how much life fed to the exigencies of language hopes for the immortality of which even at the moment of its sacrifice it cannot be certain. By death the symbol comes into being. Yet the symbol is not wholly winnowed from presence, for it hangs on presence as on the hope of its own fulfillment. Indeed synecdoche itself, that transference of meaning whereby one thing stands for another, depends upon the sacrifice of the whole to its representative part, in the name of which wholeness may be thought or imagined, but can no longer be known.

It is language, after all, that betrays our bodies stretched on a temporal rack, for it is language which adheres to temporality in its laws of sequence, progression, in its mere inability to articulate more than one thought at a time. If presence is a totality, an irreducible fulsomeness, language is piecemeal perception, one thing known at a time. Our very conventions about completed units of structure—the sentence, the paragraph, the chapter—illustrate the temporally bound dimensions in which language pauses as at repeated limitations. But the distinctions I have been adumbrating (presence as liberated from the divergence of time and space, language as the reluctant mediator between them) suffer a reversal in the lyric's wrenching apart of conventional experience. For the lyric employs language not simply to record its own limitations, but also to remedy them. In the lyric meaning gives the illusion of not having to wait upon time for its completion. Seen as if at a glance, in any case without the reader's having to lift his eyes from the page, language in the lyric dispenses with the time that threatens to destroy it. Perhaps it would be more accurate to say that its meanings are spatial rather than temporal; insofar as they can and must be extended, it is downward from one level of meaning to another (as if in a journey toward pure spatial depth) rather than outward along a temporal expanse. Thus when we want to know more about the meaning of a lyric, we do not posit a further temporal reference for it: we travel neither past the moment before its beginning (past the question of what occasions speech) nor to the moment that follows its conclusion; if we push the words at all, it is deeper, into the spaces that lie beneath the surface. The lyric's resistance to temporal extension creates the illusion of temporal wholeness, as well as of the temporal simultaneity of its moments. The dashes that punctuate Dickinson's poems do their level best to accentuate language's freedom from even the most momentary or minimal of stopping places. With no termini within the experience being narrated, articulation seems indivisible to any one of its parts, and it is conclusive not only because it comes to an end, but also because it seems through and through complete.

With the lyric's power to reverse the relative status between presence and representation, or at any rate to confuse them, presence becomes that incompletion which only words can remedy. Thus the lyric is seen as immortal not so much because it has, unlike the writer, no death to survive, but rather because it is complete/completed in and of itself, transcending mortal/temporal limits in the very structure of its articulation. Hence Dickinson can say, again, in that kerygmatic image of light: "The Poets light but Lamps—/Themselves—go out—" (P 883). Presence is the fuel fed to the wick of the lyric that enables its permanent burning not only because the poem lasts (can last) forever but also, and more important, because it is from the moment of its genesis complete. Thus it withstands, stands adjacent to, the very temporal scheme out of which it has been lifted, and in its adjacency eschews any frame of reference other than its own. The lyric occupies a position adjacent to ordinary language which likens it to presence, with this important distinction: unlike the adjacency of presence, its conditions of alterity admit of the direct scrutiny they do not seem to sanction. The lyric finds its meaning not through individual interpretations of experience—these are always relative and, as such, incomplete, incompletable—but rather in its ability to isolate meaning from time, to spatialize it:

> This was a Poet—It is That
> Distills amazing sense
> From ordinary Meanings—
> And Attar so immense
>
> From the familiar species
> That perished by the Door—
> We wonder it was not Ourselves
> Arrested it—before—
>
> Of Pictures, the Discloser—
> The Poet—it is He—
> Entitles Us—by Contrast—
> To ceaseless Poverty—
>
> Of Portion—so unconscious—
> The Robbing—could not harm—

Himself—to Him—a Fortune—
Exterior—to Time—   (P 448)

"Fortune—" inheres in the exteriority of meaning to time, as if meaning
came into being only as a consequence of its exteriority. Thus Dickinson
can talk of a distillation of "ordinary Meanings—" that depend upon
their being "Arrested," rescued from a temporality whose movement is
both unconscious and incomplete. To keep meaning from perishing is to
lift it out of the context where it is sheer mediacy, to make of mediacy
a totality and of totality a meaning. Understood in this light, we can see
the difficulty of many of the poems discussed in chapter 1: shrinking
from all connection because they fear connection means mediacy, they
fail to establish adjacent connections whose completion would spare
them from the contexts that partialize.

We have been speaking throughout of language as the refinement of
desire, that which transforms presence into transcendent symbol. Language fills the space vacated by presence, which is now only an impossible
adjacency. If we define presence, one last time, as a totality of being
immediately perceptible and direct as revelation, perhaps we can imagine
a face capable of regarding itself without the mirror, of dialogue with
God before the Covenant, of the moment of birth pausing at the first
wash of irrefutable air; we can imagine these things but we cannot see
them; we have no pictures for them and, though it is easy to forget the
fact, we never had pictures for them. Language is the picture that replaces
not presence but rather its image, different from the original and with
space intervening; for presence never was, or, if it was, it was in a history
so ancient that we could no longer recognize its true face. Lyrics are
what we make out of the badness of our memory, the mirror we hold to
our desire. Desire must be beaten into the shape of a recognizable necessity, into the human shape it both longs for and resists. Like Blake's
Tyger fashioned in the terrible furnace of unwitnessed creation and
equally invested with primitive ferocity, Dickinson's poem is mined from
the deeps of a central vision:

Dare you see a Soul *at the White Heat*?
Then crouch within the door—
Red—is the Fire's common tint—
But when the vivid Ore

> Has vanquished Flame's conditions,
> It quivers from the Forge
> Without a color, but the light
> Of unannointed Blaze.
> Least Village has it's Blacksmith
> Whose Anvil's even ring
> Stands symbol for the finer Forge
> That soundless tugs—within—
> Refining these impatient Ores
> With Hammer, and with Blaze
> Until the Designated Light
> Repudiate the Forge—   (P 365)

The first two lines with the audacity of their initial question and the preemptory relegation of vision to a position dwarfed by action specify that the speaker, like Blake's, can frame her question only in the light thrown off by the inexplicable burning. What is seen—like the light that exists in spring, like the certain slant of light, like the multiple images of light that suffuse Dickinson's poems—cannot be explained, it can only be faithfully recorded. But to whatever we take the process of spiritual refinement to correspond, it has at its heart desire and its violent transformation from red, "the Fire's common tint—," to the *"White Heat."* Desire must suffer a conversion, whether to language or to the exigencies of other loss, a last purification of passionate intensity. But the bleaching out of color is not a reduction of desire, is not the loss that its negation seems to example. In the *"White Heat"* of conversion, burning attests to the irrevocable "Blaze" of life itself, the pure light of unconsecrated existence that comes from a force that breaks, burns, blows, and ultimately makes new. This man-handling, this hammering and battering, is not, however, as it was for Donne and Hopkins, a direct heaven-handling. In the tradition of New England Puritanism, and along the lines of the Doctrine of Preparation, Dickinson's poem frames the self under its own siege of fire. In that frame it seems to insist that the conversion of desire is not its end. Conversion is no end—is process rather than end—until death (that designation for the final conversion) puts out the mortal light in the brilliance of its own inextinguishable shine. In the vision of radical transcendence at which we crouch, we witness a transformation which may, by analogy, be compared to the one which fires presence into the shape of language. For the recasting of being is a burning down to its essence, to the symbol that survives the furnace of negations. In the appalling place where presence is not, we hold to what can represent it. Language is what has the power of being in the absence of being—that which can still stand for something in the empty space whose task it is to sound with the inscrutable sweetness of its plain meanings.

V

Time and the Lyric

its not despair until time its not even time until it was
    —William Faulkner

*If it be now, 'tis not to come; if it be not to come, it will be now; if it be
not now, yet it will come.*
    —William Shakespeare

Plot is the soul of tragedy.
    —Aristotle

"CAPACITY to Terminate," Dickinson cautioned (P 1196), "Is a
Specific Grace—," and in the following pages I hope to heed the warning.
It has been my contention all along that different as Dickinson's utterances may appear from other poetry, their idiosyncrasies are really only
exaggerations of those features that distinguish the lyric as a genre, and
in this chapter I intend to submit my hypothesis to direct scrutiny. Are
Dickinson's temporal representations characteristic of an individual
style, do they reveal the influences of a certain intellectual movement,
or are they more broadly typical of any mimetic art? Perhaps the question is less likely to collapse before its own difficulty (Wittgenstein once
talked of trying to separate the strands of a spider's web with his fingers)
if we set ourselves the task of determining which temporal features are
characteristic of the Romantic movement, which of an American experience, and which of the lyric as a genre. Since, even qualified, the task
posed by the problem of discrimination is a huge one, the chapter will

constitute only a prolegomenon to a thorough study of the question. In part 2 I shall bring together the propositions about time in Dickinson's lyrics that have heretofore been relegated to marginal status. These observations, derived specifically from the particular problems generated by Dickinson's poems, will serve, when gathered in a single space, as a preface for the look in part 3, at some other Romantic lyrics and at various critical suppositions about features of Romanticism. In part 4 I shall turn to lyrics that precede the nineteenth century, in an effort to discriminate whether what is true of the Romantic lyric may equally apply to the lyric as a genre, and finally, in part 5, to a brief conclusion.

II

The complex relationship between the name for a given experience and the "timing" of the name's appearance, between phenomena and their displacement through language, utterance and an absented referentiality—Dickinson's poems return to these issues with the persistence of an *idée fixe*. In chapter 1 we examined poems in which the name for a given experience is pared from the context that generates it. The result of the isolated definitions is reduction in some instances, incoherence in others, and frequently a trivializing of experience as a consequence of the sparse definition, predicated as it is on the sacrificed memory of its own genesis. Dickinson's most complex attempts at naming shrink from the simplicity of equative representations. We recall "'Twas warm at first like Us," in which naming is by default and "It was not Death for I stood up," where not even negative equations or similes are sufficiently informed to specify the hesitations and ambiguities of a difficult reality. In these two instances, the poems themselves become names, series of predications each one of which depends for its meaning on its relationship to the whole that qualifies it. Dickinson's recognition that equative naming is frustrated by experience that cannot be so severed is nowhere as cogently demonstrated as in her dogged refusal to title—that is, to name—more than a handful of her 1775 poems, and those only indirectly. While the poems discussed in chapter 1 tag feelings and so dispense with them, those discussed in chapter 4 seek comprehension in lieu of the desired name. Thus the poet probes a feeling by describing its progressions, as in "After great pain a formal feeling comes"; knowledge is seen as a consequence of specifying qualities, as in "Pain has an Element of Blank." And sometimes, as in "It sifts from Leaden Sieves," the commonplace name must be deliberately avoided because it lies too deeply buried in the recesses of a slumbering imagination to touch a phenomenon quickened with as yet unspecified life. To understand the shape of an experience is, it would seem, to forfeit the need for an equative name.

My assertions about naming have been founded on the assumption that poems must be ordered temporally to achieve their meanings. Names are true and complex only when they establish their relationship to the dialectic out of which they arise, when they know that "Blank—" is related to "Pain" as to an origin, that "Agony" is the alternative for fear of which "Despair raves—," that the "Slant of light" gains clarity in and because of its disappearance. Thus names in search of their moment in time are in need of the very temporal movement that would partialize them in the process of conferring order. But, as we have seen, the lyric fears acknowledging that its meanings exist as a middle point between other surrounding meanings, for it fears that mediacy involves death as well as meaning. If the poems discussed in chapter 1 edge away from the dialectic that would order them temporally, the poems discussed in chapter 2 establish a dialectic that they then aggressively break into and disrupt, eschewing either specified alternative—sexuality or its renunciation, the earthly life or the heavenly life, pleasure on earth or pleasure in heaven—as inadequate. The disruptions whose specific intention is to refuse coherence, since coherence means connection, and connection, consequence and death, rage against the choices each of which catches the speaker up in its manifest unviability. All action, these poems seem to insist, and consequently all narrative and story on whose shoulders action is carried, leads to ending, leads to death. As "My Life had stood a Loaded Gun" makes overwhelmingly clear, life charged with meaning is life doomed to death; immortality, "the power to kill/Without—the power to die—," can be attained only in the reeling stance that triumphs over meaning by standing at a height dizzying in its distance from it.

Yet although all of Dickinson's poems fight temporality with a vengeance, the strategic maneuvers against time grow progressively more complex in the progressions that become clear if we arrange the poems in the groupings at which I have arrived. In the first two chapters we see that time is brought to a halt, but this is a subversive action, something that happens to the poems, not what they are directly about. In the next two chapters, however, we see the subject of the poem is time's halting, that to which attention is explicitly turned. The poems discussed in the first two chapters stagger under the weight of their own despair and under the terrible illusion that the world will subject itself to desire's reconstruction. The poems discussed in the latter chapters know, however unhappily, that the world will suffer desire only if it can pose an alternative to the limitations against which it once raged. If a poem denies the centrality of beginnings and ends, if it fails to concern itself with the accumulated sequence of a history, it must push its way into the dimensions of the moment, pry apart its walls and reveal the discovered space there to be as complex as the long corridors of historical or narrative time. For the moment is to the lyric what sequence is to the story. Even those of Dickinson's lyrics that appear to narrate more conventional stories may be seen upon closer scrutiny to throw their weight not on the plot and its end, but rather on some issue to which the end is mere preface. In "The last Night that She lived," for example, although a woman dies, death is for us (because for the speaker) not an end but rather that crucial moment around which faith is disorganized. The lyric curiosity about the moment, the vision of it as superimposed upon the long stream of moments that blur in the background to which the poem relegates them, must justify itself in a substitution of other value for the lost chronology.

So, as we saw in chapter 3, the speaker exchanges a diachronic or temporal order for a synchronic or simultaneous one. Figure and thing figured fuse and anticipate the world of projective fusion that we glimpse in "I heard a Fly buzz when I died" and "Because I could not stop for Death." Since death is regarded as categorical rather than conclusive, the impetus for journeying rather than its end, progression becomes two-directional or repetitive, the back and forth over the boundary line from life to death. With conclusion the beginning rather than the end of experience, death is an undertaking that leaves the body miraculously intact. And, as we have seen, if any change is forthcoming in the symbolic death world, it appears to be a gain, the possibility of union with the object of the speaker's desire.

The poem attempts temporal fusions or the fusion between subject and object, but it stops short of believing the two may be hazarded at the same time, for it knows that to reconstruct the world successfully is still to retain some concept of the original without which reconstruction is mere revisionary nonsense. It must acknowledge that allegorical journeys are incomplete ones, that if death is known, there yet remains some point beyond it subject merely to surmise. For although the poems on death depart from time, they are seriously bound by the strictures imposed by their own conception of it. Unlike the poems that hide from the contexts out of which their names spring, and unlike the poems that articulate a context for the purpose of disrupting it, the poems on death return to the reality they do not like. Indeed they have never left it. In their painstaking attempts to reconstruct the world, they are guided by temporal laws so integral to thought that the laws are mistaken for ideas proposed by the speaker's own imagination.

In the poems discussed in chapter 4, where the coordinate of time is recognized as space, as the difference that amounts to death, time will not stop plotting its way across existence; time *is* existence, so the speakers articulate as they learn to speak of death as the necessary sacrifice: "The General Rose—decay—/But this . . . Make Summer—When the Lady lie/In Ceaseless Rosemary—" (P 675). In these poems there is a real transformation of rage into grief: the self once maddened by the requirements of temporality against which it heaved the weight of its refusal, tearing the world apart in the conviction that no rebellion against death was too radical, is chastened in the knowledge that fury does not shatter the world, it only splinters its own reason. Action, story, and plot will not be annihilated by presence as by the vengeance of a "Loaded Gun—," for presence, the longed-for antidote to existence, is suddenly understood as a mere fable of desire.

Only when Dickinson's lyrics have established an internal order can they ever achieve the desired completion and pull themselves away from the context that partializes. When the illusion of temporality is embraced prior to the structuring of its internal elements, an utterance fragments rather than totalizes its world. If the lyric is to substitute a more satisfactory order for the dreaded temporality, the self must keep its distance from the experience it relates. Thus "A nearness to Tremendousness" and "I got so I could take his name" both record a moment in which the self is overwhelmed by the enormity of a painful experience, but in the latter instance the speaker is equivalent to her own incapacitating loss, and the poem falls prey to dramatizing what it is at a loss to know. In "A nearness to Tremendousness" the self still keeps its distance, still keeps its identity separate from the devastating power now guardedly specified as the poem's subject. Ordering even its feelings of chaos and stopped time, the self knocks windows into the wall of its incomprehension. Hence in "I felt a Cleaving in my Mind" the very sequence the speaker claims she is at a loss to reconstruct is that structure which elements the poem. In "Great Streets of silence led away" stasis is jolted into the shape of its formative progressions. Between a label for stasis and its recapitulated action, between poems that break out of temporality or ignore it altogether and those that replace temporality by synchronic order, between a self fused with an experience it can barely name and the knowledge of experience steadied by a grip on words—between these extremes Dickinson's poems vacillate. In the first instance we see atemporality embraced out of desperation; in the second, the structuring of desperation into its own alternative. Predicated on the laws of temporality, but now posed as an alternative to them—like Marvell's parallel lines which, though infinite, will never meet—the poem imitates what it desires to rise above. In the success of its imitation it earns its adjacency to ordinary, incomplete speech, as well as to the ordinary incompletions of life; or to alter my spatial picture, it transcends them.

I have suggested that the contradiction between social and personal time is the lyric's generating impulse, for the lyric both rejects the limitation of social and objective time, those strictures that drive hard lines between past, present, and future, and must make use of them. Like the second term of Dickinson's distinction between the agonizing slowness of human growth ("'Tis Ours—to wince—and weep—/And wonder—and decay/By Blossoms gradual process—") and the instantly achieved perfection of Christ's life ("He chose—Maturity—/And quickening—as we sowed—/Just obviated Bud—/And when We turned to note the Growth—/Broke—perfect—from the Pod—" (P 567), the poem is a sequence that conceals its progressions, or synthesizes them so that it appears a completion no process could have prepared for. Dickinson's propensity to describe movement not as a series of progressive steps but rather as a synthesis is most obvious in her depiction of the hummingbird:

> A Route of Evanescence
> With a revolving Wheel—
> A Resonance of Emerald—
> A Rush of Cochineal—
> And every Blossom on the Bush
> Adjusts its tumbled Head—
> The mail from Tunis, probably,
> An easy Morning's Ride—   (P 1463)

Motion is equivalent to the discrete colors that fail to fuse even in the flash of their disappearance. The synthesis not of one color with another, as we might expect in such a fanfare, but rather of color with movement—

the two become the apotheosis of "A Route of Evanescence"—reveals the exactitude with which loss imprints itself on the abandoned imagination. Temporal fusions are a consequence of the way in which past and future rise to meet the present on its own ground. Given the desire to frame the present in the stasis of perception, it is easy to see why the lyric confuses present tense with the presence that, distinguished from action or story, will bring them to a halt. Unlike the story, novel, or drama, the lyric enjoys an independence from authorial interruption (those breaks in the action that remind us all action inevitably ends), and it is free as well from the speech and thought of other characters. As pure unmediated speech it lies furthest of all the mimetic arts from the way we really talk. Lyric speech might be described as the way we would talk in dreams if we could convert the phantasmagoria there into words. But as the present is neither the past nor the future, as desire is not equivalent to the object of its longing, as there is a space predicated between the landscape and the human subject who regards it, between language and what it hopes to word into being, so the same radical inequality is manifested between lyric speech and the voice or voices it represents.

For lyric speech is not the recognizable voice of its author, and if we conceive of it as issuing from an anonymous speaker, we are still far from ascertaining its mysterious source. Neither speech nor thought as we know it, not simply different in kind of language but also in function, lyric speech is not a remembrance of the diverted or altered presence, but a distinct contradiction of the reality from which it diverges. At the center of the contradiction rises the lyric's choral voice, however disguised under the cloak of a customary first-person speaker; and in Dickinson's utterances, choral voice is emphasized by the hymn meters that structure her poems (meters that imply a union of many voices), and by the frequent existence of multiple pronouns within a given poem.[1] In addition, like the several motions blurred to the synthesis of a single sweep in "A Route of Evanescence" and like the depiction of Christ's life, which achieves maturity in the simultaneity of an instant, vision in the lyric is often pluralistic, the perception of many moments distilled into one, which having burst upon the reader as a unitary phenomenon will then extend its hold on his perception by burrowing into the surrounding space, deepening it to the meaning that is the poem. Perhaps a poem's meaning might even be seen as equivalent to this process of rooting a group of perceptions whose color brightens to one solitary configuration in the single space that is the lyric's most deceptive soil. The proposition of lyric vision and speech as pluralistic is most compelling when we recall, on the one hand, the lyric's affinity with the chorus of the Greek drama,[2] and on the other, some of its more recent spokesmen, as for example, the self-professed pluralistic speaker of Whitman's poems who is nothing if not multiple.

Could our thoughts be pitched as the lyric's, we might in fact shatter time with the determined voice of our musings. But we speak in a single voice whose pitch the lyric always rises above or drops below. The lyric's collective voice, or more accurately the voice of its collective moments, bound together as if one, is not equal to a human voice, and J. Hillis Miller, speaking about the identity of narrative voice, offers insight into this immense inequality:

> The reader may experience the impossibility of deciding, in a given passage, who is speaking, the author, the narrator, or the character, where or when, and to whom. Such a passage in its undecidability bears the indelible traces of being a written document, not something that could ever be spoken by a single voice and so returned to a single *logos*. There is always, in such passages, something left over or something missing, something too much or something too little. This forbids translating the written text back to a single mind, imagined or real. In one way or another the monological becomes dialogical, the unitary thread a Möbius strip.[3]

The lyric posits a speaker whose identity is even more contingent upon economic difference—the more or less than reality that the poem presents—because his origin remains deliberately unspecified, unlike that of characters in narratives, whose first task is to particularize themselves. Lyric speakers do not even have names, and in their shirking of name they diverge from real persona or rather from single persona. Thus the lyric is a departure not only from temporality but also from the finite constrictions of identity.

Perhaps the evasion of single identity helps account for the bizarreness of speech in poems like "I heard a Fly buzz when I died" and "Because I could not stop for Death," where the expectations of a living speaker exist alongside of, but uncontradicted by, the more knowledgeable experience of one who has survived death. What would qualify those expectations in the apprehension of a single mind need only be seen as simultaneous in the conjoining of two perspectives that are not to be

reduced to a unity since they have not, in the first place, been generated
by one. Similarly, in the poems that lament the loss of sequence by
structuring the occurrence of loss sequentially, we have two perspectives
rather than one, and since they radiate from different origins—whether
we care to designate those differences as author/speaker, the moment
before sequence/the moment after it, the memory of sequence/the
experience of its loss, or as the attempt to cross/cross out perception by
the possible ways of noting it at once—we must somehow account for
plurality of voice.

Voice living beyond itself is the subject of a poem the source of whose
popularity (its assertion of the identity of beauty and truth) has diverted
attention from what I take to be a more powerful claim to interest, the
capacity of voice to survive its limitations, hyperbolically figured in the
apparent survival of its own death:

> I died for Beauty—but was scarce
> Adjusted in the Tomb
> When One who died for Truth, was lain
> In an adjoining Room—
>
> He questioned softly "Why I failed"?
> "For Beauty", I replied—
> "And I—for Truth—Themself are One—
> We Brethren, are", He said—
>
> And so, as Kinsmen, met a Night—
> We talked between the Rooms—
> Until the Moss had reached our lips—
> And covered up—our names—   (P 449)

The conversation between anonymous persons, the obscuration of whose
names in the last stanza is a second or further blurring of an identity
that was never clear in the first place, reveals several important facts.
Voice becomes pluralistic, speech a passageway between separate spaces,
as a consequence of the same death that deprives it of a name. Although
the poem explicitly has two speakers, they survive individual identity
and the singularity of given names and become one voice ("Themself"
who are "One—") in the inauspiciously dropped quotation of the last
stanza. All of identity is translated into voice—a phenomenon characteristic of every lyric—and in this particular poem voice comes to an end,
or says it does, in that haunting intersection of two pictures: of the moss

that grows outside along the tombstone and obscures the speakers' names and the moss that grows underground or inside the tomb, along their bodies, silencing the speakers' words. The crossing of parallel pictures, of interior and exterior, leads to the weird intersection at which the two come together and *still* escape the single point of reference that the poem's ending claims. For although the voice tells us what silences voice, it is still talking, is *after* its end relating its end. If the lyric voice continues past its own end (with *end* defined as limitation as well as identity) it thereby represents division not by the ceding of territory to different characters (this is the way narratives and dramas represent division), but rather, as we have seen in all the proleptic utterances, by the contradiction that lies at its heart: action that is completed and yet survives, a speaker who says "I" and yet is pluralistic, a succession of moments long past the point at which succession is possible. I have suggested that finished actions constitute the predicate of utterance, its stable ground, and that all lyrics are referential in their harking back to an earlier moment. What they refer to is what they seek to convert—the fixity of time and of the single identity conferred by time.

Although language is the most painful reminder of temporality, as it struggles to relate one thing at a time, language is also what converts differences to references, and it teaches us to tell the very differences it has worked so hard to dispel. This central contradiction lies at the heart of mimetic art, of speech that is the same thing but something different, contingent upon its desire to slow time even as it is caught up in the momentum of temporal advance. We shall return to a discussion of the temporal contradiction at the heart of the lyric, but first we must ask how these generalizations follow directly from Romanticism.

III

Propositions about Romanticism have sprung up and multiplied to such a plenty that it is sometimes difficult to see the phenomenon beneath the banners of its most ardent spokesmen. As early as 1963, Rene Wellek recognized the need to take the definitional plurality in hand and to coordinate the multiple assertions that flourished as if in genial tolerance of one another.[4] Since then, of course, propositions have mushroomed into books, and new theorists, often with only a cursory nod to their predecessors, have taken upon themselves the task of redefinition. Perhaps the preemptive dismissal of others' conceptions is itself a

Romantic gesture which, to get the object right, must get it wholly on its own terms.[5] In any case there are certain family resemblances between the many definitions to which the literature, notwithstanding its particular quibbles, diligently returns, and we might find it useful to recall some of them here. In "The Drunken Boat: The Revolutionary Element in Romanticism," an essay that stands as one of the finest attempts to delineate Romantic characteristics, Northrop Frye writes, "What I see first of all in Romanticism is the effect of a profound change, not primarily in belief, but in the spatial projection of reality."[6] In a post-Newtonian world, divinity is not "placed" above or outside of the self as it was for Milton or Dante but, Frye postulates, it is relocated within and moved downward.

The correlative of space is time, and if one feature of Romanticism is spatial dislocation, we expect a corresponding distortion in temporal perception. In "Timelessness and Romanticism," Georges Poulet attends to this change, observing that temporal divisions blur because of a tendency toward paramnesia (perception that appears to be recollected) and, alternately, because of true recollection that mistakes itself for original sight. Perhaps the primary characteristic of Romantic timelessness may be located in the apparitional sense that "duration is not successive but permanent."[7] The Romantic embrace of eternity is not endlessness, Poulet tells us: "It is 'a simultaneous full and perfect possession of interminable life.' It is simultaneously possessed, TOTA SIMUL. In it there is neither present, nor past, nor future."[8] And in *Creative Evolution*, Henri Bergson speaks of a related nineteenth-century desire to root perception in concrete duration: "The advent of the moral sciences, the progress of psychology, the growing importance of embryology among the biological sciences—all this was bound to suggest the idea of a reality which *endures* inwardly, which is duration itself."[9] Bergson's remark reveals the point of intersection between TOTA SIMUL and spatial internality, and it foreshadows Starobinski's observations about the marriage of past and interiority.[10] The conjunction of temporal permanence with spatial internality raises the inevitable question about the relationship between subject and object. For as Emerson writes, "Therefore is Space, and therefore Time, that man may know that things are not huddled and lumped, but sundered and individual."[11] If, however, time and space conspire to smudge the sundered points of individual experience, the result is fusion. Rene Wellek writes, "What is called Romanticism in England and on the Continent is . . . the concern for the reconciliation of subject and object, man and nature, consciousness and unconscious-ness."[12]

Though Frye and Wellek are understandably more concerned with establishing Romantic characteristics than with working out their rela-tionships, we may speculate that timelessness raises the central question about what fusions will withstand individuating resistance and what fu-sions must succumb to it. The fusion between subject and object, if com-plete, results in death, and long before Freud this observation was voiced by Emerson in "Experience": "It is a main lesson of wisdom to know your own from another's."[13] "Two human beings are like globes, which can touch only in a point. . . . Life will be imaged, but cannot be divided nor doubled. Any invasion of its unity would be chaos."[14] Before Emer-son, the great psychologist Jonathan Edwards, in yet stronger language, spoke of the prohibition against fusion: "Disagreement or contrariety to Being, is evidently an approach to Nothing, or a degree of Nothing; which is nothing else but disagreement or contrariety of Being, and the greatest and only evil: And Entity is the greatest and only good. . . . Two beings can agree one with another in nothing else but Relation; because otherwise the notion of their twoness (duality) is destroyed, and they become one."[15] That the simultaneous perception of diverse temporal states leads to the desire for fusion between subject and object, and this, in turn, to a longing for death that will facilitate it, is a progression that, once recognized, seems obvious. Thus Frye's assertion that "in many Romantic poems, including Keats's nightingale ode, it is suggested that the final identification of and with reality may be or at least include death"[16] fails to focus its insight at the significant point of an explana-tion. In the nightingale ode, death is desired not for its own sake, not even because it brings the highest knowledge, as Frye suggests, but rather because it is the means of fusion with the immortal bird.

The concerns voiced above provide a convenient recapitulation of the temporal characteristics we have noted in the poems discussed in the last four chapters: the struggle to exempt language from the temporal pro-gressions it fears will submerge it (chapter 1), the blurring of distinctions between subject and object (chapter 3), the propensity to spatialize and internalize experience, and the subsequent effects of timelessness (chap-ters 2, 4). In the next few pages we shall look at the way in which other Romantic lyrics create worlds similar to those we have witnessed in Dick-inson's poems, worlds that have been characterized by our theorists as essentially atemporal (presenting past, present, and future as copresent), spatially dislocated, and concerned with problems of fusion and death.

Perhaps of all the Romantics, Blake most directly conceives the problematic object relations that follow from temporality. In his unqualified temporal division between unlapsed and fallen states, the *Songs of Innocence and Experience* (half of the lyrics denying succession blindly, the other half trapped in a conception of time so bitter as to wall out all memory of what has been lost), we see Blake as a true Dickinsonian progenitor. If we recall two of the paired poems, "The Lamb" and "The Tyger," we remember that the speaker of the former has enough sense of time to query origin, but so naively as to miss its point. Speaking of Christ to the lamb, the persona says, "He is called by thy name/For he calls himself a Lamb." The speaker, who invokes questions of origin for the purpose of transferring identity ("He became a little child./I a child, & thou a lamb/We are called by his name"), imagines the whole world as stalled in the benign fiction of equivalence. Origin, then, as the speaker inadvertently defines it, does not imply divergence (self from the God who generated it, one moment from those that follow), but the dubious blessing of mere repetition. The self at one with God conceives of neither time nor loss, and it is these two dimensions of experience that are introduced into the world of "The Tyger."

Although the speaker of "The Tyger" has a profounder sense of mythological time (of the elusive "when the stars threw down their spears"), he is so overwhelmed by the grief of this moment that he sees all created forms that differ from himself as framed by incomprehensible malevolence. The absent God is conjured into presence, but the imagination can only understand the necessity for such conjuring (for the replacement of palpable object by its image) as murderous:

> And what shoulder, & what art,
> Could twist the sinews of thy heart?
> And when thy heart began to beat,
> What dread hand? & what dread feet?

As Harold Bloom suggests in *The Visionary Company*, this is not vision, it is projection; the speaker's own mortal eye is framing the tiger in darkness.[17] Presence *is* personification; it can only be that, and the speaker takes this fact, underlined as it is by the inescapable difference between moment of origin and present moment, between creator and created, as evidence of a world in which loss and difference equal death itself. His incredulous question, "Did he who made the Lamb make thee?" is posed at the heart of despair over forms that have neither the same shape nor the same name, over the difference from the self that he thinks will annihilate it.

Nowhere is the terror of time and difference recorded with such hallucinatory violence as in Blake's "The Tyger," but many other Romantic lyrics also confess the central problematics of their temporal orientation. In Keats's "La Belle Dame sans Merci," the confusion is heightened by the question of the speaker's identity, for although the poem begins as a narrative, in the fourth stanza the "I" of the persona has shifted to the knight's response, and since it has done so without signaling quotation marks, we might almost suppose a covert continuity between speaker and knight, as if the whole poem were a lyric by default, the knight's dramatic rendering of a self-interrogation.[18] In "La Belle Dame sans Merci," the dilemma of dream is to ascertain what has been envisioned and what the vision means. But all the knight can repeat of the lady's discourse is aggravated by nagging reservations about his role as interpreter: "She looked at me as she did love,/And made sweet moan." Does "as" mean "while" here, or "as if"? We never learn, and it is clear from the knight's lament that he does not know. Even the more direct report of speech, "And sure in language strange she said/'I love thee true,'" undercuts its own certainty by stressing it. In addition, the poem is baffled by an indeterminacy of landscape and a narrative that fails to acknowledge the lapse between one moment and the next:

> "She took me to her elfin grot,
>   And there she wept, and sighed full sore,
> And there I shut her wild wild eyes
>   With kisses four.
>
> "And there she lullèd me asleep,
>   And there I dreamed,—Ah! woe betide!
> The latest dream I ever dreamed
>   On the cold hill's side.

Between the "elfin grot" and the "cold hill's side" where the knight dreams and ultimately awakens, there lies the discrediting absence of unaccounted-for time and space. How he got from grot to hill's side, whether the dream is the dream he thinks it is, of "pale warriors, death-pale," or whether it is a larger dream of the whole experience, of La Belle Dame herself—the nightmare extrapolated from its context and made to seem self-generating—these questions remain unanswered, and it is the poem's purpose to pose them at the center of temporal and spatial indeterminacy. Where the nightmare occurs is thus a question of what the nightmare is. In the temporal and spatial unhinging of the speaker's vision (an unhinging that is perfectly illustrative of Frye's proposition about spatial displacement in Romantic literature), meaning truly does "loiter" outside of all fixed territory.

We can observe a similar propensity to displace experience in two of Keats's odes. In "Ode to Psyche," the speaker dreams of Psyche and Cupid; to transform the fleeting vision into permanence, he must internalize it, construct a sanctuary for it in his mind. As he does so, natural and psychological landscape fuse, and "branched thoughts, new grown with pleasant pain,/Instead of pines . . . murmur in the winds." The speaker of "Ode to a Nightingale," for whom "but to think is to be full of sorrow," exchanges his thoughts for the nightingale's song, which for the duration of the dream brings sorrow to an end by literally re-placing it. Problems of stasis and interiority come together in "Ode on Melancholy," where the appropriate response to sorrow is to "feed" on its meanings, for when the speaker looks at his mistress, he recognizes the inevitable transubstantiation of pleasure into the poison of loss: "She dwells with Beauty—Beauty that must die/And Joy, whose hand is ever at his lips/Bidding adieu." Thus action, when it exists at all, *is* interiorization, in this case, the conversion of joy into melancholy's eternal image.

We see the intersection of stasis and interiority more simply defined as memory in Keats's "In drear-nighted December":

I
In drear-nighted December,
  Too happy, happy tree,
Thy Branches ne'er remember
  Their green felicity:
The north cannot undo them
With a sleety whistle through them;
Nor frozen thawings glue them
  From budding at the prime.

II
In drear-nighted December,
  Too happy, happy Brook,
Thy bubblings ne'er remember

Apollo's summer look;
But with a sweet forgetting,
They stay their crystal fretting,
Never, never petting
About the frozen time.

III
Ah! would 'twere so with many
A gentle girl and boy!
But were there ever any
Writh'd not of passed joy?
The feel of not to feel it,
When there is none to heal it,
Nor numbed sense to steel it,
Was never said in rhyme.

The poem is a lament for human memory which records temporal loss without being able to reverse it. Unlike the natural states wintered by tree and brook, joy is not cyclical, not a recurrent present, and that spectacularly Dickinsonian line, "The feel of not to feel it," enacts the negated presence which is the poem's subject. Doomed to a past he must experience as past, the speaker mourns the frozenness that nature submits to without feeling at all. In the pivotal lines, "were there every any/Writh'd not of passed joy," the question is fixed in the form of the negation it registers, and the twisting of feeling around the space of its own loss is in complete contrast to the direct reversion of insensate world to natural, uncomplicated plenty.

In Shelley's "To a Skylark" we see interiority not as memory but rather as the conflation of subject and object, as the speaker first frames the bird by his series of metaphors for it, and then, in the last stanza, desires a self-transcendence through the being he has voiced. A similar projection concludes Coleridge's "Kubla Khan," whose speaker dreams of a "pleasure dome" only to replicate the dream by imagining himself as its object:

I would build that dome in air,
That sunny dome! those caves of ice!
And all who heard should see them there,
And all should cry, Beware! Beware!
His flashing eyes, his floating hair!

> Weave a circle round him thrice,
> And close your eyes with holy dread,
> For he on honey-dew hath fed,
> And drunk the milk of Paradise.

To preserve the image is to internalize it, to become oneself an image for others to internalize.

I have been speaking thus far of High Romantic lyrics and of their working out of object relations, of discontinuities, of the problem of time itself. Perhaps it should be added by way of footnote here that the Romantics often frame their lyrics in narrative settings; they show a resistance to the full temporal disembodiment exemplified in more modern poems. Thus one interpretation of the first and last stanzas of "La Belle Dame" is that the knight does not tell his story directly to us, but rather to the speaker of the poem, and as a consequence of the narrative enclosure, the knight's disorientation is tempered by the confines of a larger, more stable text. The mediation of lyric speech, the framing of it by narrative, is often dispensed with in later Romantic works, to be replaced by direct image, which is presented as that recurrence or inevitability that contradicts story, narrative, and sequence itself. Thus if image is framed in Keats's lyric, in many of Yeats's poems it seeps much like an ink spot to the borders of the poem, which it then dominates as a totality.[19] We see the obsessive dominance of image in "The Cold Heaven," where an impenetrable sky yields to the severity of meaning, and suddenly riddles the speaker with guilt for the past: "And I took all the blame out of all sense and reason." In "The Cold Heaven" the glimpse of the sky generates a proleptic vision of punishment at Judgment Day in its image and predicts the reading of all life's experiences by the light of unmitigated blame. Here, as in many of Yeats's poems, meaning remains affixed to an image's value as it breaks through the mundane reality, enlightening reality with terror. The crossing of experience by its atemporal reference point or source is clearly demonstrated in "A Deep Sworn Vow":

> Others because you did not keep
> That deep-sworn vow have been friends of mine;
> Yet always when I look death in the face,
> When I clamber to the heights of sleep,
> Or when I grow excited with wine,
> Suddenly I meet your face.

In poems like "The Magi," "Leda and the Swan," or "The Second Coming," image is controlled by the hysterical exaggerations of hypnogogic vision. In "A Deep Sworn Vow," the image at the end compels the same rapt attention, but it is for reasons opposite its intimated familiarity. Although between the third and last line efforts at unconsciousness intervene, they are unsuccessful in obscuring the too-close bond between the two lines: "Yet always when I look death in the face . . . Suddenly I meet your face." As image accosts the speaker, frustrating all efforts to subdue it, as it springs from the very unconsciousness behind which the mind has barricaded itself, we see that the pivotal word in the poem is "meet." It is its power to stun that gives the image power at all, and the poem is as if swayed or thrown off balance by the hard fact of its last line. Rising against the one-directional sweep of temporal reality that moves in stubborn defiance away from the past, the image is an uprising that shatters temporal progression, bringing it back to the still point of meaning.

Sometimes, in the modern lyric, a poem's subject is its own self-consciousness about the reprieve it grants from temporality, as we see, for example, in one of Auden's songs, which begins:

> Lay your sleeping head, my love,
> Human on my faithless arm;
> Time and fevers burn away
> Individual beauty from
> Thoughtful children, and the grave
> Proves the child ephemeral:
> But in my arms till break of day
> Let the living creature lie,
> Mortal, guilty, but to me
> The entirely beautiful.

The reprieve from inconstancy (including that of the speaker, who is anxious to inform us that "Certainty, fidelity/On the stroke of midnight pass/Like vibrations of a bell") depends upon the "time out" that is the poem and in which the lover is sheltered not from the inevitability of time's passage but rather from its horror. Woven into the fabric of the consolation are the very snags on which it will catch—the speaker's faithlessness, the lover's guilt. But that consolation must endure in the toughness of the conditions which legislate against it is the source from which such consolation seemingly derives its strength. The lover is "mortal, guilty" but, stripped thus of virtue and perfection, still "to me the entirely beautiful." Yet if the poem is a cry against time to which it concedes full power, for what purpose does the speaker hold this night as compensation for its fleeting disappearance? How does the poem stop the carnage it claims to accept as inevitable? The last stanza begins:

> Beauty, midnight, vision dies:
> Let the winds of dawn that blow
> Softly round your dreaming head
> Such a day of sweetness show
> Eye and knocking heart may bless,
> Find the mortal world enough;

The speaker ushers the lover from the world into retreat with him, which is, on another level, into the poem, but when he relinquishes the lover—at the end of night, at the end of vision, at the end of speech, even perhaps at the end of love—it is to that very temporality from which the latter no longer appears to need protection. The world that begins where vision ends is the world he would have sanctify love. Not vision that blesses, not the poem, but "eye and knocking heart" that "Find the mortal world enough."

Although extolling the world, the poem clearly rises above it. The vision may be regarded as a suspension of time that makes time bearable, as it superimposes one image upon another, a double take or double exposure: the night of vision and the world against which the night is set. The lover, for all practical purposes, sleeps through the speaker's meditation, summoned and then relinquished, as will-less as a character in someone else's reverie. This is not to suggest that Auden wishes us to visualize the person addressed as unreal, but reality is a function of the speaker's projection. The lover is with the speaker as a dream and only awakens to a moving reality that breathes, sees, blesses when allowed to drift back into the flux of temporal passage; thus the poem, despite assertions to the contrary, seems like an embrace of stasis, word set against the world that eventually dissolves into its flow. Indeed the poem demonstrates how compliant the object of the speaker's beholding remains. As much a projection as Stevens's Mrs. Pappadopoulos, that apparition summoned and dismissed at the esthete's will, the lover in Auden's poem has only the subordinate life characteristic of a figure addressed in the lyric who neither talks nor exists in his own right, but remains always only what the speaker can make of him. The one-directional connection between

subject and object in the lyric is elevated to self-conscious prominence
in the Romantic lyric, where the speaker's problematic relation to what
lies outside of his perceptual boundaries is frequently the focus of the
poem. Hence Keats's nightingale, Wordsworth's Lucy who "could not
feel/The touch of earthly years," Blake's Tyger, Yeats's Helen—all these
remain figments not exactly of the speaker's imagination, but rather of
his will, figures personalized in the image of their maker. Auden's poem
reveals the way in which the lyric relationship between subject and object is voyeuristic, projectional, and requires the cessation of time, for
animation would liberate these characters to independence.

   While some Romantic lyrics stall temporal flow, others rearrange it,
subordinating true sequence to an imaginary configuration, as, for example, Dylan Thomas does in "The Conversation of Prayer":

> The conversation of prayers about to be said
> By the child going to bed and the man on the stairs
> Who climbs to his dying love in her high room,
> The one not caring to whom in his sleep he will move
> And the other full of tears that she will be dead,
>
> Turns in the dark on the sound they know will arise
> Into the answering skies from the green ground,
> From the man on the stairs and the child by his bed.
> The sound about to be said in the two prayers
> For the sleep in a safe land and the love who dies
>
> Will be the same grief flying. Whom shall they calm?
> Shall the child sleep unharmed or the man be crying?
> The conversation of prayers about to be said
> Turns on the quick and the dead, and the man on the stairs
> Tonight shall find no dying but alive and warm
>
> In the fire of his care his love in the high room.
> And the child not caring to whom he climbs his prayer
> Shall drown in a grief as deep as his true grave,
> And mark the dark eyed wave, through the eyes of sleep,
> Dragging him up the stairs to one who lies dead.

Temporal lines cross in Thomas's poem so that the child inherits the
man's grief (in his dream awareness of the reality of death) and, like the
child, the man discovers love momentarily severed from the contemplated

affliction of its loss (as he reaches the woman at the top of the stairs whose life he has prematurely mourned). Whether or not the woman in the situation is the same for man and child (wife to one, mother to the other) is irrelevant, and in fact one tends to doubt she is, since the intersection presented by the poem is not of two simultaneous realities but rather of two successive states of feeling. The poem records a fated reciprocity, as grief remembers its genesis in the love that impassioned it and love learns grief in the shuddering intimation of an inevitable end. The conversation of prayer between "one not caring to whom in his sleep he will move" and "the other full of tears that she will be dead" takes place in the intersection of those dotted or imaginary lines that project our fates away from the solitary incompletion of the individual moment. Man and child may even be regarded as parts of the same person, each representing a temporal incompletion that totalizes itself in its antithesis, in the other half of the fragmented figure, and, as if to complete the fusion toward which the poem climbs, we note that in the title "prayer" is singular. Though, as in Auden's poem (or as in Dickinson's "I died for Beauty but was scarce"), we are presented with two central figures, they quickly reduce to the totality of one, and this reduction which lies beneath the surface of appearances means that both parts of the whole must be projected to a spatial completion, the man brought to "his love in the high room" and the boy dragged "up the stairs to one who lies dead." In the conflation of figures, it almost seems as if the boy is the one who lies dead in the mature grief to which the man is destined. For the moment by itself is a mere seed that flowers only in the crossing of present and future, only in the conversation whose both sides heard together means coherence.

The poems we have examined thus far have not taken time as their explicit subject, nor have their temporal features been extraordinarily flamboyant. Nonetheless, they have each accomplished the stalling of time that Poulet notes as a characteristic of Romanticism (as Yeats's images do when they cut across temporal progressions, or as Thomas's images do in their juxtaposition of successive states of feeling), the confusion between phenomenal and psychological space that Frye observes as a characteristic of Romanticism (as we have seen it in "Ode to Psyche" and "Kubla Khan"), the fusion between subject and object described by Wellek (between man and creator in "The Lamb," speaker and bird in "To a Skylark"), and, even if only by way of hint, the relationship between fusion and death (as we intuit it in "Ode to a Nightingale,"

"Conversation of Prayer," and "A Deep Sworn Vow"). Different as all the poems we have looked at are, one feature binds them together: the speakers and the objects of their attention (the Tyger and the Lamb, the tree and brook of Keats's "In drear-nighted December," and the lovers in "A Deep Sworn Vow") all manifest a static relationship to each other. Once the relationship comes fully into being, it has already defined its limitations.[20] Thus the knight in "La Belle Dame" remains baffled by his experience; retelling the dream fails to yield him further comprehension of it. The man in "Conversation" is left at the bottom of the stairs despite the cogency of the speaker's happier projections for him. The lover in Auden's song sleeps and wakes within the framework of the speaker's limited directive. The TOTA SIMUL that Poulet describes, the radical sameness the images retain despite the transformations to which they are subjected, creates the illusion of a static present. Although these poems do not represent the only type of English Romantic lyric, they seem notably different from the American Romantic lyric as it is written by poets like Whitman, Hart Crane, and Wallace Stevens.

In *The Design of the Present*, John Lynen discusses characteristic versions of time in American literature, and he argues compellingly for the theory that in American literature, temporal reality is often depicted as a duality, the present moment seen in abrasive juxtaposition to an eternal reference.[21] Although he concedes that English Romantic poets also strive to bring past, present, and future into relationship, he notes the following distinctions between Whitman and Wordsworth:

> In a representative passage from *The Prelude* we see Wordsworth working to suppress the very contrasts Whitman's style depends upon. The event Wordsworth describes is not a sudden realization; it is a smooth, progressively developing flow of perception into meaning. . . . For to Wordsworth time is a continuum in which the past evenly advances toward the present. . . . Wordsworth does not project himself directly into the time remembered or relive it as if it were present; he sees it as what it *was*. . . . For Whitman . . . instead of a temporal continuum, there is a continuous movement on the part of the poet, . . . [which] commits him to endless commutation between the now and other times markedly distinct from it. . . . Whitman uses collage rather than blending.[22]

Lynen's distinction between temporal continuity and temporal contrast, as he sees it differentiate English and American literature, with

Whitman and Wordsworth as representative spokesmen, provides an interesting explanation for the static relationship between subject and object we have observed in the English Romantic poets glanced at above. For if the past is fixed as past, remembered but in no way reexperienced, the relationship between subject and object is likely to remain suspended in the initial terms of the proposed status quo, or, if it is redefined, the redefinition is regarded as a stable or singular one. If, on the other hand, in the poetry of Whitman, Crane, and Stevens, temporal categories are flexible, even fluid, we have a provocative hypothesis for why the relationship between subject and object is transformed by violent perceptual shifts. Indeed the intention of these American poets seems to be to posit a relationship between subject and object that the poem then almost axiomatically submits to redefinition. The subsequent transformations are as abrupt as they are generative of temporal leaps and lapses, for as Lynen suggests, when progressions occur in American literature they are characteristically not continuous or sequential but are rather emblematic or epidometic. We must of course be wary of categorizing either literature without sufficient qualification. It is admittedly difficult to differentiate the English Romantic lyric from its American counterpart, especially in the twentieth century when the two have had the opportunity to learn from each other, and all distinctions must survive the test of their exceptions. Although, for example, Lynen intimates that English Romantic literature manifests a continuity between present and past, the observation is more apt for Wordsworth than for Keats or Blake, and it is not really true for those poems by Auden and Thomas at which we looked above. Thus it is not only important to distinguish between the English and American lyric before they have begun to exert mutual influences, but between individual writers, and Lynen's argument is correctly couched in terms of particular poets. The distinction here really rests its case on degree, and as we shall see if we give ourselves the leeway of even the most scrupulous of generalizations, the younger and bolder American lyric, under the influence of Whitman, and shaped precisely by those temporal juxtapositions of the present with its eternal reference point, is more fluid in its depiction of the present's transcendence of itself and in the fusions it posits between subject and object. It is to Whitman, Crane, and Stevens we therefore turn in order to discover how Romanticism is modified in some American lyrics.

"Language begins only with the void," Maurice Blanchot writes,

"Plenitude and certitude do not speak."[23] In Whitman's poems, where there is an abundance of language, the implications of Blanchot's statement seem appalling. Yet if we look at two of Whitman's most beautiful and characteristic lyrics, "Crossing Brooklyn Ferry" and "As I Ebb'd with the Ocean of Life," we see how plenitude and absence arise from the same source. In "Crossing Brooklyn Ferry," the speaker gazes into the water and sees the shimmer of humanity projected from his image: "Diverge, fine spokes of light, from the shape of my head, or any one's head, in the sunlit water!" In "As I Ebb'd" the speaker hovers at "The rim, the sediment that stands for all the water and all the land of the globe," and his vision is not moving but static: "I too but signify at the utmost a little wash'd-up drift." In "Crossing Brooklyn Ferry" water is magnificent, the "eternal float of solution," that liquid which pours, converts, moves between, connects, and finally merges identities. In "As I Ebb'd with the Ocean of Life," "the measureless float" funnels to "but a trail of drift and debris," to death itself: "see, from my dead lips the ooze exuding at last." But although the poems present opposite images, of center and rim, plenitude and impoverishment, water as float of life and ooze of death, they share several significant features. In both instances the speaker relinquishes the constrictions of mortal body to assume the fluid identity of water: "myself disintegrated, every one disintegrated yet part of the scheme." In both poems life and death are the shared experience whereby finite identity is transcended and the individual becomes composite: "You furnish your parts toward eternity/ you furnish your parts toward the soul."

Many of Whitman's lyrics embrace eternity by outright temporal defiance, not just moving counterclockwise (as, for example, "Prayer of Columbus" does, where the vision of harmony is really a divination, Whitman's attempt to intuit the present as if it were future, from the imagined perspective of a figure in the past), they eschew clocks altogether. Again and again, the lyric speakers tell us the earth is to be "spanned" so that "All these separations and gaps shall be taken up and hook'd and link'd together" ("Passage to India"). As we are reminded in "Prayer of Columbus," it is the explorer's dream that "the hemisphere be rounded and tied, the unknown to the known," and this feat is to be accomplished not by encircling the world from the outside, guided by temporal-spatial laws, but by cutting through it as if in a giant cross-section a line that runs straight through its heart. Although Whitman is capable of visionary ecstasy that displaces the world as we know it by the beatific claims made in its name ("The sleepers are very beautiful as they lie unclothed,/They flow hand in hand over the whole earth . . . as they lie unclothed"),[24] the complexity of his temporal-spatial transcendence is rooted in the particularity that gives it life.[25] In "Passage to India," the speaker talks of "Something swelling in humanity now like the sap of the earth in spring." The second part of the comparative term converts abstraction to bonded proof, the generative blood to which man can testify because it is pumped, as through one system, from the earth into the pulsing veins of a bodied humanity.

In "Crossing Brooklyn Ferry," where the crossings are multiple (between self and the unknown in time present, and between self and the unknowable in time future, in the imagined retrospect of a future time in which the present could be recollected as a true past), just as vision is about to exhaust itself from soaring, the speaker dives into the heart of its engendering truth: "What is more subtle than this which ties me to the woman or man that looks into my face?/Which fuses me into you now, and pours my meaning into you?"—into the exchange of glances between two people who read and intimate meaning in the luxury of true apprehension, between whom meaning "pours" in Whitman's more generous word.

Not only the particularity that teaches in these cautionary few lines, but also the fluency of meaning as it transcends the necessary specificity of its embodiment. Thus "It avails not, time nor place—distance avails not" is no fanciful assertion based on the speaker's desire to importune other worlds into the shape of this one; it is rather a glimmering of the truth that real connection is atemporal, impalpable, unembodied. It pours from the void into the shape of a glance, a word, a momentary feeling, those ties that cross between us mediating the bare space. Although we tend to think of Whitman (even the Whitman of the lyrics) as expansive, digressive, writing in a form that opens in ever larger circles outward, in reality his insight always plunges back into the center from which movement was propelled in the first place, back to those intersections or crossings between people at the heart of which relationship is defined. Thus if the space in his lyrics looms large—the whole of created and uncreated worlds alike brought together—we must see this partly as an effort to remedy the terror at space that remains unmediated; space must be thought into being in a place where primary laws transcend the temporal-spatial ones, for in a world of temporality, precious little mediation is possible.

To fix the moment of relationship above time, to replace the clock's tick-tock and all the accompanying spatial limitations, requires violence, and it is hence no accident that in Whitman's world words barrage the empty or inadequate space as if in an effort to fill it with "plenitude and certitude," with an energizing meaning. Insofar as words must obliterate the static objects, must shock them into relationship, it is no wonder Whitman designates the spirit who engenders his poems as "electric." Perhaps nowhere in the history of poetry do we see such a savage re-arrangement of the world's temporal laws. When Whitman's poems concede to the laws of this world, as at the end of "As I Ebb'd With the Ocean of Life," we see the grief against which the other poems rage:

> Me and mine, loose windrows, little corpses,
> Froth, snowy white, and bubbles,
> (See, from my dead lips the ooze exuding at last,
> See, the prismatic colors glistening and rolling,)
> Tufts of straw, sands, fragments,
> Buoy'd hither from many moods, one contradicting another,
> From the storm, the long calm, the darkness, the swell,
> Musing, pondering, a breath, a briny tear, a dab of
>   liquid or soil,
> Up just as much out of fathomless workings fermented
>   and thrown,
> A limp blossom or two, torn, just as much over waves floating,
>   drifted at random,
> Just as much for us that sobbing dirge of Nature,
> Just as much whence we come that blare of the cloud-
>   trumpets,
> We, capricious, brought hither we know not whence, spread
>   out before you,
> You up there walking or sitting,
> Whoever you are, we too lie in drifts at your feet.

Ceding territory and amassing it—if Whitman's poems may be said to have a characteristic rhythm, an ebb and flow, perhaps this is it, though, as we have noted, rarely does he stay "at the rim" or at any one spot long enough to inspect the minutiae of broken things out of which de-spair weaves its lament. That things cannot be made whole, that "straw, sands, fragments," all the shored debris of "As I Ebb'd" remain irretriev-ably severed, justifies the address in the last line where the tone of appeal reverberates from the soundings of the angered ocean and from the walls of accumulated observation. Much of the power of the colloquial plea is that it seems to catch the speaker off-guard; his lament which has been directed downward and then inward spins him around and moves him to look up, a direction that, from the drift of the poem thus far, seemed as unlikely as irrelevant. That it becomes relevant, that the pantheistic cry gleans its origins outside of nature, outside of anything to which it can see itself as comparable, and far beyond what it knows how to mend, is the conclusion that focuses mourning at a source. While the pummeling of the waves against the sand offers one explanation for the flatness of the speaker's vision, the last line provides another, or rather it provides the perspective on incompletion, leveling, brokenness that, amplifying it in the light of a lapsed connection, alters its terms.

For Whitman's successor, Hart Crane, the world was more "broken" than Whitman had dreamed possible, and Crane's efforts to span and convert the separations lodged against a less hospitable time and space. In *The Bridge*, as movement flows back and forth from historical figure to idealized myth, from Rip Van Winkle to Pocahontas, from Columbus to Walt Whitman, from woman to continent, Indiana to Virginia to New England, from airplane to subway tunnel, the prayer remains steady: "Lug us back lifeward—bone by infant bone."

The desire for a bridge between past and present, for the bleeding of one into the other so that all temporal divisions might blur, culminates in the beseeching question at the end of "Recitative": "In alternating bells have you not heard/All hours clapped dense into a single stride?" In his yearning to escape boundaries the speaker in "Voyages" places himself at the center of the sea, of "rimless floods":

> Bind us in time, O Seasons clear, and awe.
> O minstrel galleons of Carib fire,
> Bequeath us to no earthly shore until
> Is answered in the vortex of our grave
> The seal's wide spindrift gaze toward paradise.

The longed-for derangement of sensibility that will drive our minds clean of sense in order to deprive us of temporality, exemplified here by the seal's moony state, is as chilling a way out of time as Crane ever seizes upon, and, with a backward glance to the issues discussed in the last chapter, we might speculate that this is the shape presence would take could it literalize itself in an expression. For the seal's "wide spindrift gaze" represents oneness with the natural world as a draining away of self, a collapse into the idiot-silence of dreamless indifference. The object of the sacrifice is clear. To be bound in time and awe is to be spellbound in eternity, to be centered in the "rimless" eye of the world. But however ecstatic mystical experience, putting the mind clairvoyantly in touch with a unity before which distinctions buckle, it eventually returns man to the routine limitations of a human world. For the world no longer protean, rimmed by time and space, the speaker mourns and, as is often the case, his grief takes the form of imagining its own alternative:

> The imaged Word, it is, that holds
> Hushed willows anchored in its glow.
> It is the unbetrayable reply
> Whose accent no farewell can know.

The "imaged Word" spelled out in the picture of illuminated stasis and set against the world from which it differs "holds," but only in the gleanings of a transparent imagination. For the speaker sees clearly enough that if "the unbetrayable reply" exists, it is not in the word made flesh, not in the mortal world. His desire for permanence thus forces him out of the world of persons, a leavetaking so egregiously extreme that grief seems at a loss to further specify it.

The speaker in "The Broken Tower" reverses this decision, breaks himself into an identity as, no longer drifting at sea, he falls upon the mercy of the earth:

> The bell-rope that gathers God at dawn
> Dispatches me as though I dropped down the knell
> Of a spent day—to wander the cathedral lawn
> From pit to crucifix, feet chill on steps from hell.
>
> Have you not heard, have you not seen that corps
> Of shadows in the tower, whose shoulders sway
> Antiphonal carillons launched before
> The stars are caught and hived in the sun's ray?
>
> The bells, I say, the bells break down their tower;
> And swing I know not where. Their tongues engrave
> Membrane through marrow, my long-scattered score
> Of broken intervals . . . . And I, their sexton slave!

Oval encyclicals in canyons heaping
The impasse high with choir. Banked voices slain!
Pagodas, campaniles with reveilles outleaping—
O terraced echoes prostrate on the plain! . . .

And so it was I entered the broken world
To trace the visionary company of love, its voice
An instant in the wind (I know not whither hurled)
But not for long to hold each desperate choice.

My word I poured. But was it cognate, scored
Of that tribunal monarch of the air
Whose thigh embronzes earth, strikes crystal Word
In wounds pledged once to hope—cleft to despair?

The steep encroachments of my blood left me
No answer (could blood hold such a lofty tower
As flings the question true?)—or is it she
Whose sweet mortality stirs latent power?—

And through whose pulse I hear, counting the strokes
My veins recall and add, revived and sure
The angelus of wars my chest evokes:
What I hold healed, original now, and pure . . .

And builds, within, a tower that is not stone
(Not stone can jacket heaven)—but slip
Of pebbles—visible wings of silence sown
In azure circles, widening as they dip

The matrix of the heart, lift down the eye
That shrines the quiet lake and swells a tower . . .
The commodious, tall decorum of that sky
Unseals her earth, and lifts love in its shower.

"God is a circle whose center is everywhere and whose circumference nowhere," St. Augustine wrote, and "The Broken Tower" may be conceived as a speaker's flight from a world where no rim converts brokenness to the grace of a spiritual whole. The fall from the tower is a fall into time, and the poem tries to replace its own original understanding of spatial-temporal lines with another order entirely, signified by "the visible wings of silence sown/In azure circles, widening as they dip/The matrix of the heart." The transformation demands a revised perception of space (rather than ascend the tower, the speaker will embrace it: "Not stone can jacket heaven"), and a shift from archetypal world to personal world, from "crystal" divinity before whom one's words, poetic or otherwise, can never be certainly "cognate" to words that "pour" regardless, from clamorous sound to "widening" silence. But different as these alternatives seem, both the protective enclosures of the cathedral, at the poem's beginning, and of the mystical vision, at its end, wall out the experience of the fragmented phenomenal world that puts the speaker most closely in touch with the central rhythm of life.

How much "The Broken Tower" depends upon the antiphony of its movements (like Whitman's ceaseless conversation between the vast expanses of time-space and the specificity of a particular mediation, between the body and those disembodied connections that gird the world) is immediately apparent if we look at the precipitous balance of its contrary movements.[26] Although the first six stanzas commemorate the fall into a broken world—of time, of intervals, of experience ransacked by pain, of things separate—and the last four stanzas revive the speaker to the visionary wholeness in which love engenders love, the poem's beginning is seared by beauty (Yeats would have called it a "terrible beauty") that seems to cut itself from agony, while the peace of its conclusion is retarded and qualified by the many subordinate clauses, the complicated predication, syntax circling around itself in a pacing that can only be described as tortuous. The first six stanzas are separated from each other by end-stopped lines, and the feel of the words themselves, their frenzied insistence ("Have you not heard; have you not seen; The bells, I say, the bells break down their tower"), is in direct contrast to the poem's fluid conclusion, whose one long sentence unites—though it does not have the power to still—the profound disturbances of a broken world. The poem derives its power from those antagonisms between beauty and pain that in so much of Crane's work surface only in relationship to each other, and long before the turning resolution in the last four stanzas, we note that its movement is not progressive but is rather synchronic, a daring venture in catachresis.

Though the harrowing drop to experience is a conventional enough subject for a religious poem (man sent away from God to be tried by the severative charge of experience), even in the first line, "The bell-rope that gathers God at dawn," we sense the violence of words at work against each other. In the synecdochic literality of the focused-upon bell-rope (which seems an idiomatic shorthand for "gathers people at dawn to worship God"), as in the literal attempt to gather in one place an essence that is flung out across the entire universe, we have as if encapsulated the impetus for both the poem's violence and its beauty. Something about the impossible abundance of summoned presence as it bursts out of the confines of its allotted space touches a string of beauty, and it is that which the speaker returns to play upon. Nothing else can explain the rapture of the second stanza except its association with the poem's first line, and the stanza is particularly thrilling as it issues from a revised understanding of the bells' calling, which had heretofore and mistakenly dispatched the speaker rather than summoned him. In the dawn rung in by the bells during which "The stars are caught and hived in the sun's ray," the swarming of fragmentary radiance to a honey-colored whole literalizes on another, natural level the gathering of plenitude to one entity. Image here is liquid, and its wild epiphanic rapture is like nothing before in the poem, and like nothing that will follow it either.

In fact it is the gathering of the stars to the mass of the sun that overflows the bounds of conceptual fullness and compels the "breaking" in the next stanza. The release from permanent form, the spilling of plenty back into the world, leads to the dissolution of wholeness, to "broken intervals." It is important to realize that the world at the moment of its breaking is richer, more stunningly seductive than it will ever be in any unity, including that of the poem's conclusion, for from this paradox comes the power of the individual stanzas. The world breaks out of its profusion—because of, as well as away from—it cannot totalize profusion except in the intersection of contrary impulses; the voices "slain," "outleaping," and "terraced" perhaps even suggest the contradictory echoes of one voice at three separate intervals. The "Oval encyclicals," moved from tower to plain, have been humanized by their agony, but though the fourth stanza asks us to see the bells as imitative of humankind smitten prostrate by the inadequacy of its efforts to rise to the tower of grace, pain is transcended in its own rapturous lyricism: the voices on the plain catch at the circle of wholeness, live at its center, however powerless they are to comprehend its circumference.

The stanza that mediates between the lament over brokenness and the celebration of its mending is ushered in by a somber assessment of pain as past tense:

And so it was I entered the broken world
To trace the visionary company of love, its voice
An instant in the wind . . .

Rising above the antagonists on the plain, severing itself from the chorus
of voices almost as a soloist's recitative would, the stanza demonstrates
Crane's extraordinary ability to register multiple points of view and, at
the same time, to lay bare their common genesis, for the fifth stanza is
removed from the preceding as a past is removed from a present, or as a
moment of reflection casts itself aside from the pain that has bodied it.
Perhaps the most significant feature of the aside is its recognition of the
voice that hushes the turmoil on the plain by being harkened to even in
its absence: of love that is momentary ("an instant in the wind"), subject
to sudden departure ["(I know not whither hurled)"], and never palpable ("company" for which the mind must make space inside of itself).
The sudden perception of love as "visionary" is the true rejoinder to the
voices on the plain as they aspire to the impossibility of both wholeness
and presence. Relationship exists in the absence of the concrete, in the
stone of the mind's affections as they allow themselves to be carved by
the certain passage of ephemeral presence. Only in its absence is wholeness conceived and made palpable. Thus although the "healing" of the
poem's conclusion provides us with a more unified conception of the
world, with the throwing off of violence beatitude disappears also, and,
as I mentioned before, the long tributary sentence of the last four
stanzas, in praise of completion and singularity, is syntactically troubled,
as if to dissuade us from mistaking the ease of any such resolution, for
in brokenness there is plurality, connection, life.

   Jonathan Edwards, who wrote so much about the dilemma of perceiving presence in the void of its palpable manifestations, and whose
"Dissertation Concerning The End For Which God Created The World"
the last stanza of Crane's poem seems almost to suggest,[27] concluded the
seventh section of that essay with the staunch assertion: "It is no solid
objection against God's aiming at an infinitely perfect union of the
creature with himself, that the particular time will never come when it
can be said, the union is now infinitely perfect."[28] In the space between
the poem's fifth stanza and its conclusion, Crane seems to sacrifice a
comparable knowledge. "The visionary company of love" transformed
to the real blood and flesh of the woman offers to unit the "brokenness"
and to permit the ecstasy of union with God. Yet it is in the earlier

demarcation of an impossible rising, of a vision of love aspired to, lost, and aspired to once again, that the multiple voices of the poem choir the rich contradictions of the world as we know it.

The brokenness that Crane laments occasions Wallace Stevens's celebration. The pleasures of merely circulating, the thirteen ways of looking at a blackbird, the jar that, set against the wilderness in Tennessee, orders it—these are jokes on the world, provocative ways of viewing its temporal-spatial possibilities, and they are instigated by a more than marginal insistence that order is always both provisional and alternative. The polar terms of Crane's world (either the fixed time-space or the fluid perception that fuses all into a simultaneity) in Stevens's poems are flung against the ground and shattered to smithereens. Thus in "The Glass of Water" the chemical states of ice and liquid between which water shuttles are proposed as analogues for the mind's transformations. But ice and water are merely poles; between, "the refractions,/The *metaphysica*, the plastic parts of poems/Crash in the mind." Crane desired perception to simplify itself to a unity, and he despaired of the fact that, except in rare moments, it could not do this. For the Stevens of "Poems of Our Climate," even assuming such unity "stripped one of all one's torments, concealed/The evilly compounded, vital I," one would still long for the affliction of disorder, because:

> The imperfect is our paradise.
> Note that, in this bitterness, delight,
> Since the imperfect is so hot in us,
> Lies in flawed words and stubborn sounds.

In "This Solitude of Cataracts" we are told that to know the earth separate from our versions of it, to stand without being swayed by "the oscillations of planetary pass-pass," is to become a "bronze man." Thus permanence is conceived not as the world synthesized to a grand stasis, but rather as the self made statue, and Stevens therefore promotes those changes that Crane's anguish only compels him to record. Indeed Stevens's boisterous delight in plurality and transformation, his gaudy intellectual propositions, much like Whitman's exuberant claims of bonded identity, often appear to shortchange any perception of loss or limitation. Buoyed up by the extravagance of their claims (Whitman's to defy space-time by positing an existence in the future as well as in the past, and Stevens's to convert the thing endlessly beyond its recognition), both can seem

curiously hardened against all real grief, and we might note, parentheti-
cally, that this is in direct contrast to Dickinson's unprecedented ability
to make pain and grief the very ground of the metaphysical reach and of
lyric self-consciousness. The manipulative intercession in temporal-
spatial law by rotations that whirl the object to the blur of imaginary
stasis effectively annihilates time-space and raises man, lordly, above
transformation itself. Whitman accomplishes such fluidity by his serial
propositions, Stevens by his series of analogies. But if we doubt that
Stevens understands the meaning of transformation, we have only to
turn to "Prologues to What is Possible," where analogy, powerful as
instinct and often as profoundly buried, rises to a recognition that
touches the world with the magnitude of human change:

I

There was an ease of mind that was like being alone in a boat at sea,
A boat carried forward by waves resembling the bright backs of
    rowers,
Gripping their oars, as if they were sure of the way to their destina-
    tion,
Bending over and pulling themselves erect on the wooden handles,
Wet with water and sparkling in the one-ness of their motion.

The boat was built of stones that had lost their weight and being no
    longer heavy
Had left in them only a brilliance, of unaccustomed origin,
So that he that stood up in the boat leaning and looking before him
Did not pass like someone voyaging out of and beyond the familiar.
He belonged to the far-foreign departure of his vessel and was part
    of it,
Part of the speculum of fire on its prow, its symbol, whatever it was,
Part of the glass-like sides on which it glided over the salt-stained
    water,

As he traveled alone, like a man lured on by a syllable without any
    meaning,
A syllable of which he felt, with an appointed sureness,
That it contained the meaning into which he wanted to enter,
A meaning which, as he entered it, would shatter the boat and leave
    the oarsmen quiet
As at a point of central arrival, an instant moment, much or little,

Removed from any shore, from any man or woman, and needing
   none.

II

The metaphor stirred his fear. The object with which he was
   compared
Was beyond his recognizing. By this he knew that likeness of him
   extended
Only a little way, and not beyond, unless between himself
And things beyond resemblance there was this and that intended to
   be recognized,
The this and that in the enclosures of hypotheses
On which men speculated in summer when they were half asleep.

What self, for example, did he contain that had not yet been loosed,
Snarling in him for discovery as his attentions spread,
As if all his hereditary lights were suddenly increased
By an access of color, a new and unobserved, slight dithering,
The smallest lamp, which added its puissant flick, to which he gave
A name and privilege over the ordinary of his commonplace—

A flick which added to what was real and its vocabulary,
The way some first thing coming into Northern trees
Adds to them the whole vocabulary of the South,
The way the earliest single light in the evening sky, in spring,
Creates a fresh universe out of nothingness by adding itself,
The way a look or a touch reveals its unexpected magnitudes.

"Prologues to What is Possible" moves toward an understanding of
how analogy transforms the world into the astonishments of meaning.
It begins, however, as far from that point as self-consciousness can
strike a pose, in an analogy that substantiates itself only by a backward glance to a part of its own artificial proposition: an "ease of
mind" is "like being along in a boat at sea," but the waves of the sea
"resembl[e] the bright backs of rowers." Enacting the very obscurity
it is trying to work its way through, the first section catches the subject at various unsatisfactory angles, in the synchrony of several proposed meanings, for though the man "is part of" the boat, "whatever
it was," his exact relationship to it remains deliberately unspecified.
To journey in analogy is to await the moment of "central arrival"
when the vehicle will fall away, leaving the subject in the clear air of

its own light: "A meaning which, as he entered it, would shatter the boat and leave the oarsman quiet."

In Part II, in the shying away of the central figure from the foreignness of the previously proposed analogies, the problem is laid out along the central grid of knowledge. What is connection? What renders it farfetched? How are things comparable? What are the connections between things not comparable? In the wonderful image of "The this and that . . . On which men speculated in summer when they were half asleep," Stevens proposes an analogue for incompletion: the persistent strangeness of dream symbols and the meanings they insinuate while manifestly concealing. So the figure "lured on by a syllable without any meaning" comes home to rest in its newly recognized correspondence with the self's relation to its own unconscious. But it is not enough that Stevens indicate two sides of analogy catching sight of each other's meaning; the poem's conclusion enacts the recognition and, as we might expect, it does so by way of analogy.

If, momentarily, we stand back from the last stanza and see the whole poem in a theoretical framework, we may take its devotion to the miraculous power of analogic conversion as an unintentional gloss on the larger pattern of American figuration from Puritan literature to those poems by Whitman, Crane, and Stevens that I have discussed. Correspondence "between . . . things beyond resemblance"—whether they be the disjoint circles of different ages inaugurated and brought into alignment by the fine eye of Whitman's atemporal reverie or the dissonant voices of brokenness harmonized in Crane's lament and pitched to the ecstasy of a still unviolated conception of wholeness, or whether they be Stevens's subjects in search of their freedom from figuration, who must first pass through figuration as through the trials of a faltering imagination—this is as persistent a strain in American poetry as any subject. Its tensions give way to the fluid passage between two terms of analogy that converts them to a unity, either by synthesis (as Lynen describes it and as we have seen it in Crane and Whitman) or, as in the last stanza of "Prologues to What is Possible," by the sudden transformation of one into the other. The poem works its way through the progressive paring away of propositions as deftly as if its movement were a bonafide free fall. Like those made in dream, its connections are dramatic, allusive, emphatically self-referential, and precipitous as the withholding of meaning. Like dream, too, the poem moves with deceptive randomness toward its own understanding, and when it comes, in the

flush of sudden comprehension, it overwhelms the poem with the abundance of its clarity, utterance growing voluble, getting a grip on the
vision that evaded it.

The last stanza is drenched with the bounty of its life-bestowing additions, and it is not for nothing that Stevens has worked to show up the
multiple and artificial efforts at figuring an analogy, for only at the point
of "central arrival" is that strained-after oneness alluded to in the first
stanza achieved with true ease. Perhaps the first fact to strike us about
the final stanza is how the "flick," the barely perceptible difference of
addition, is no longer separate from the world that it transforms and
how, at the same time, it teeters on the word-thin, world-engendering line
of perception before which the universe is bequeathed the miraculous
gift of life. The wonder of these analogies is how unambiguously they
convert the world into its own redemptive alternative, rescuing it from
the poverty that precedes true relationship, and leaving behind as almost
unimaginable the long arduous process through which discovery fought
its way free. This is creation as we might have witnessed it in Genesis,
and the poem closes with the authority of a history or fable, a story
almost beyond repeating because of the god-given generosity with which
it specifies the continuousness of life itself:

> A flick which added to what was real and its vocabulary,
> The way some first thing coming into Northern trees
> Adds to them the whole vocabulary of the South,
> The way the earliest single light in the evening sky, in spring,
> Creates a fresh universe out of nothingness by adding itself,
> The way a look or a touch reveals its unexpected magnitudes.

In the synecdochic conversion that such addition implies, the two
terms of analogy are joined at the moment when "some first thing
coming into Northern trees" is seen to contain "the whole vocabulary of
the South," and the figure, whether bird or leaf or sheer symbol, uncom-
mitted to designated form, weaves between its possibilities under the
weight of an almost unbearable compression. "Vocabulary" is just the
right word to convey the infinity of the additions as they spill outward
from the single, unspecified, yet clearly finite form. In fact the line
enacts the very conversion from nothing to one thing to multitudinous
meaning that, on another level, we may take to be its subject by making
the reader query the form of the proposed figure much as the eye might
try to catch hold of it. In the teasing out of possibilities that do not

allow themselves to be eliminated, the figure unburdens its wealth, and the poem's final two examples escape the parallelism into which the verbal patterning seems to push them, precisely because they remain subordinate to that initial image whose language, learned, generated them. In the disarmingly simple image of the final line, Stevens rests his case on a vision of human correspondence, of intimacy unexpectedly arrived at, resonating with the earlier accretions of both luminosity and plenty, and still reeling from the suggestion—as outrageous in one sense as it is true in another—that life breaks into flower out of nothing but recognition of its own being: "Creates a fresh universe out of nothingness by adding itself." Tinged by the light of these previous suggestions and reiterating them in its unbalance of a barely palpable addition to the flooding of the world with subsequent fullness, the last line drifts outward in a motion as expansive as the water of the poem's initial analogy, but no longer awash in an artificial boat, riding now on its bare, its beneficent meaning: "The way a look or a touch reveals its unexpected magnitudes."

Whitman and Crane would have approved of this reading of experience by its atemporal reference point. We recall that despite the ventures into ages past and future, Whitman's speakers always return to the insistent question: "What is more subtle than this which ties me to the woman or man that looks into my face?/Which . . . pours my meaning into you," and that for Crane, too, brokenness may be patched by relationship: "Is it . . . sweet mortality [that] stirs latent power?" The plunge into meaning, either serially, as Whitman does it, or by a series of analogies, as we have seen it in Stevens, is in Crane's work carried to the perplexed revisionary extremity that yields meaning at a cost greater than either Whitman or Stevens imagined. For Crane's speakers seem to covet the world-splintering brokenness when they think it will sanction a world rearrangement, and they sometimes even dream that the ultimate atemporal revision might, by risking death, reverse it. Thus in "Voyages," all temporal rendings and dismemberings are transcended in the sea change of the ocean whose apotheosis is heralded by a metamorphosis in language, a "transmemberment" in which the striking out of the negative prefix "dis" and affixing to the word a substitution that reverses its meaning claims that death is no negation; it

> Presumes no carnage, but this single change,—
> Upon the steep floor flung from dawn to dawn
> The silken skilled transmemberment of song;

Neither Stevens nor Whitman cared to risk such a misreading of experience, though both stand on its verge by their insistence on the fluid transformations of temporal sequence to which the world must submit itself in its search for recognizable shape. Whitman and Stevens may in fact be said to play with the temporal violations that Crane committed in earnest and, in this respect, as in the driven intensity with which death in his poetry assumes the curiosity of meaning, we see his strange kinship to Dickinson. Crane referred to Dickinson twice in his poetry. Once in *The Bridge* he spoke of "that stilly note/Of pain that Emily, that Isadora knew," and again, in a memorial sonnet to Dickinson, of the deprivation left in the wake of "Some reconcilement of remotest mind—." As he seemed to understand the phrase, and as we might apply it to his own work, Crane read prophecy in the breaking and fragmenting of temporal order, finally even dreaming he might budge the most intractible manifestation of time, death itself. From the extremity of this Romanticism we now turn in order to discover how the connection between atemporality and death reveals its roots in the generic struggle to reconcile temporal disparity and meaning, a struggle we may presume to be equally overt in its efforts to sabotage the terrible rigor of chronology.

IV

We cannot know the phenomenal world, Kant's first *Critique* insists; all we can attest to are its manifestations. Thus while the object itself is "transcendental," lies beyond our sensible intuition, it may be perceived and ordered within the temporal-spatial grid upon which rests our apprehension of the whole world. Time and space are real not as objects but rather as modes of perceiving objects, and Kant's "Transcendental Aesthetic" is given over to demonstrating the relationship between the duration, succession and coexistence of objects and of events.[29] For our purposes two features of Kant's exposition are important; the first concerns temporal mediacy, the second, temporal permanence. Kant writes:

> Just as I can say *a priori* that all outer appearances are in space, and are determined *a priori* in conformity with the relations of space, I can also say, from the principle of inner sense, that all appearances whatsoever, that is, all objects of the senses, are in time, and necessarily stand in time-relations. . . . Certainly time is something real, namely, the real form of inner intuition. . . . Time is therefore to be

regarded as real, not indeed as object but as the mode of representation of myself as object.[30]

and

Only in the permanent are relations of time possible. . . . For change does not affect time itself, but only appearances in time. . . . in all appearances there is something permanent, and . . . the transitory is nothing but determination of its existence.[31]

Kant's efforts to prove that the temporal world is mediate (that through which the self knows itself and other objects) and permanent (has, underlying all transitions, the fixed point of its totality) are, as we have seen in the last two chapters, "proofs" equally sought by the lyric. We have spoken about the way in which the self totalizes itself by seeking an equation with the words that spell it out. The transformation of life into words compresses the very meanings it totalizes, and in this reduction, it asserts its claim to permanence.

All mimetic art depends upon compression. The novel is shorter than the life that it records, and must remain shorter, by a good deal, if the reader is to make time for it within his own life; even the Greek drama scrupulously adhering to the unities of a day is confined, more severely, by the theatrical limits of a few hours. But despite these abbreviations, which we might designate as proportional, the scaling down of action to manageable space, both drama and novels expand rather than compress the individual moments of their stories. We see this expansiveness in a soliloquy as the moments of plot are squeezed apart to make room for the luxury of articulated self-reflection, in the apprehension of several characters' proximate thoughts at the apparent simultaneity of a given moment, in a novel's landscape as it is sculptured to the dimensions of observable shape; we see as we do not in life, because what we see has been magnified, given prominence, and lengthened. Novels and dramas teach us by such cuing: they unravel meaning, shake it loose, insist we make it visual—give it spatial as well as temporal depth—and because they do so, we may liken the drama or narrative to motion picture which, in so many respects, often tries to liken itself to them. In contrast, the lyric is a still life, and even that metaphor is misleading unless we qualify it by adding that the picture it presents is not representational, but contracts its own meaning. Although lyric verbs often record temporal change, they also collapse their progressions so that movement is not consecutive but is rather heaped or layered. This stacking up of movement, temporal forays cut off from linear progression and treated instead as if they were vertically additive (very much as we have seen Dickinson's "Great Streets of silence led away" demonstrate), is quite opposite to the way in which meaning "unfolds" in novels or in the drama. The least mimetic of all art forms, the lyric compresses rather than imitates life; it will withstand the outrage of any complexity for the sake of being able to present sequence as if it were a unity.

Anticipating objections to the hard line of my distinction brings us up short against the bias of this section. It may be argued that my definitions accommodate only the most conventional novels and could be contradicted by twentieth-century novels or dramas, which set out to tamper with fictional conventions; that my assertion about temporal indeterminacy in the lyric, while accurate enough as our theorists have told us and as we have seen, if applied to the Romantic lyric, are just that—a phenomenon prompted by Romanticism and therefore historical in nature. But while it is true that contemporary novels, or even the eighteenth century's *Tristram Shandy*, violate the very laws of sequence by a subversion that I have been insisting comprises a generic distinction, those violations depend upon the reader's recollection of the conventions that have been displaced. Thus when it occurs, a novel's ousting of progression is a reference to its own generic history, which it now wishes to write anew. Such a rewriting is both self-referential and historically generated, and this is claim that could be proved easily enough by noting when the novel's treatment of time begins to tamper so conspicuously with linear sequence, that is, when the novel begins to assume lyric features. Alternately, however, the premise that the lyric compression of temporality is similarly generated by the Romantic movement does not bear up under the scrutiny of lyrics written in the sixteenth and seventeenth centuries, or even in fact earlier. For as we shall see, the displacement of speech from a definitive context, the namelessness of the lyric speaker and the gratuitousness of her history, the lyric's travel backwards and forwards restlessly over the same ground—all these features that unhinge time from its fixtures and reduce it to a unity—are present in the earliest lyrics we can examine.

An important qualification is, however, in order here. The generic claims I have made for poems throughout the course of these chapters are predicated on certain *tendencies* of lyric speech, possible in no other genre but not necessarily inevitable in, or made explicit by, a particular lyric. These tendencies may be summarized as follows: (1) the manifest concern with direct questions about temporality and with the object relations that are its consequence; (2) the accomplishment of predictable substitutions (voice for action, synchrony for diachrony, plural meanings for singular ones); (3) the collapse of opposites into a single third term; and (4) the parodic rendering of temporal conflict through verbal formulations so extreme that they seem to enact the conflict they also specify. But while all lyrics share these tendencies, those lyrics that make them explicit may be said to constitute a separable tradition in the history of the lyric (a tradition that Dickinson helps to change as well as to define when her poems exploit the violence of temporal conflict still further). These are poems of exaltation or trauma, where time has been stopped dead, or exploded, where it has been reinvented according to more generous conceptual specifications, and where verbal sequence is itself alert to temporal rearrangement and is sometimes even imitative of it. One characteristic of this lyric strain then is strain itself, a fretting against or pushing back or outright violation of the normal limits of the lyric, whether it takes the form of temporal improbability, structural self-consciousness, or psychic extremity. Indeed this lyric strain may be defined partially by the single-mindedness with which it converts all conflict into the temporal dilemmas that underlie it, and in choosing to locate the origin of conflict in temporality, the drastic terms of its formulation—life and death—are set against each other in an active engagement of battle. But while the poems that comprise this lyric strain often push their alternatives as far apart as conception will tolerate, they also wildly compress the oppositions they have isolated, and we thus see lyric compression—the pushing apart of alternatives for the sake of bringing them together anew—as radically different from the forms of compression practiced by novelistic or dramatic art forms. Novels and dramas compress action by abbreviating it; lyrics winnow alternatives from action and then compress them to a single identity. Novels and dramas stylize temporality; lyrics transform it.

I shall have more to say about this transformation in a moment, but I want first to differentiate by example the poems I have defined as constituting a subcategory of lyric speech from those lyrics whose temporal conflict is implicit, or that merely specify what the more distraught lyrics enact. The speakers in Keats's "When I Have Fears" and in his "Bright Star" both quest for permanence, but in the latter instance, the life-and-death alternatives that would stall time to a stasis are so close to the surface of the poem that when they erupt in its last line ("And so live ever—or else swoon to death"), we see a verbal fulfillment of slowed time, "living ever" and "swooning to death" being one and the same strategy for temporal transfiguration. Similarly, while Herbert's "Easter Wings" and "Church Monuments" imply, respectively, an escape from temporality and a fall to its inevitable completion, only the first poem dramatizes the upward movement of its flight. While Yeats's "Leda and the Swan" and his "The Magi" allude to moments of conception and birth with the intention of baffling our ordinary ideas of generation, in "Leda" the orgasmic spasm is described in terms of what it will produce, and what it will produce is death ("A shudder in the loins engenders there/The broken wall, the burning roof and tower/And Agamemnon dead"). "The Magi," on the other hand, prodded by the disquieting adjectives of its last line ("The uncontrollable mystery on the bestial floor"), unsettles without really shifting our ideas about conception. While "Tintern Abbey" laments the passage of time, and Tennyson's "Tithonus" laments its failure to pass with any personal consequences, neither dramatizes their protest against temporality; Keats's "Ode to a Nightingale," however, under the pressure of the subject-object conflict (the desire to fuse with the ecstasy of song), enacts at its center the stopped time that is the poem's subject.

All lyrics posit speech outside of the action from which they exempt themselves, and such a retreat is inevitably bound up in ideas about the revision of temporality. Romanticism exaggerates the temporal self-consciousness I have been discussing, but timelessness is a generic concern, and, as we shall see from the following examples, we can observe it best in those poems that comprise a subcategory of the lyric because of the boldness with which they lay their conflict before us and polarize it in life-and-death terms.

In the words of Sir Walter Ralegh, many lyric speakers desire to be "filled with immortality," and they are equally conscious of death, which subverts desire every time the speaker casts his thoughts on the necessity of his end. "In what estate so ever I be/*Timor mortis conturbat me*"—so begins the anonymous fifteenth-century lyric, and continues by observing that death's liminal disturbance lies in its capacity to lurk beneath the most routine phenomena:

> Wake I or slepe, ete or drynke,
> Whan I on my laste ende do thynke,

> For greet fere my soul doth shrynke:
> *Timor mortis conturbat me.*

I have spoken of compression as a lyric feature, and we are now in a better position to see that what it compresses is not just language or action, but, underlying them, a proposition about immortality as it presses upon the prophetic understanding of a speaker's own death. Many lyrics present a conversion experience, transforming death into immortality or vice versa, and the poles of death and immortality are thus those states that poetic language shuttles between. Tichborne, trying to catch the instantaneousness of the conversion, spelled it out in paradox:

> I sought my death and found it in my womb,
> I looked for life and saw it was a shade,
> I trod the earth and knew it was my tomb,
> And now I die, and now I was but made;
> My glass is full, and now my glass is run,
> And now I live, and now my life is done.

The compression of death and immortality, one slipping into the other, with slippage always a subversion, is not only frequently the lyric's subject but also often dictates one of its characteristic structures which, seen close up, looks very much like the paradigmatic scheme of Tichborne's elegy or, alternately, looks like the scheme proposed by Dickinson's "Behind Me—dips Eternity—/Before Me—Immortality—/Myself—the Term between—" (P 721). Neither especially subtle nor complex, it must seek a formal reconcilement of forms that remain opposite, a phenomenon we see most clearly in Medieval and Renaissance lyrics. It is implicit in the hair-tearing contradictions of Wyatt, Sidney, and Surrey. Shakespeare with his characteristic boldness makes it explicit, as love discovers its lament in the desire for immortality and the knowledge of its negation. Shakespeare's sonnets are strewn with references to hours, days, seasons, as with memento mori, and they often appear transparently easy, even vacant of subject, because the subject so closely adheres to, seems like a doubling or repetition of, what I have called a lyric structure. Donne's love poems are as formally disguised as Shakespeare's are obvious, yet underneath the disguise we may discern those contradictions and compressions of death and immortality that lie at the heart of the metaphysical conceit. In "A Sun Rising," "The Canonization," and "A Valediction: Forbidding Mourning," compression wields its accomplishments in the service of temporal distortion; it would wrench the moment out of temporal sequence and raise it above "the hours, days, months, which are the rags of time." As the moment is elevated to its atemporal resting place, we see the consequence of lifting it from its context is a compression that transforms it to an essence. Thus when the lover in "The Canonization" imagines the jealous laity to praise love's accomplishments, he projects the praise in these terms:

> You, to whom love was peace, that now is rage;
> Who did the whole worlds soule contract, and drove
> Into the glasses of your eyes
> (So made such mirrors, and such spies,
> That they did all to you epitomize)
> Countries, Townes, Courts: Beg from above
> A patterne of your love!

In Donne's poetry, as in Shakespeare's, the soul's contraction epitomizes its recoil from a world-devouring temporality, and it does so by besting temporality on another level, by compensating for what it lacks in duration with an unparalleled breadth. The lover's boast that "We can dye . . . if not live by love,/And if unfit for tombes . . . We'll build in sonnets pretty roomes" is a clever enough admission that sonnets are not simply alternate dwelling places, they are also radically other temporal schemes in which words offer sanctuary that does not admit of ordinary death. Exacerbated by the petty exactions of a commonplace temporality, the boast of immortality is provoked time and again in Donne's poems, but we must recall that for Donne, as for Dickinson, refuge in language is predicated on the departure of presence. Seen in this context, the comfortable alternative phrasing of "We can dye . . . if not live by love" sheds all its charm in the hardening of "can" into "must." Consigning their lives to words, the lovers lose them, for, as I discussed in the last chapter, and as the following observation by Maurice Blanchot reiterates, words equal the death of presence:[32]

I say: "this woman," and immediately I dispose of her. . . . No doubt, my language kills no one. However, when I say "this woman," actual death is announced and is already present in my language; my language says that this person, who is there, now, can be detached from herself, subtracted from her existence and her presence and plunged suddenly into a nothingness of existence and presence; my language signifies essentially the possibility of this destruction; it is, at every moment, a resolute allusion to such an event. My language kills no one. But, if that woman were not really capable of death, if she were not at every moment of her life menaced by death, bound and united to it by a tie of essence, I could not accomplish this ideal negation, this deferred assassination that is my language.[33]

Words assassinate and they immortalize, and they do both as a consequence of the death of presence. Blanchot's observations have spoken words in mind, and all words must of course come to terms with the ambivalent forces that have generated them, but for the most part this task is an unconscious one. It *becomes* conscious in the lyric (hence the obsessive thematic dominance of time and immortality in the lyric as in no other verbal art form) and it manifests its consciousness partly by the resolute shiftiness we note if we try to pin the lyric down to a discrete time and place. We catch sight of a poem's temporal indeterminacy when we see that its speech both issues out of a specific occasion and, at the same time, rises above it, floating somewhere between designated motive and less-circumscribed intentions, which it indicates but stops short of specifying.

"A Lyke-Wake Dirge" clues us to indeterminacy by the contradiction posed in the poem's first line. Recalling that "ae" means "one" in Middle English, "This ae night, this ae night" isolates a particular moment in time that is immediately thereafter raised to a plurality:

> This ae night, this ae night,
> *Every night and all,*
> Fire and sleet and candle-light,
> *And Christ receive thy saul.*

Words uttered over a particular corpse to warn the soul that it may be in danger of suffering the deprivation afforded by its lack of generosity:

> If ever thou gavest hosen and shoon,
> Sit thee down and put them on:
>
> If hosen and shoon thou ne'er gavest nane,
> The whins shall prick thee to the barest bane:

and words spoken across five centuries to us who still have time to choose or eschew generosity, words mediate between the two—mortal words about mortality that nonetheless escape it in the transcendent ambiguity of the "Thou" who is addressed.

"Western Wind," the anonymous four-line lyric also from the fifteenth century, is even less affixed to a particular time and place; in fact it takes its own temporal indeterminacy as its subject:

> Westron wind, when will thou blow?
> The small rain down can rain:
> Christ, if my love were in my arms
> And I in my bed again!

Does the wind bring the rain or take it away? Is love generative of loneliness or solace to it? What is the relationship between the sacred longing and the sexual one?[34] Insofar as the experience described is one predicated on tension and contradiction, any effort to "place" it exactly misses the point. Because the experience translates temporal fixture (the "when" of the first line) into a question about itself, sequential reasoning leaves obvious dissatisfactions, the most striking of which comes to light in the attempt to connect the third and fourth lines, to understand the progression from the contemplated presence of the lover to the solitary consequence, "And I in my bed again!" Diverting our attention from sequence to broader questions about generation and change, the poem insists on the totalization of nothing but loss.

Lyric features of compression and temporal indeterminacy come together and figure in the recognition that the beginning of a poem is often only arbitrary, a moment apprehended as a beginning not because it has sequential priority but rather because it has dramatic priority. In this respect, Dickinson's concentration of tension at the beginning of a poem is really an exaggeration of a generic feature. For if beginnings are, by definition, the fullest rather than the first moments of entry, they may be revised, and indeed Herbert's "Affliction (I)" attempts to do just that as it starts itself twice, first in the initial line, "When first thou didst entice to thee my heart/I thought the service brave," and later in the nineteenth line, as the complaint about God's service catches more sharply at the specificity of its negated pleasures: "At first thou gav'st me milk and sweetnesses;/I had my wish and way."[35]

As I have suggested, a poem frequently imitates structurally the temporal compression it takes as its subject, as for example, Donne's "At the round earths imagin'd corners, blow" does, or Vaughan's "They Are All Gone into the World of Light!" or as does Fulke Greville's "Sion lies waste, and thy Jerusalem,/O Lord, is fallen to utter desolation." In the last instance, the body of the poem chronicles the temporal desecrations that Judgment Day will end, and it so equates its enumeration of sin

with sin's actual occurrence that it seems to believe verbal completion
may coincide with a temporal one. Thus although the plea in the concluding stanza implores that Israel's plagues not be eternal, it really desires they not be present, that God "fill up time" as the speaker has filled
up the poem, that He collapse it to instantaneous Presence:

> Yet, Lord, let Israel's plagues not be eternal,
> Nor sin forever cloud thy sacred mountains,
> Nor with false flames, spiritual but infernal,
> Dry up thy mercy's ever springing fountains.
>   Rather, sweet Jesus, fill up time and come
>   To yield the sin her everlasting doom.

It is no accident divine presence is a lyric concern and that, for example,
we have a religious lyric rather than a religious novel or drama,[36] for it is
not surprising that the lyric, whose province is by nature the annihilation
of a severative temporality, and which can compress space in its own restorative design, should seek to mediate the most profound space of all.

We have some sense of how daring the mediation can be if we recall
one of its most extraordinary instances, Donne's "Goodfriday, 1613,
Riding Westward." It is characteristic that a poem which cuts backward
into time, utterly annihilating the fixture of a past, also insists upon a
date in its title, for the insistence underlines the reality of temporal reversal even as it affixes it to the specific moment in time that is the
poem. The title also indicates the other contrariety of the speaker's direction as, obsessed by the terror of contemplated vision, he rises away
from the scene of the crucifixion:

> . . . .
> Yet dare I'almost be glad I do not see
> That spectacle, of too much weight for mee.
> Who sees Gods face, that is selfe life, must dye;
> What a death were it then to see God dye?
> . . . .
> If on these things I durst not looke, durst I
> Upon his miserable mother cast mine eye,
> Who was Gods partner here, and furnish'd thus
> Halfe of that Sacrifice, which ransom'd us?
> Though these things, as I ride, be from mine eye,
> They're present yet unto my memory,

> For that looks towards them; and Thou look'st towards mee,
> O Saviour, as Thou hang'st upon the tree;
> I turne my backe to thee, but to receive
> Corrections, till thy mercies bid thee leave.
> O thinke mee worth thine anger; punish mee,
> Burne off my rusts, and my deformity,
> Restore thine Image, so much, by thy grace,
> That thou may'st know mee, and I'll turne my face.

The speaker is turning away from the crucifixion, carried first, and most directly, by a literal advance of time, which specifies the sacrifice as the advent of temporal calculation, and in a second, breathtakingly double, even opposite and more idiomatic sense of turning away, he is refusing to witness a sight that could be seen for the looking at, and apparently must be seen even in its absence. Just as these two temporal senses contradict each other (one asserting distance from the mythical event, the other a terrible proximity), so vision doubles when the speaker's knowledge of the crucifixion is suddenly emended into a "memory" of it. The farther he travels from the image, the more sharply it projects itself against his mind, until he acknowledges it in (because of) the cross of relationship: "Though these things, as I ride, be from mine eye,/They're present yet unto my memory,/For that looks towards them; and Thou look'st towards mee." Only when he sees himself as seen can the speaker admit the sacrifice's reversion from myth to reality, and in the shadow of the subsequent immediacy, he cannot seem to bear what he was afraid of all along; he cannot bear Divinity in the human shape of pain. Although the speaker claims he will not countenance God's image because he is sinful, the poem offers barely submerged evidence that vision is intolerable precisely as it transforms Christ the God into Jesus the man.

Thus the plea in the last line, "Restore thine Image," is both reference to the Biblical depiction of man as made in God's image (reference to the speaker) and, less obviously, a literal reference to Christ Himself: "Restore thine Image"; allow me to see You as God rather than Jesus, as Lord rather than suffering man. Recognition therefore depends upon resurrection, for not God's image which, seen, brings death, but rather Jesus', the agony of the sacrifice that, close up, cannot be borne. The power of the last few lines depends upon the doubling of the restoration—man's into a state of grace, Jesus' into a divinity distanced from the horrible presence of suffering—and the phrase that intimates knowledge,

"That Thou may'st know mee," weirdly reverses itself in the uncanny echoes of an unspoken but resonant second sense, "That I may'st know Thee." The speaker can turn only when there is guaranteed space between himself and God, and this interpretation, which seems stressed by the shock of the conditional last lines, throws into relief the degree to which apprehension has personalized myth into a memory and then rendered it intolerable by the experience of it as present. Thus vision is renounced in lieu of the very mediating space that it has been the explicit intention of speech to abridge, and the poem offers an extreme example of how the religious lyric can so subvert time and space, so rewrite itself into prior history, that it is left shuddering from the reality it has called into being.

The lyric abridgment of temporality, of womb and tomb, to recall Tichborne's formulation, results, as we have seen, in a poem's ambiguous and indeterminate temporal status (the mist of its surrounding geography, the unclarity of its motive for speech, the plurality of its audience); it results in the apparent assumption that beginnings may be modified into middles, and that even ends—the past tense of the crucifixion itself—subjected to solicited reversal. The lyric frequently enacts the conflict between a psychological state and a natural one, between the mind's dominance and the dominance of the world; underlying the conflict is the pervasive fear of death. In Dickinson's "My Life had stood a Loaded Gun" and Marvell's "The Mower's Song," we observed the lyric equation between meaning and death. We must now turn to "Damon the Mower" to see how the lyric imagines death when it is embodied in man's image.

Marvell's five "mower" poems chronicle the relationship between displacement, doubleness, and death. Doubleness is a consequence of displacement—woman torn from man's ribs, so the story goes, literally halving paradise,[37] and man torn from the natural world, unable any longer to see by its light, as "The Mower to the Glo-Worms" complains:

> Your courteous Lights in vain you wast,
> Since *Juliana* here is come,
> For She my Mind hath so displac'd
> That I shall never find my home.

"Damon the Mower," perhaps the most baffling of the garden poems, evades the correspondence between natural world and world of feeling that its central character tries to establish. Though Damon suffers from the world's failure to encourage his identification with it, his suffering

seems curiously devoid of any knowledge of consequences. In Damon's
belief that he may rise from the dead (since death is, after all, conceived
as only a figure in his own image) we recognize the dumb confident features of our own credulous faces:

I

Heark how the Mower *Damon* Sung,
With love of *Juliana* stung!
While ev'ry thing did seem to paint
The Scene more fit for his complaint.
Like her fair Eyes the day was fair;
But scorching like his am'rous Care.
Sharp like his Sythe his Sorrow was,
And wither'd like his Hopes the Grass.

II

Oh what unusual Heats are here,
Which thus our Sun-burn'd Meadows sear!
The Grass-hopper its pipe gives ore;
And hamstring'd Frogs can dance no more.
But in the brook the green Frog wades;
And Grass-hoppers seek out the shades.
Only the Snake, that kept within,
Now glitters in its second skin.

III

This heat the Sun could never raise,
Nor Dog-star so inflame's the dayes.
It from an higher Beauty grow'th,
Which burns the Fields and Mower both:
Which made the Dog, and makes the Sun
Hotter then his own *Phaeton*.
Not *July* causeth these Extremes,
But *Juliana's* scorching beams.

IV

Tell me where I may pass the Fires
Of the hot day, or hot desires.
To what cool Cave shall I descend,
Or to what gelid Fountain bend?
Alas! I look for Ease in vain,

When Remedies themselves complain.
No moisture but my Tears do rest,
Nor Cold but in her Icy Breast.

V

How long wilt Thou, fair Shepherdess,
Esteem me, and my Presents less?
To Thee the harmless Snake I bring,
Disarmed of its teeth and sting.
To Thee *Chameleons* changing-hue,
And Oak leaves tipt with hony due.
Yet Thou ungrateful hast not sought
Nor what they are, nor who them brought.

VI

I am the Mower *Damon*, known
Through all the Meadows I have mown.
On me the Morn her dew distills
Before her darling Daffadils,
And, if at Noon my toil me heat,
The Sun himself licks off my Sweat.
While, going home, the Ev'ning sweet
In cowslip-water bathes my feet.

VII

What, though the piping Shepherd stock
The plains with an unnum'red Flock,
This Sythe of mine discovers wide
More ground then all his Sheep do hide.
With this the golden fleece I shear
Of all these Closes ev'ry Year.
And though in Wooll more poor then they,
Yet am I richer far in Hay.

VIII

Nor am I so deform'd to sight,
If in my Sythe I looked right;
In which I see my Picture done,
As in a crescent Moon the Sun.
The deathless Fairyes take me oft
To lead them in their Danses soft;

And, when I tune my self to sing,
About me they contract their Ring.

IX

How happy might I still have mow'd,
Had not Love here his Thistles sow'd!
But now I all the day complain,
Joyning my Labour to my Pain;
And with my Sythe cut down the Grass,
Yet still my Grief is where it was:
But, when the Iron blunter grows,
Sighing I whet my Sythe and Woes.

X

While thus he threw his Elbow round,
Depopulating all the Ground,
And, with his whistling Sythe, does cut
Each stroke between the Earth and Root,
The edged Stele by careless chance
Did into his own Ankle glance;
And there among the Grass fell down,
By his own Sythe, the Mower mown.

XI

Alas! said He, these hurts are slight
To those that dye by Loves despight.
With Shepherds-purse, and Clowns-all-heal,
The Blood I stanch, and Wound I seal.
Only for him no Cure is found,
Whom *Julianas* Eyes do wound.
'Tis death alone that this must do:
For Death thou art a Mower too.

The last two lines of the second stanza suggest Marvell might have been remembering the words of Donne's speaker in "Twicknam Garden": "And that this place might thoroughly be thought/True Paradise, I have the serpent brought." But although we find ourselves in another garden, Damon's lament is that of postlapsarian man, severed from nature and woman alike. In fact the poem shows up a series of discrepancies: between the green world and Juliana who scorches it, the heat of July and the unnatural heat of desire, between the self-inflicted wound of Damon's

carelessness and the death wound anticipated as cure.[38] Analogue is the
means whereby correspondence is most adamantly sought, and from the
first stanza we see how powerless it is to bring mind and world into alignment. The speaker may announce that "ev'ry thing did seem to paint/
The Scene more fit for his complaint," but the next lines make clear that
analogue is incommensurate with the complexity of human feeling, for
"Fair" and "scorching" reveal no true similitude. Thus although the first
stanza establishes a connection between human and natural world
("Sharp like his Sythe his Sorrow was/And wither'd like his Hopes the
Grass"), the ninth stanza points out the problem with taking it literally
("[I] with my Sythe cut down the Grass,/Yet still my Grief is where it
was"). In his assumption that an action extending outward in time and
space could really be the visible reflex of an interior transformation,
Damon makes the profound mistake of confusing the natural world with
the psychological one. At its best, the consequence is narcissism that
converts the world into subservient slave: "And, if at Noon my toil me
heat,/The Sun himself licks off my Sweat"; at its worst, the inability to
distinguish the self from other images except as they are self-replicating:
"Nor am I so deform'd to sight/If in my Sythe I looked right;/In which
I see my Picture done,/As in a crescent Moon the Sun." For Damon distinction is blurred as much by pun as by analogy; so we hear in the
equative echo of "Sighing I whet my Sythe and Woes."[39] Damon projects a distinction between the time of the year (July) and the untimely
and "unusual" heats of desire. Because the distinction is displaced, made
to seem supernatural (the world fired to an intolerable heat that lurks
above and causes it to wither), it distracts from the mower's bizarre inability to distinguish himself from the natural world. His failed perception reminds us this is no conventional pastoral: the naive shepherd has
been metamorposed into a mower, and the death-dealing fury with
which he "depopulate[s]" the world, masked as it is by the boisterous
cheer of the rhymed couplets, issues from his rage at the difference between himself and these natural objects to which he keeps making such
desperate comparative reference.

We cease to laugh at his confusion as sorrow, not knowing its own
bounds, honed by analogue, grows scythe-like, draws its sharpness out into an exterior, palpable, world-annihilating form and, like Blake's 'Poison Tree," which also started from a mere nothing, comes to have power
to kill. Though Damon narrates his acts of destruction, it is clear they
never penetrate his mind and that evil, as he conceives it, lies outside of

him in the cruelty of Juliana's indifference. Even the recital of his presents to her escapes knowledge of their manifest venom, partly by the strategic dissociation of the malignancy of the "Snake . . . within," as it is described in the second stanza, from its innocuousness, as it is understood in the fifth. Venom has not been lost; it has simply been internalized. Just as sorrow is drawn from the self and, in its exteriorization, sharpened into a weapon that cuts down the whole discernible world, so in the parallel inverse action the snake's poison is extracted and sucked inward. This is the consequence of failing to distinguish between phenomenal and psychological worlds—projection, on the one hand, and the incorporation of poison, on the other.

Sexuality and death are brought together in the symbol of the snake, and the connection is reiterated by Damon's mowing, which at first seems to subvert sexuality and then in stanza ten to parody it. But although Damon never acknowledges the parching heat as his own, he is the dominant, perhaps even the only, figure in the poem; Juliana, the disembodied bitch-goddess, is a mere heat on the landscape, and the speaker, interpolating action and framing it by his narrative, is hardly distinguishable from the pokerfaced Damon whom we might otherwise be inclined to see him as ridiculing. That knowledge of death and sexuality should need to be self-referential before it can be anything else at all, something experienced as separate from the world, is an idea the poem exploits for its comic possibilities until the tenth stanza makes clear in the fall of sexuality (in the fall to death) that these experiences alone resist the impulse for fusion with the world and, at the same time, legitimately establish their natural connection to it.

The poem plays with the idea of death as revenge against an inhospitable sexuality, as mimetic parody of sexuality, and finally as an ordeal the mower survives intact. That he survives it by trivializing it (pops up to assure us he is still waiting to be mowed down by the real thing) is a reduction that seems clearly inappropriate after the sober and seemingly conclusive description given us by the speaker in the tenth stanza, whose scrupulous attention to detail (opposed as it is to Damon's more impressionistic style) shows us the death-dealing scythe in the naturalistic terms of the dangerous weapon it is. Damon the mower parodies death the mower, and Damon is right to appreciate the difference between the two. Death is cure for sexuality only insofar as it cuts down real, palpable flesh. Damon could do the same, could seek the body for what he has so consistently defused into the landscape, and this would eventually mean raising sexuality to consciousness, acknowledging desire as his own. While the latter would not be cure, it would at least be contact with a world whose boundaries he has so displaced that Juliana is no more to him than an extract of heat, and he no more to himself than sorrow sharply externalized. But Damon is still dreaming of immortality, of a prelapsarian world in which flesh is one with the grass before rather than after or as a consequence of death. Prior to the fall, the words "All flesh is grass" might have indicated man's oneness with the natural world in a metaphor we are no longer in a position even to understand. After the fall, its import is clearly that all flesh can be mowed as grass, die the death of grass. Isaiah tells us:

> A voice says, "Cry!"
> And I said, "What shall I cry?"
> All flesh is grass,
>   and all its beauty is like the flower
>   of the field.
> The grass withers, the flower fades,
>   when the breath of the LORD blows
>   upon it;
>   surely the people is grass.

The mower's mistaking of flesh for grass literalizes the Biblical emblem,[40] on one level, and, on another, makes it more explicit; flesh mowed as grass is flesh that bleeds, and for a moment the stanza threatens a consequence as irrevocable as it is private. But natural man is exactly what Damon does not wish to become, for to be one with nature after the fall is to be dead. Once again lifting himself out of the mortal world, the mower is made whole by a process of magical regeneration. Still believing himself unfallen, a part of the garden world, he is healed botanically by the balm of the wonderful green. This is a cure with a vengeance, a cure that walls out the meaning of death and sexuality alike, those two manifestations of a fallen world, in the cataclysmic repression of all mortal loss.

Marvell's poem locates the myth of immortality at the moment of its genesis in man's refusal to comprehend the irrevocability of the Fall, and he suggests immortality is really an idea about Eden, an effort to reify those memorial vestiges of it as they assert their presence in desire and in dream. "Damon the Mower" reads very much like a dream that has not yet woken to the fact it is a dream. Damon cannot tell the difference between interior and exterior, prelapsarian and postlapsarian, flesh and grass, sexuality and death, and this blurring of opposites may be explained by analogy to dream's immediate conversion of wish into its own fulfillment. In a form as mercifully reversible as it is fluid, dream seems to promise that the heat of sexuality and the sharpness of sorrow may be escaped once the mortal world is exchanged for immortality. The disassociation we perceive as we read the poem is a consequence of the inability of meaning to register its finality in the mind of either Damon or the speaker, for although the speaker is different from Damon—an example of the plurality of persona about which I spoke earlier—he seems curiously unaffected by Damon's story. Meaning's failure to register is thus a metaphor for a larger incompletion, death conceived of minus its finality: like the clown in comedy who rises from his fall, Damon stands up unharmed. So the unconscious dreams existence out of the severative hazards of time. So lyrics drowse and dream fantastic dreams of origins. In fact the interpretation of lyrics, like the interpretation of dreams, depends upon the conversion of timeless symbols to those temporal sequences, those stories that will make sense of symbol.

We are left to reflect on one final fact about Damon, namely his family resemblance. Father Time, as Erwin Panofsky tells us in his *Studies in Iconology*,[41] is an image that fuses the classical Aion with the medieval Saturn. Representations of him differ throughout the Renaissance, but he is characteristically recognized by his scythe and, almost as often, by a snake or dragon that either encircles him in its coils or is depicted biting its tail at his side. It is surely no accident that Marvell's mower, who cuts and reaps, who harvests his own death, should represent the very temporality against which he lodges his comic protest. Time harvests death, though, as we have seen, it does not necessarily reap death's consequences. For the poem provides the framework of permanence in which figures in time/of time move within the brackets of a legislated status quo. All the transformations to which they are subject are fixed as surely as the figures on Keats's Grecian Urn. To recall Kant's words: only in the permanent are relations of time possible. And to alter them: in the appearance of the poem there is something permanent; the transitory (those temporal transformations to which poems submit themselves) is nothing but determination of its existence. All time converges upon the poem in whose one space splintered temporal fragments lodge and totalize. The poem lifts the fragments out of a severative reality. It prolongs, exaggerates, speeds up, subordinates, and, simultaneously, seals its moments off from the world so that, unlike the sand in the proverbial hour glass, they do not sift through. Thus while in one context Damon is the self-approbating fool who does not know when he is beaten, in another metaphoric context (like Dickinson's survivors of the dead), he is a personification of the lyric speaker whose actions need not add up to any reductive conclusion. For the lyric records loss while not feeling obliged to register it as final; the poem totalizes itself and understands by its totalization the continued presence of all its phenomenal aspects, whatever their temporal priorities. In so doing, it totalizes the representative self. Again, to adopt Kant's words: the lyric is not real as object but rather as the representation of "myself" as object.

"Plot is the soul of tragedy," for things happen in time and are lost irretrievably to it; things happen in time that can be neither forestalled nor reversed. "If it be now, 'tis not to come; if it be not to come, it will be now; if it be not now, yet it will come." The squaring calculation that reaches its conclusion in Hamlet's courageous "Let be," is the hardest lesson drama has to teach us. Lyrics lay the lesson aside. Afflicted by the same knowledge of an exacting temporality from which springs the grief of so many conclusions, lyrics hold to the contradictions that contain, even if they do not openly sanction, the regressive movement whose doing over might mean difference. Ultimately what is at stake here is an idea about change, and because the final change would humanize death by having it suffer the conversion of overwhelming forgiveness, the lyric is always on the verge of folding under the preposterousness of its propositions. Damon gets up from his fall because he thinks he can. The poem, running its action backward, frames him at this moment.

V

In the past five chapters, we have looked at the features of Dickinson's poems in the structural light of the generic characteristics they lead us to infer, and at the same time, learned something about those characteristics in their own right. The sixteenth- and seventeenth-century lyric, goaded by its desire for immortality, strongarms temporal sequence, as its speakers are sent into the past, even to the Good Friday of the crucifixion, and forward into the future, even to the finale of a contemplated Judgment Day, for the major space annihilated by the early lyric exists between the speaker and an absent God. Romanticism secularizes this temporal and spatial abridgment in its concern with more immediate object relations—object relations that the English lyric tends to regard as stable, and that many American lyrics, especially more modern ones, represent as serial and subject to revision. Dickinson's poems figure here and take a mediating position because they are equally concerned with immortality and with those object relations whose revisions might secure it.[42] In addition, her poems help us to define a subcategory of lyric speech, particularly apparent in the Romantic era but, as we have seen, sending its roots back to the very origins of the lyric, in which temporal conflict is posed in the extremity of life-and-death terms, and dramatized with the belief that temporal constraints might loosen to the exception that would liberate. Religious lyrics are especially vulnerable to such a belief, predicated as they are on that violation of time/space which will bring their speakers into yearned-for relation with God. Dickinson's lyrics are in fact conceived within a tradition of utterance that imagines redemption itself to rest upon a speaker's ability to fight free of the grip of this world, and to embrace instead that unthinkable space whose time exacts no separations.

My discussion of the American Romantic lyric has steered clear of contemporaneous and colonial poets and has not tried to make a case for their influence on Dickinson's poetry; it is not clear one could be made.[43] It is true that the Romantic belief (espoused by Coleridge, and adamantly embraced by Emerson and Thoreau) that held the generating idea of a poem to dictate its exterior form was adopted as wholeheartedly by Dickinson as by her American counterparts, and the departure of her poetry from the strictures of traditional form (like the varying degrees of formlessness in their poetry) might profitably be studied with reference to this seminal idea.[44] It is no accident that Dickinson and Whitman both pull away from the pentameter line, Whitman by lengthening it, Dickinson by eliding it to sixes and eights. But Dickinson stands apart from the "tradition" of American experiments about which she could not possibly have known, in this respect: the treatment of time in her poems strikes a balance between the stasis-making representation of subject and object, as we have seen it in at least one strain of the English lyric, and the serial and sequential transformations, as recorded by the American Romantic lyric, with Whitman as its earliest and most extreme spokesman. Dickinson's poems do record progressions, but they are clearly of a finite nature, and are in fact most often limited to the relationship between three terms. We see the characteristic triad in "Behind

Me—dips Eternity—/Before Me—Immortality—/Myself—the Term between—'' (P 721); in the picture presented by "Our journey had advanced," which predicates choice three ways: "Retreat—was out of Hope
—/Behind—a Sealed Route—/Eternity's White Flag—Before—/And God—
at every Gate—"; we see it in the stages that come after great pain:
"First—Chill—then Stupor—then the letting go—." The triad of terms
that situates Dickinson's poems between the fixed relations of English
Romanticism and the more serial progression of a later American Romanticism schematizes, even exaggerates, the shape of the lyric endeav-
or: the collapsing of eternity into immortality in the designated space of
the present.

Elemented by what Stevens would have called "flawed words and
stubborn sounds," Dickinson's poems attempt to stall time to a stasis,
and, as we have seen, they accomplish their enterprise with varying degrees of success. But however primitive the methods, the generative conception is not. "To live, and die, and mount again in triumphant body
. . . is no schoolboy's theme!" (L 184), Dickinson remarked long before
she could have known how much of her own writing would require the
testiness of this defense. The deathless world of no time is a world we
lose by merely waking up. Dickinson's poems articulate the loss and, like
all lyrics, they attempt to reverse it. If she dreamed this reversal bolder
than most lyrics do, throwing into relief the shape of the lyric struggle
itself, she also knew more profoundly the shocking certainty of its disappointment.

Notes

INTRODUCTION

1. Texts for Dickinson's poems and letters are from the editions by Thomas H. Johnson, *The Poems of Emily Dickinson*, 3 vols. (Cambridge, Mass.: Harvard University Press, Belknap Press, 1955), and *The Letters of Emily Dickinson*, 3 vols. (Cambridge, Mass.: Harvard University Press, Belknap Press, 1958), abbreviated here as "P" and "L" respectively. "PF" stands for Prose Fragments. Poems and letters are cited by the numbers assigned to them in the Johnson editions. When I use Dickinson's first lines as titles, I omit the punctuation of the Johnson text.

2. Dates of the poems and letters, as specified by the Johnson texts, are often approximate.

3. Immortality will be "When from a thousand skies/On our *developed* eyes/Noons blaze!" (P 63). It will be "Centuries of noon" (P 112).

4. The longed-for immortality is often not heaven but earthly pleasures made permanent, and the speaker in P 636 makes a distinction between the two when she says, "I . . . sigh for lack of Heaven—but not/The Heaven God bestow—."

5. Dickinson often focuses her attention on contained moments of transition during which something palpable lapses into the void from which no observation can pry it. When in P 1420 she asks, "Why Birds, a Summer morning/Before the Quick of Day/Should stab my ravished spirit/with Dirks of Melody," the answer lies in closer scrutiny of that ambiguous time, "the Quick of Day," at the arrival of which the flood of music abruptly ceases. In the same spirit of observing boundary lines, she trains her eyes on the horizon, and there are a fair number of early poems especially taken by the cyclical motion of the sun's rising and setting from which she thought she could learn. See, for example, P 1349, P 152, P 291, P 290, P 228, and P 552.

6. Charles R. Anderson suggests that the pun might have come from one of the definitions of "physiognomy" in her lexicon: "Her Lexicon, after defining physiognomy in the usual sense, has a bracketed note: 'This word formerly comprehended the art of foretelling the future fortunes of persons by indications of the countenance.' Yet it is clearly this obsolete sense, connected with astrology and magic, that she has resurrected for her poem on the spider. He spins out his inner self into his web, a figurative extension of his face. If his design corresponds to his soul then this is his 'Strategy' for comprehending 'Immortality,' but not revealing it." *Emily Dickinson's Poetry: Stairway of Surprise* (Garden City, N.Y.: Doubleday & Co., 1966), p. 143.

7. "The Private World," in *The Recognition of Emily Dickinson: Selected Criticism since 1890*, ed. Caesar R. Blake and Carlton F. Wells (Ann Arbor: University of Michigan Press, 1968), p. 302.

8. In L 342b, Higginson reports Dickinson's comment to his wife.

9. *This Was a Poet: A Critical Biography of Emily Dickinson* (New York: Charles Scribner's Sons, 1938; reprint ed., Ann Arbor: University of Michigan Press, 1957), p. 97. Of the first three major biographies, Whicher's is the most comprehensive, notwithstanding Thomas H. Johnson's

important chapter, "The Valley," on Dickinson's connection to the traditions of the Connecticut Valley (in *Emily Dickinson: An Interpretive Biography* [Cambridge, Mass.: Harvard University Press, Belknap Press, 1955]) and Richard Chase's discussion of the achievement of status as the single most symbolic act in the poems (in *Emily Dickinson* [New York: William Sloane Associates, 1951]).

10. (New York: Columbia University Press, 1968), p. 230.

11. 2 vols. (New Haven, Conn.: Yale University Press, 1960; reprint ed., New York: Archon, 1970).

12. *Emily Dickinson's Reading: 1836–1886* (Cambridge, Mass.: Harvard University Press, 1966).

13. *After Great Pain: The Inner Life of Emily Dickinson* (Cambridge, Mass.: Harvard University Press, Belknap Press, 1971). In summary of the earlier studies Klaus Lubbers writes: Side by side with sober biographical research the quest for the identity of the lover continued. Rebecca Patterson retraced the steps of Kate Scott, a close childhood friend of Susan Dickinson, and believed she had found in her an answer to the riddle. . . . Later, two critics elevated Samuel Bowles to the rank of a lover. David Higgins supposed that the small group of 'Daisy' letters was addressed to Bowles; Winfield Scott went further by trying to show that all dates and allusions which had earlier been connected with Hunt, Gould, and Wadsworth, would apply as well to the editor of *The Springfield Republican*. . . . In a group of love poems Griffith saw an unconscious fear of everything male. . . . A year later Anna Mary Wells made an amateurish attempt to render the poet's life in the form of a clinical report to prove that she was for a time psychopathic and was treated in Boston for this. . . . In *Ancestor's Brocades*, which was often far removed from the pretended 'objective factual account' . . . Millicent Todd Bingham . . . first played off Susan Dickinson against Lavinia and then Lavinia against Mrs. Todd, and . . . unveiled both sister and sister-in-law of the poet as furies filled with irreconcilable hatred for each other. (*Emily Dickinson: The Critical Revolution* [Ann Arbor: University of Michigan Press, 1968], pp. 167–68).
Suppositions about the lover's identity have been continued in Ruth Miller's *Emily Dickinson's Poetry* (Middletown, Conn.: Wesleyan University Press, 1968).

14. Richard Chase calls her aphorisms "one of the striking mementoes of American inventiveness, like Whitman's free verse or Melville's combination of American folk language with traditional English forms" (*Emily Dickinson*, p. 105), and David Higgins speaks of her prose as so original that the closest approximations of her style are Emerson's journals, "which she cannot have read" (*Portrait of Emily Dickinson: The Poet and Her Prose* [New Brunswick, N.J.: Rutgers University Press, 1967], p. 74).

15. In an unpublished dissertation, "Dramatic Poses in the Poetry of Emily Dickinson" (Stanford University, 1962), Thomas Arp comments on the connection between familiarity and formal strategy when he notes an abrupt change in Dickinson's letters to Higginson after their first meeting: "The closer she grew to him personally, hinged as that growth was on their two meetings, the more impersonal her letters to him. He might have the illusion of understanding her private life, because of the many reports of domestic event, but her mind delivered to him contrived and bombastic comments on life, death, and immortality which have apparently little reference to her own psychological state, and which even contradict themselves on occasion" (p. 52).

16. *The Voice of the Poet: Aspects of Style in the Poetry of Emily Dickinson* (Cambridge, Mass.: Harvard University Press, 1968), pp. 19–27.

17. Lubbers, *Critical Revolution*, p. 214. This book presents an excellent discussion of the various phases of critical reception.

18. "New England Culture and Emily Dickinson," in Blake and Wells, *Recognition*, pp. 153–67.

19. *Emily Dickinson: The Mind of the Poet* (Cambridge, Mass.: Harvard University Press, 1965), p. 91.

20. *Stairway of Surprise*, p. 76.

21. *Circumference and Circumstance*, p. 157. See also Johnson (*Interpretive Biography*), who, in regarding Dickinson's poetry as bound to the traditions of the Connecticut Valley, would agree with Sherwood.

22. "Emily Dickinson Was a Poetess," *College English* 34 (October 1972): 67. At times efforts to individuate Dickinson run the risk of overt ahistoricism. Chase writes, "Emily Dickinson's eschatological cast of mind, on the whole a departure from New England Puritanism, was entirely a personal vision of life and has no direct historical or social implications. . . . she lived with a loose and sometimes mutually contradictory complex of ideas historically akin to Calvin-

ism, Romanticism, Transcendentalism, Stoicism, Gnosticism, and even a revolutionary Futurism. Philosophically considered, it is a hopelessly confusing creed" (*Emily Dickinson*, pp. 186–7). On p. 225, however, Chase seems to take it back when he asserts: "Amherst was not exempt from the large operations of history. The poet lived in the last decadence of a religious culture."

23. "Emily Dickinson and the Limits of Judgment," in Blake and Wells, *Recognition*, p. 187.

24. "Emily Dickinson's Notation," in *Emily Dickinson: A Collection of Critical Essays*, ed. Richard B. Sewall (Englewood Cliffs, N.J.: Prentice-Hall, 1963), p. 80.

25. "Emily Dickinson," in Blake and Wells, *Recognition*, p. 103.

26. The distinctions are Blackmur's. In 1937 he wrote, "Without benefit of comparative scholarship it is impossible to determine whether a given item is a finished poem, an early version of a poem, a note for a poem, a part of a poem, or a prose exclamation" ("Emily Dickinson: Notes on Prejudice and Fact," in Blake and Wells, *Recognition*, p. 201).

27. For discussions of Dickinson's punctuation and capitalization, see R. W. Franklin, *The Editing of Emily Dickinson: A Reconsideration* (Madison: University of Wisconsin Press, 1967), pp. 117–28; Edith Perry Stamm, "Emily Dickinson: Poetry and Punctuation," *Saturday Review* 66 (30 March 1963): 26–27, 74; Austin Warren, "Emily Dickinson," in Blake and Wells, *Recognition*, pp. 268–86; David T. Porter, *The Art of Emily Dickinson's Early Poetry* (Cambridge, Mass.: Harvard University Press, 1966), pp. 140–45, and on style generally, pp. 125–55; and Brita Lindberg-Seyersted, *Voice of the Poet*, pp. 180–96.

28. *Editing of Emily Dickinson*, p. 128.

29. See Franklin's discussion in *Editing of Emily Dickinson*, pp. 131–43. In an address before the English Institute, 1951, Johnson discusses the problems of editing the texts; he concludes by explaining why it is so difficult to determine which variants of a given poem are definitive ones:

In one instance I thought she herself had provided a solution. One of the poems which she copied into a packet had several suggested readings for eight different words in the course of the five stanzas, but with no indication of her choice. . . . Then I found the same poem included in a letter to Higginson with choices made in every instance. Here, then, seemed proof that she had established her final version. But in another letter to another correspondent, written at substantially the same time, she has included the same poem—also evidently a final version—wherein she adopted six of the choices made in the Higginson letter, but selected two from among her variants in the remaining instances. If any conclusion is to be drawn from this citation, it would seem to be that there are no *final* versions of the poems for which she allowed alternate readings to stand in the packets. Franklin, *Editing of Emily Dickinson*, p. 130.

30. Inder Nath Kher (*The Landscape of Absence: Emily Dickinson's Poetry* [New Haven, Conn.: Yale University Press, 1974], p. 5); Warren ("Emily Dickinson," p. 271); Herbert Read ("The Range of Emily Dickinson," in Blake and Wells, *Recognition*, p. 174); David Porter (*Art of Emily Dickinson's Early Poetry*, p. 175); and Charles Anderson (*Stairway of Surprise*, p. xii) are some of the many critics who speak of lack of development in the poems. Robert Sherwood and Thomas W. Ford regard Dickinson's work as falling into distinct periods, but they don't characterize them similarly. See Sherwood, *Circumference and Circumstance*, pp. 23–67, and Ford, *Heaven Beguiles the Tired: Death in the Poetry of Emily Dickinson* (Alabama: University of Alabama, 1966), pp. 68–71.

31. Porter writes: "In the years from 1850 to 1862 she succeeded in refining genuine and effective expressions of feeling from a clutter of commonplace ideas and syntaxes. Perhaps the principal reason for her early success is that she addressed herself again and again to a single theme" (*Art of Emily Dickinson's Early Poetry*, p. 174).

32. F. O. Matthiessen calls her a "private poet" ("The Private Poet: Emily Dickinson," in Blake and Wells, *Recognition*, p. 224).

33. *Stairway of Surprise*, p. 70.

34. "Notes on Prejudice and Fact," p. 215.

35. Weisbuch's study, *Emily Dickinson's Poetry* (Chicago: University of Chicago Press, 1975), along with Charles Anderson's *Emily Dickinson's Poetry: Stairway of Surprise* and David Porter's *The Art of Emily Dickinson's Early Poetry* is one of the finest book-length contributions to Dickinson scholarship, and what he has to say both about the scenelessness of her poetry and the confusion of its categories leaves the reader of Dickinson's poems profoundly indebted to the clarity of this way of conceiving of them.

I read the Weisbuch study when my own book was well along toward completion, and I was struck by the parallels between parts of my third chapter and his similar sense of death utterances as figural in nature, a coincidence that I took to be a reassuring gauge of the accuracy of the perception. Though, finally, Weisbuch and I use the explanatory apparatus of type and antitype for different purposes, I have returned to several passages of my book, and where I have observed similarities between the two discussions, I have acknowledged them after the fact with footnotes.

36. Weisbuch, *Emily Dickinson's Poetry*, p. 19. While Weisbuch makes the astute observation that the analogic language of the poem exists parallel to the world of experience, one would like him to distinguish still further between analogies that parallel experience when experience is inadequate (as, for example, in the poems whose speakers survive death in order to secure knowledge of it) and poems that parallel experience when experience, itself perfectly adequate, lacks adequate vocabulary in which to articulate itself (as for example, in "It was not death for I stood up").

37. *Emily Dickinson*, p. 107.

38. Weisbuch offers the poem as an example of a typical "analogic collection," though he makes more sense of it than perhaps it deserves, when he writes, "The poem may be thought of as a wild and disconsolate rewriting of Wordsworth's Immortality Ode, a dirge to lost powers, a dirge in which mere intimations of the thing itself torture rather than console" (*Emily Dickinson's Poetry*, pp. 20–21).

39. *Art of Emily Dickinson's Early Poetry*, p. 99. For the most complete discussion of Dickinson's syntax, see Brita Lindberg-Seyersted, *Voice of the Poet*, pp. 214–60, and for a wonderful discussion of the precedents for Dickinson's bizarre verb forms, see Grace B. Sherrer, "A Study of Unusual Verb Constructions in the Poems of Emily Dickinson," *American Literature* 7 (March 1935): 37–46.

40. For a discussion of Dickinson's diction, see William Howard, "Emily Dickinson's Poetic Vocabulary," *PMLA* (March 1957), p. 236. The three primary idiosyncrasies in Dickinson's diction, as singled out by Howard, are "her ratio of 5:12:8 for adjectives, nouns, and verbs; the small number of words—only 17—that she uses 8 or more times per 1,000 lines; and her occasional use of many words in a somewhat singular way, e.g., the use of a noun to denote a quality possessed by the thing for which the noun stands" (p. 248).

Howard makes the excellent point that we call a word rare or unusual if our own linguistic experience of it is a limited one. In fact, many words that strike us as odd in Dickinson's poetic vocabulary ("attar," or "cochineal," for example) were in common usage in the early nineteenth century. "Cochineal" occurs as the name of a food coloring in recipes of the period (see p. 231). See also J. V. Cunningham's discussion of metonymy or the proximate word in "Sorting Out: The Case of Dickinson," *The Southern Review* 5, no. 2 (Spring 1969): 436–56.

41. "Emily Dickinson," in Blake and Wells, *Recognition*, p. 285.

42. Robert Weisbuch amplifies such distinctions in his discussion of the "willful confusion of categories" in the poems (*Emily Dickinson's Poetry*, p. 13).

43. *Years and Hours of Emily Dickinson*, 1: xxi. On the subject of confusion and ambiguity, see also Dolores Dyer Lucas, *Emily Dickinson and Riddle* (DeKalb: Northern Illinois University Press, 1969).

44. *Mimesis: The Representation of Reality in Western Literature*, trans. Willard R. Trask (Princeton, N.J.: Princeton University Press, 1953), pp. 17–18.

45. *The Unnamable* (New York: Grove Press, 1958), p. 4.

46. Vladimir Nabokov, *Lolita* (New York: Berkeley Medallion, 1955), p. 97.

47. *Poetic Closure: A Study of How Poems End* (Chicago: University of Chicago Press, 1968), p. 20.

48. "The Avoidance of Love: A Reading of *King Lear*," in *Must We Mean What We Say: A Book of Essays* (New York: Charles Scribner's Sons, 1969), p. 330.

49. "Avoidance of Love," p. 334.

50. *The Confessions of St. Augustine*, trans. John K. Ryan (Garden City, N.Y.: Image Books, 1960), book 11, chapter 14, pp. 285–86.

51. Augustine, *Confessions*, book 11, chapter 11, p. 285.

CHAPTER I

1. In *I. A. Richards: Essays in His Honor*, ed. Reuben Brower, Helen Vendler, and John Hollander (New York: Oxford University Press, 1973), p. 173.

2. For discussions of the relationship between pain and atemporality in Dickinson's poems, see Charles R. Anderson, *Emily Dickinson's Poetry: Stairway of Surprise* (Garden City, N.Y.: Doubleday & Co., 1966), p. 230; Inder Nath Kher, *The Landscape of Absence: Emily Dickinson's Poetry* (New Haven, Conn.: Yale University Press, 1974), pp. 23 and 82; David T. Porter,

The Art of Emily Dickinson's Early Poetry (Cambridge, Mass.: Harvard University Press, 1966), p. 155; George Frisbe Whicher, *This Was a Poet: A Critical Biography of Emily Dickinson* (New York: Charles Scribner's Sons, 1938; reprint ed., Ann Arbor: University of Michigan Press, 1957), p. 302; and Richard Wilbur, "Sumptuous Destitution," in *Emily Dickinson: A Collection of Critical Essays*, ed. Richard B. Sewall (Englewood Cliffs, N.J.: Prentice-Hall, 1963), p. 128.

3. *Disease, Pain and Sacrifice: Toward a Psychology of Suffering* (Chicago: Beacon Press, 1968), p. 77.

4. "Literature as Equipment for Living," in *Perspectives by Incongruity*, ed. Stanley Edgar Hyman (Bloomington: Indiana University Press, 1964), p. 106.

5. For a discussion of how a verbal community determines response, see B. F. Skinner's "The Tact" in *Verbal Behavior* (New York: Appleton-Century-Crofts, 1957), pp. 81–146.

6. *The Complete Works of Ralph Waldo Emerson*, ed. E. W. Emerson, Centenary Edition, 12 vols. (Boston: Houghton, Mifflin, 1903), 2: 109.

7. For an excellent summary of the history of views on the function and nature of definitions, see Raziel Abelson's discussion in *The Encyclopedia of Philosophy*, 8 vols., ed. Paul Edwards (New York: Macmillan, 1967), 3: 314–24. Abelson gives a brief and critical history of the three major philosophic positions on the problem of definition: the essentialists, who believe that definitional knowledge is that of essences; the linguistic philosophers, who assert that it is knowledge of language usage; and the prescriptivists, who maintain that definitions contain no knowledge of any kind. Abelson concludes: "An evaluation of a definition must begin with the identification of the point or purpose of the definition, and this requires knowledge of the discursive situation in which the need for the definition arises" (p. 322).

8. Millicent Todd Bingham, *Ancestors' Brocades: The Literary Discovery of Emily Dickinson; The Editing and Publication of Her Letters and Poems* (New York: Harper, 1945; reprint ed., New York: Dover, 1967), p. 311.

9. *This Was a Poet*, p. 305.

10. "Emily Dickinson: Notes on Prejudice and Fact," in *The Recognition of Emily Dickinson: Selected Criticism since 1890*, ed. Caesar R. Blake and Carlton F. Wells (Ann Arbor: University of Michigan Press, 1968), p. 223.

11. Blackmur, "Notes on Prejudice and Fact," p. 215. David Porter, in *The Art of Emily Dickinson's Early Poetry*, also mentions Dickinson's habitual use of emphatic opening and closing lines.

12. "Aphasia as a Linguistic Topic," in Roman Jakobson, *Selected Writings*, 6 vols. (The Hague: Mouton, 1971), 2: 232, 254.

13. In "Precision and Indeterminacy in the Poetry of Emily Dickinson," Roland Hagenbüchle also discusses the relationship between Dickinson's use of metonymy and aphasia. *ESQ, A Journal of the American Renaissance*, 20, no. 1 (1974): 33–56.

14. Jakobson, "Aphasia as a Linguistic Topic," p. 236.

15. Roman Jakobson, "Two Aspects of Language," in *Selected Writings*, 2: 251.

16. *Modern American Poetry, MidCentury Edition*, ed. Louis Untermeyer (New York: Harcourt, Brace, 1950), p. 7.

17. In "Structural Patterns in Emily Dickinson's Poetry," *Emerson Society Quarterly, A Journal of the American Renaissance*, no. 44 (1966), pp. 12–17, Carroll Laverty specifies the single sentence as one of eight basic patterns in Dickinson's poetry.

18. Donald E. Thackery, "The Communication of the Word," in Sewall, *Emily Dickinson*, p. 51.

19. "Aphasia as a Linguistic Topic," p. 237.

20. Albert J. Gelpi, *Emily Dickinson: The Mind of the Poet* (Cambridge, Mass.: Harvard University Press, 1965), p. 145.

21. In *Emily Dickinson's Poetry* (Chicago: University of Chicago Press, 1975), Robert Weisbuch discusses a similar phenomenon in Dickinson's definitional poems when he observes that they sometimes propose analogues that the rest of the poem revises or even overthrows (see pp. 63–71).

22. *Disease, Pain and Sacrifice*, p. 65–66.

23. *Marxism and Form: Twentieth-Century Dialectical Theories of Literature* (Princeton, N.J.: Princeton University Press, 1971), p. 85.

24. "A Note on Dialectic," *Marxism and Art: Essays Classic and Contemporary*, ed. Maynard Solomon (New York: Alfred A. Knopf, 1973), pp. 534–35.

25. "The Antithetical Sense of Primal Words" in Sigmund Freud, *On Creativity and the Unconscious* (New York: Harper & Row, Publishers, 1958), p. 60.

26. *Psychiatry and Anti-Psychiatry* (London: Tavistock Publications, 1967), p. 8.

27. Ludwig Wittgenstein, *Philosophical Investigations*, trans. G.E.M. Anscombe, 3rd ed. (New York: Macmillan, 1958), p. 46.

CHAPTER II

1. Sigmund Freud, "Fragment of an Analysis of a Case of Hysteria," in *Collected Papers*, 5 vols. (London: The Hogarth Press, 1949), 3: 25.

2. "Freud and Dora: Story, History, Case History," *Partisan Review* 41, no. 1 (1974): 92.

3. *Swinburne: An Experiment in Criticism* (Chicago: University of Chicago Press, 1972), p. 169.

4. *Swinburne*, p. 170. For another description of poetic distraction from the centrality of story, see Geoffrey Hartman's essay on Valéry's "Fable of the Bee" in *The Fate of Reading and Other Essays* (Chicago: University of Chicago Press, 1975). Hartman speaks of that poem as being drained of story or event, purified to a melodic line: "The most brilliant thing in Valéry is indeed this melodic élan, never quite determined by a content it half-creates. It purifies its own movement toward closure, rendering all figures figures of speech, all terms charms of language. The author will not close the sense for us, by insisting on sense" (p. 231). What is interesting about both Hartman's and McGann's descriptions is the attention each pays to the deviations from story, and to the alternative ways of conceiving of poetic completion. For the Dickinson poems under discussion in this chapter, such alternative explanations often bequeath the only sense these poems can be said to make.

5. Soren Kierkegaard, *Repetition: An Essay in Experimental Psychology*, trans. Walter Lowrie (New York: Harper & Row, Publishers, 1941), p. 33.

6. *Repetition*, pp. 52–53.

7. Wayne C. Booth, *A Rhetoric of Irony* (Chicago: University of Chicago Press, 1974), pp. 1–31.

8. In "Dickinson's 'My Life had stood—a Loaded Gun,'" *Explicator* 21 (November 1962), item 21, Laurence Perrine discusses this fusion between gun and body.

9. Robert Weisbuch's discussion of "My Life had stood a Loaded Gun" identifies the poem's subject as that of the relationship between power and freedom, nothingness and "self-realization through subservience" (p. 27), but because he considers the analogies it employs as almost infinitely extendable, the discussion seems close to suggesting that the poem is about everything or nothing, as Weisbuch himself acknowledges. Such hospitality to diverse interpretations is carried to its furthest extreme when Weisbuch offers one of Dickinson's letters that employs similar imagery as a new gloss on the poem, suggesting (as I think the poem does not) that this may be a poem about the power of writing poetry. Despite the improbability of the latter speculation, Weisbuch's willingness to look below the surface of the poem's images, as few critics before him have, allows him to see its problematic posing of the dilemma of power and identity, of "transcendence at the cost of freedom or freedom at the cost of meaning" (*Emily Dickinson's Poetry* [Chicago: University of Chicago Press, 1975], p. 32).

10. "The Storyteller: Reflections on the Works of Nikolai Leskov," in *Illuminations*, ed. Hannah Arendt, and trans. Harry Zohn (New York: Schocken Books, 1973), p. 94.

11. "Storyteller," pp. 100–101.

12. Robert Scholes and Robert Kellogg, *The Nature of Narrative* (New York: Oxford University Press, 1966), pp. 214–35.

13. "The Voice of the Shuttle: Language from the Point of View of Literature," in *Beyond Formalism: Literary Essays, 1958–1970* (New Haven, Conn.: Yale University Press, 1970), p. 348.

14. *Emily Dickinson's Poetry: Stairway of Surprise* (Garden City, N.Y.: Doubleday & Co., 1966), p. 320.

15. Tzvetan Todorov, *The Fantastic: A Structural Approach to a Literary Genre*, trans. Richard Howard (Ithaca, N.Y.: Cornell University Press, 1975), p. 166.

16. *The Fantastic*, p. 159.

CHAPTER III

1. "The Inside and the Outside," *Hudson Review* 28, no. 3 (Autumn 1975): 334.

2. "Sorting Out: The Case of Dickinson," *The Southern Review* 5, no. 2 (Spring 1969): 454.

3. "The Rhetoric of Temporality," in *Interpretation: Theory and Practice*, ed. Charles S. Singleton (Baltimore, Md.: The Johns Hopkins University Press, 1969), p. 206.

4. "Rhetoric of Temporality," pp. 207-8.

5. *"Figura"* in *Scenes from the Drama of European Literature: Six Essays* (New York: Meridian Books, 1959). Tracing the semantic development of the word *figura*, Auerbach tells us that as it evolved with Augustine's usage, it came to designate two historical and real events, the first predictive of the second, the second fulfilling the first, and both promising a third ultimate fulfillment at the end of the world. The primary purpose of figural interpretation was to demonstrate the way in which the Old Testament prefigured the New Testament and its providential history.

6. Any general reader of poetry who wants to know more about Dickinson's consistent attempt to dramatize typological relationships as a way of knowing the unknowable should turn to Robert Weisbuch's *Emily Dickinson's Poetry* (Chicago: University of Chicago Press, 1975), which offers a complete discussion of Dickinson and the typology of death. The Dickinson reader has, I assume, long ago found his way there with appreciation. Weisbuch invokes the typological apparatus to suggest the multiple relationships of prefigurement in Dickinson's poems: the type of death's anticipation and the antitype of its reality, the type of experience and the antitype of eternity, the type of separation and the antitype of the death of affection, to name a few of the most important patterns that are discerned and discussed. Weisbuch argues that the typological pattern is a shifting one in Dickinson's poetry, the terms of anticipation and its fulfillment fleshed out in different forms, although he sees each attempting to invert, internalize, or otherwise transform a traditional Christian typology. My own use of the typological theme is a limited one: to specify the way in which despair in these poems comes to anticipate death and, at the same time, to epitomize it.

7. *"Figura,"* p. 58.

8. "Time as Succession and the Problem of Duration," in *The Voices of Time: A Cooperative Survey of Man's Views of Time as Expressed by the Sciences and by the Humanities*, ed. J. T. Fraser, and trans. Francesco Gaona (New York: G. Braziller, 1966), p. 39.

9. "Et in Arcadia Ego: Poussin and the Elegiac Tradition," in *Meaning in the Visual Arts: Papers in and on Art History* (Garden City, N.Y.: Doubleday & Co., 1955).

10. Panofsky refers to Poussin's second composition on this subject.

11. Panofsky, "Poussin and the Elegiac Tradition," p. 316.

12. "Poussin and the Elegiac Tradition," pp. 316-17.

13. *Emily Dickinson's Poetry: Stairway of Surprise* (Garden City, N.Y.: Doubleday & Co., 1966), pp. 230-34.

14. See Hartman, "The Voice of the Shuttle: Language from the Point of View of Literature," in *Beyond Formalism: Literary Essays, 1958-1970* (New Haven, Conn.: Yale University Press, 1970), p. 349, Weisbuch, *Emily Dickinson's Poetry*, p. 51, and Bloom, *Wallace Stevens: The Poems of Our Climate* (Ithaca, N.Y.: Cornell University Press, 1977), p. 19.

15. Another way of conceiving of the "Fork" of "Eternity—" is to see it composed of the separate possibilities of salvation and damnation, possibilities whose distinction ceases to matter as the speaker turns all her attention to the more immediate fact of death.

16. *Stairway of Surprise*, p. 263.

17. See, for example, Anderson, *Stairway of Surprise*, p. 263, Ford, *Heaven Beguiles the Tired*, pp. 113-14, and Weisbuch, *Emily Dickinson's Poetry*, p. 101.

18. *Cosmos and History: The Myth of the Eternal Return*, trans. Willard R. Trask (New York: Harper & Row, Publishers, 1959), p. 86.

19. In *The Savage Mind* (Chicago: University of Chicago Press, 1966), p. 263, Claude Lévi-Strauss writes:

> The characteristic feature of the savage mind is its timelessness; its object is to grasp the world as both a synchronic and a diachronic totality and the knowledge which it draws therefrom is like that afforded of a room by mirrors fixed on opposite walls, which reflect each other (as well as objects in the intervening space) although without being strictly parallel. A multitude of images forms simultaneously, none exactly like any other, so that no single one furnishes more than a partial knowledge of the decoration and furniture but the group is characterized by invariant properties expressing a truth. The savage mind deepens its knowledge with the help of *imagines mundi*. It builds mental structures which facilitate an understanding of the world in as much as they resemble it. In this sense savage thought can be defined as analogical thought.

20. In "The Inside and the Outside," Jean Starobinski speaks, in fact, of the Fall as that

moment which delivers us to our inheritance of temporal consciousness: "The fall is not just a migration from the inside out but the fulcral moment that dooms man to perceive, in constant pain and awareness, the points of contact or of transition between the corporeal inside and hazardous outside" (pp. 344–45).

21. See Rudolf Bultmann, *The Presence of Eternity: History and Eschatology (The Gifford Lectures 1955)* (New York: Harper & Brothers, 1957), pp. 37–155.

22. *Christ and Time: The Primitive Christian Conception of Time and History*, trans. Floyd V. Filson, rev. ed. (Philadelphia: The Westminster Press, 1951), p. 39. Consonant with Eliade's distinction discussed above, Cullman suggests that while for primitive Christianity the symbol of time is the line, the Greek idea of time is symbolized by the circle: "The Greek conception of [redemption] is thus spatial" (p. 52). For an exploration of these temporal conceptions in relation to fiction, see Frank Kermode, *The Sense of an Ending: Studies in the Theory of Fiction* (New York: Oxford University Press, 1966).

23. *The Confessions of St. Augustine*, trans. John K. Ryan (Garden City, N.Y.: Image Books, 1960), book 11, chapter 20, p. 293.

24. Augustine, *Confessions*, book 11, chapter 28, pp. 301–2.

25. In Joyce's *Ulysses*, for example, the world of *kairos* masquerades as *chronos* (the careful selection of detail presuming to be random), and in Robbe-Grillet's fiction we see the opposite impulse, *chronos* replacing *kairos* (meaningless events where meaning should be).

26. Alain Robbe-Grillet, *For a New Novel: Essays on Fiction*, trans. Richard Howard (New York: Grove Press, 1965), p. 155.

27. In "Spatial Form in Modern Literature" (*Criticism The Foundations of Modern Literary Judgment*, ed. Mark Schorer, Josephine Miles, and Gordon McKenzie, rev. ed. [New York: Harcourt, Brace and Company, 1958]), Joseph Frank suggests that it is precisely this fusion of temporal categories and the accompanying representation of experience as if it existed all in one place with no dimension or depth that is characteristic of modern literature: "For when . . . objects are presented in one plane, their simultaneous apprehension as part of a timeless unity is obviously made easier" (p. 391). But Erich Auerbach's description of the Homeric world is strikingly similar: "The Homeric style knows only a foreground, only a uniformly illuminated, uniformly objective present" (*Mimesis: The Representation of Reality in Western Literature*, trans. Willard R. Trask [Princeton, N.J.: Princeton University Press, 1953], p. 7). Such foregrounding, it could be argued, is as characteristic a symptom of the lyric as a genre as it is of either modernity or the Homeric world.

28. One possible exception to these assertions is the narrative lyric. See Robert Langbaum, *The Poetry of Experience: The Dramatic Monologue in Modern Literary Tradition* (New York: W. W. Norton & Co., 1957).

29. "Emily Dickinson and the Limits of Judgment," in *The Recognition of Emily Dickinson: Selected Criticism since 1890*, ed. Caesar R. Blake and Carlton F. Wells (Ann Arbor: University of Michigan Press, 1968), p. 192.

30. "New England Culture and Emily Dickinson," in Blake and Wells, *Recognition*, p. 161.

31. Anderson, *Stairway of Surprise*, pp. 274–77, Richard Chase, *Emily Dickinson* (New York: William Sloane Associates, 1951), p. 250, and Weisbuch, *Emily Dickinson's Poetry*, pp. 114–15, also note this progression.

32. *Allegory: The Theory of a Symbolic Mode* (New York: Cornell University Press, 1964), p. 177.

33. *Form and Fable in American Fiction* (New York: W. W. Norton & Co., 1961), p. 248.

34. *American Renaissance: Art and Expression in the Age of Emerson and Whitman* (New York: Oxford University Press, 1941), pp. 242–313.

35. Matthiessen, *American Renaissance*, p. 250.

36. "Rhetoric of Temporality," p. 191.

37. *PMLA* 89, no. 3 (May 1974): 563–79. Many of the observations in my previous paragraph, though applied here to Dickinson, Wright also makes about the lyric generally.

38. "The Lyric Present," p. 573.

39. "The Lyric Present," p. 573.

40. "The Lyric Present," p. 563.

CHAPTER IV

1. See P 322, P 474, and P 664 for examples.

2. The term is borrowed from Ernest Becker, *The Denial of Death* (New York: Free Press, 1973).

3. In a letter to Mrs. Holland and in reference to Kate Holland's marriage, Dickinson encloses a poem that seems to envision the union as the annihilation of time: "The Clock strikes one that just struck two—/Some schism in the Sum—/A Vagabond from Genesis/Has wrecked the Pendulum—" (P 1569).

4. *Speech and Phenomena and Other Essays on Husserl's Theory of Signs*, trans. David B. Allison (Evanston, Ill.: Northwestern University Press, 1973), pp. 142-43.

5. *Speech and Phenomena*, p. 153.

6. For a similar equation between a speaker's loss and her identity, see P 1123: "A not admitting of the wound/Until it grew so wide/That all my Life had entered it/And there were troughs beside. . . ." For the psychoanalytic explanation of how a lost object becomes identified with the self, see Freud's "Mourning and Melancholia," in *Collected Papers*, 5 vols., ed. James Strachey (New York: Basic Books, 1959), 4: 152-70.

7. For examples of paradoxical formulations, see: "Success is counted sweetest," (P 67); "A Wounded Deer leaps highest," (P 165); "By a departing light," (P 1714); "The Zeroes taught us Phosphorus," (P 689); "'Tis Opposites entice," (P 355); "As by the dead we love to sit," (P 88); "For each ecstatic instant," (P 125); and "To learn the Transport by the Pain," (P 167).

8. Anthony Wilden's distinction between repression as a potentially reparable tear in the fabric of memory and foreclusion as an original and therefore irreparable *béance* (in the notes to Jacques Lacan's *The Language of the Self: The Function of Language in Psychoanalysis*, trans. Anthony Wilden [New York: Delta, 1975], p. 98) suggests my terminology in this paragraph, although, as is obvious, I adopt the rhetoric in a wholly different context and without regard or reference to his distinction.

9. *The Years and Hours of Emily Dickinson*, 2 vols. (New Haven, Conn.: Yale University Press, 1960; reprint ed., New York: Archon, 1970), p. xxi.

10. See Charles Anderson's reading of the poem in *Emily Dickinson's Poetry: Stairway of Surprise* (Garden City, N.Y.: Doubleday & Co., 1966), pp. 222-23.

11. Inder Nath Kher, *The Landscape of Absence: Emily Dickinson's Poetry* (New Haven, Conn.: Yale University Press, 1974).

12. See "Emily Dickinson: Notes on Prejudice and Fact," in *The Recognition of Emily Dickinson: Selected Criticism since 1890*, ed. Caesar R. Blake and Carlton F. Wells (Ann Arbor: University of Michigan Press, 1968), pp. 214-17.

13. The choice alluded to in the last stanza may be construed as a directive to the reader, albeit not an especially fortuitous one, to select which depiction of violence he fancies greater.

14. "Negation," in *Collected Papers*, 5: 184.

15. "The Insistence of the Letter in the Unconscious," in *The Structuralists from Marx to Lévi-Strauss*, ed. Richard and Fernande DeGeorge (Garden City, N.Y.: Doubleday & Co., 1972), p. 319.

16. See Lacan's *Language of the Self*.

17. "Insistence of the Letter," p. 318.

18. "The Question of the Subject: The Challenge of Semiology," trans. Kathleen McLaughlin, in *The Conflict of Interpretations: Essays in Hermeneutics*, ed. Don Ihde (Evanston, Ill.: Northwestern University Press, 1974), p. 242.

19. *Systematic Theology: Reason and Revelation, Being and God*, 3 vols. (Chicago: University of Chicago Press, 1951), 1: 133.

20. *Disease, Pain and Sacrifice: Toward a Psychology of Suffering* (Chicago: Beacon Press, 1968), p. 124.

21. *Disease, Pain and Sacrifice*, p. 127.

22. *Speech and Phenomena*, pp. 151-52.

23. For a discussion of the importance of the circle in American literature, see R. A. Yoder, "The Equilibrist Perspective: Toward a Theory of American Romanticism," *Studies in Romanticism* 12, no. 4 (Fall 1973): 705-40.

24. Samuel Beckett, *The Unnamable* (New York: Grove Press, 1958), p. 143.

25. "The Crucial Experience in Emily Dickinson's Poetry," *ESQ: A Journal of the American Renaissance* 20, no. 4 (1974): 281. Porter also alludes to the way in which space widens as it replaces temporality in the "aftermath," and he attributes some of the lexical deformations we have been discussing to the same phenomenon.

26. *Studies in Human Time*, trans. Elliott Coleman (Baltimore, Md.: The Johns Hopkins University Press, 1956), p. 346.

27. *The Discovery of the Mind: The Greek Origins of European Thought*, trans. T. G. Rosenmeyer (1953; reprint ed., New York: Harper & Brothers, 1960), p. 57.

28. Ralph W. Rader records an interesting observation on the complex relationship between past and present in the lyric when he writes: "Our sense that the experience in the dramatic lyric is real is directly contradicted by the fact that the poem gives it to us as actual in the present. This logically denies it any connection with reality since a real event of this kind could only be reported to us as a memory of something in the past" ("The Dramatic Monologue and Related Lyric Forms," *Critical Inquiry* 3, no. 1 [Autumn 1976]: 143). Like George T. Wright (see his observations recorded in chapter 3), Rader seems to regard the lyric present as the primary symbol of its fiction.

29. "Three Uses of the Present: The Historian's, the Critic's and Emily Dickinson's," *College English* 28 (November 1966): 133.

30. This sentiment was expressed cantankerously, if well, by Lisa Foley in an undergraduate paper "Emily Dickinson" at Boston University.

31. "Sorting Out: The Case of Dickinson," *The Southern Review* 5, no. 2 (Spring 1969): 455.

32. *Time and Free Will: An Essay On the Immediate Data of Consciousness*, trans. F. L. Pogson (1910; reprint ed., New York: Harper & Row, Publishers, 1960), p. 79.

33. *Time and Free Will*, p. 95.

34. Bergson, *Time and Free Will*, p. 101.

35. Bergson, *Time and Free Will*, p. 128.

36. Bergson, *Time and Free Will*, p. 130. Interestingly enough, Bergson, unlike Paul de Man (see the discussion in chapter 3), views reality as generative of fusion, and symbolic construction as the arbitrary splitting of the whole into its discrete parts. However, the disagreement between the two, at least on this issue, may be reduced to the semantic level at which it really exists, for both speak, most importantly, of the confusion that results when a perceptive state alters what is there.

37. "The Subject and His Landscape," in *Romanticism and Consciousness: Essays in Criticism*, ed. Harold Bloom (New York: W. W. Norton & Co., 1970), p. 61.

38. Van den Berg, "Subject and His Landscape," p. 64.

39. Yeats's "Sailing to Byzantium" and Keats's "Ode on a Grecian Urn" would, I suppose, be a third major strain in the tradition of such poems, suggesting, as they do, the magical world in which mutability is negated, just as Stevens's "Sunday Morning" might be seen as the response to that alternative, an impassioned disagreement about the necessity for magic.

40. For an interesting comparison of these two language philosophers, see Marjorie Grene's "Life, Death, and Language: Some Thoughts on Wittgenstein and Derrida," *Partisan Review* 43, no. 2 (1976): 265–79.

41. "Question of the Subject," p. 252. For an excellent discussion of the critical and historical relationship between structuralism and the phenomenology practiced by Ricoeur, see Gerald L. Bruns, *Modern Poetry and the Idea of Language: A Critical and Historical Study* (New Haven, Conn.: Yale University Press, 1974).

42. Ricoeur, "Question of the Subject," p. 265.

43. *Speech and Phenomena*, p. 159.

44. *Creation and Fall: A Theological Interpretation of Genesis 1-3*, trans. John C. Fletcher (New York: Macmillan, 1959), pp. 49–50.

45. *Creation and Fall*, p. 51.

CHAPTER V

1. On the subject of pronouns and plurality, see Emile Benveniste, "Relationship of Persons in the Verb," in *Problems in General Linguistics* (Miami, Fla.: University of Miami Press, 1971), pp. 195–204. Benveniste suggests that the distinction between singular and plural should be replaced by a more accurate distinction between "*strict person* (= 'singular') and *amplified person* (= 'plural')" (p. 204), for "'we' is not a multiplication of identical objects but a *junction* between 'I' and the 'non-I'" (p. 202). Thus "the verbal person in the plural expresses a diffused and amplified person," (p. 203). Benveniste's distinction is central, for in poems the speaker is most accurately not several voices at once, but rather an amplified voice, larger than the individual; and, we might speculate, it is just this amplification that commands our attention. It should

be noted however, that in Dickinson's poems the very amplification of voice contains those contradictions which make it appear plural. Thus in the body of my discussion I have stuck to my description of voice as "plural."

2. Although one is tempted to say that lyric speech is related to the epic as to an origin, Gregory Nagy (*Comparative Studies in Greek and Indic Meter* [Cambridge, Mass.: Harvard University Press, 1974]) tells us differently when he insists that the lyric is independent of epic versification: "The rigid phraseological correspondences between [Sappho's] pentameter and the epic hexameter are due to parallel inheritance of related formulas from related meters. But . . . Sapphic pentameter is actually far more archaic in structure than Homeric hexameter" (p. 134). For discussion of these meters, see the entire chapter "The Metrical Context of κλέος ἄφθιτν in Epic and Lyric," pp. 103–39.

3. "Ariadne's Thread: Repetition and the Narrative Line," *Critical Inquiry* 3, no. 1 (Autumn 1976): 73.

4. "Romanticism Re-Examined," in *Romanticism Reconsidered: Selected Papers from the English Institute*, ed. Northrop Frye (New York: Columbia University Press, 1963).

5. See Wystan Curnow's discussion of the effects of Romanticism on criticism in "Romanticism and Modern American Criticism," *Studies in Romanticism* 12, no. 4 (Fall 1973), pp. 777–99.

6. *Romanticism Reconsidered*, p. 5.

7. Georges Poulet, "Timelessness and Romanticism," *Journal of the History of Ideas* 15, no. 1 (January 1954): 6.

8. "Timelessness and Romanticism," pp. 6–7.

9. *Creative Evolution*, trans. Arthur Mitchell (New York: Henry Holt and Co., 1911), p. 334.

10. See the discussion of Starobinski in my third chapter, pp. 91–92.

11. Ralph Waldo Emerson, "Nature," *Selections from Ralph Waldo Emerson: An Organic Anthology*, ed. Stephen Whicher (Boston: Houghton Mifflin Co., 1957), p. 37.

12. "Romanticism Re-Examined," pp. 129–30.

13. In *Selections from Ralph Waldo Emerson*, p. 271.

14. Emerson, "Experience," in *Selections from Ralph Waldo Emerson*, p. 270.

15. "Notes on the Mind," in *Selections*, ed. Clarence H. Faust and Thomas H. Johnson, rev. ed. (New York: Hill and Wang, 1962), pp. 33–34.

16. *Romanticism Reconsidered*, p. 19.

17. *The Visionary Company: A Reading of English Romantic Poetry* (Garden City, N.Y.: Doubleday & Co., 1963), pp. 33–38.

18. In "Keats's Lady, Metaphor, and the Rhetoric of Neurosis" (*Studies in Romanticism* 15, no. 2 [Spring 1976]), David Simpson discusses the gap between these two stanzas as an "ontological blurring" (p. 275). Simpson writes, "The gap between consciousness and knowledge, which Kant chooses to fill with the moral imperative, is the gap which Freud will try to fill with the analysis of the dream and the unconscious, and the gap which the dramatic experience of Keats's poem has begun to plot in its own way" (p. 285). For an excellent discussion of metaphor and dream, see Simpson's entire essay (pp. 265–88).

19. For a thorough study of the way in which the image is distinguished from action, rational power, and ordinary temporality, see Frank Kermode, *The Romantic Image* (New York: Vintage Books, 1957).

20. Even in Yeats's work, while the image expands to dominate the poem, it reveals its meaning without radically transforming itself, or if it undergoes a transformation, it is a single rather than a serial one.

21. *The Design of the Present: Essays on Time and Form in American Literature* (New Haven, Conn.: Yale University Press, 1969). Lynen sees the juxtaposition between present and eternal as converting action into a stasis, a conclusion I take issue with, for it seems more accurate when applied to the English lyric. In fact we have observed the static relations between subject and object in poems by Keats, Yeats, and Thomas, who tend to focus or freeze the apparition or image. Even a poet like Wordsworth, for whom Lynen stipulates that progressions are all, focuses meaning around defined "spots of time." My disagreement may, however, be at least partly terminological, since any of Lynen's descriptions of American poetry (as, for example, that Whitman's technique is one of collage) sound exactly right.

22. *Design of the Present*, pp. 328–31.

23. Gerald L. Bruns, *Modern Poetry and the Idea of Language: A Critical and Historical Study* (New Haven, Conn.: Yale University Press, 1974), p. 200.

24. "The Sleepers."

25. If we look at the best of Whitman's movements from the speck of self-hood to its aggrandizement into a universality, we see how logical, how psychologically valid the steps between the two are, when he takes the time to spell them out for us. In "There Was a Child Went Forth," for example, we are shown how being augments itself, first through the knotted intimacies of a looming familial figure:

> The father, strong, self-sufficient, manly, mean, anger'd, unjust,
> The blow, the quick loud word, the tight bargain, the crafty lure,

then in the equivocating world-conclusion, as yet uncertain of the accuracy of its instincts:

> the sense of what is real,
> the thought if after all it should prove unreal,
> The doubts of day-time and the doubts of night-time, the curious whether and how,
> Whether that which appears so is so, or is it all flashes and specks?

finally, in the hard-won confidence of mature speculation:

> Men and women crowding fast in the streets, if they are not
> flashes and specks what are they?

26. The bell-rope of the church and the bell-like movement of blood pulsing through the speaker's veins, the "crystal Word" and the mortal world, Christ of the crucifix and God "The tribunal monarch of the air," the pagodas of the east and the campaniles of the west, the voices "heaping/The impasse high" and those that are struck to earth "slain," the "pledge to hope" and its defilement in despair, the tower of pebbles and the stone tower—these are some of the obvious antiphonal movements. In *The Poetry of Hart Crane: A Critical Study* (Princeton, N.J.: Princeton University Press, 1967), R.W.B. Lewis points to further verbal patterning, to "near repetitions and internal rhymes which thicken the poem's texture: 'I know not where . . . . I know not whither,' 'strikes . . . . strokes,' 'hold . . . . healed,' and so on" (pp. 410–11).

27. Both poem and treatise are concerned, and in almost the same language, with an upward and infinite rising toward God: "The emanation . . . of the divine fulness . . . has relation to God as its fountain" (Edwards, "Notes on the Mind," in Faust and Johnson, *Selections*, p. 344).

28. Edwards, "Notes on the Mind," in Faust and Johnson, *Selections*, p. 348.

29. For a discussion of "The Transcendental Aesthetic," see W. H. Walsh, "Kant on the Perception of Time," in *The First Critique: Reflections on Kant's Critique of Pure Reason*, ed. Terence Penelhum and J. J. MacIntosh (Belmont, Calif.: Wadsworth Publishing Company, 1969), pp. 70–88, and Norman Kemp Smith, *A Commentary to Kant's "Critique of Pure Reason"* (New York: Humanities Press, 1962).

30. Immanuel Kant, *Critique of Pure Reason*, trans. Norman Kemp Smith (London: Macmillan & Co., 1964), pp. 77, 79.

31. Kant, *Critique of Pure Reason*, pp. 214–15.

32. For a discussion of death and the word in Wordsworth's poetry, see Thomas Weiskel, *The Romantic Sublime: Studies in the Structure and Psychology of Transcendence* (Baltimore, Md.: The Johns Hopkins University Press, 1976), pp. 167–205.

33. Bruns, *Modern Poetry*, p. 199.

34. For interesting answers to these questions, see Charles Freh, "Interpreting 'Western Wind,'" *ELH* 43, no. 3 (Fall 1976): 259–78.

35. For a discussion of the poem's two beginnings, see Barbara Harman, "George Herbert's 'Affliction (I)': The Limits of Representation," *ELH* 44, no. 2. (Summer 1977): 267–85.

36. In am discounting medieval drama (the Miracle and Mystery plays) in which the answers to all questions are implicit, and suffering, if it exists at all, is momentary.

37. See Stanza VIII of "The Garden," where Marvell tells us "Two paradises 'twere in one/To live in paradise alone."

38. For a discussion of these and other discrepancies in the poem, see Donald M. Friedman, *Marvell's Pastoral Art* (Berkeley: University of California Press, 1970), pp. 93–147.

39. For a discussion of other puns in the poem, see Rosalie L. Colie, *"My Ecchoing Song": Andrew Marvell's Poetry of Criticism* (Princeton, N.J.: Princeton University Press, 1970).

40. For discussions of this literalization, see Geoffrey Hartman, "Marvell, St. Paul, and the Body of Hope," *ELH* 31 (1964): 175–94.

41. "Father Time," in *Studies in Iconology: Humanistic Themes in the Art of the Renaissance* (New York: Harper & Row, Publishers, 1972), pp. 69–94.

42. See Allen Tate's definition of the situation for poetry in the 1850s and '60s in "Emily Dickinson," *Collected Essays* (Denver, Colo.: The Swallow Press, 1959).

43. In *Emily Dickinson's Reading: 1836–1886* (Cambridge, Mass.: Harvard University Press, 1966), Jack L. Capps documents the fact that Dickinson's knowledge of Shakespeare and the

Bible, as well as of the religious and English Romantic poets, was an influence more dominant than any American counterpart. Although it is true that the the Dickinson library contained poetry volumes by Bryant, Longfellow, and Whittier, and probable that she read, in addition, Thoreau, Lowell, and Holmes (see *Emily Dickinson's Reading*, and also "Books and Reading" in Vol. 2 of *The Life of Emily Dickinson*, ed. Richard B. Sewall, 2 vols. [New York: Farrar, Straus & Giroux, 1974] 2:668-705). Dickinson's writing defines its space at such a boldly experimental distance from theirs that it seems hardly comparable. Even Emerson's poetry (which Dickinson read and loved, and to which among all other nineteenth-century American writers her work is most frequently compared) is similar only in the allusiveness of certain phrasing and in a gnomic fashion of rendering philosophic statement, but not really in the substantive treatment of given subjects.

Capps tells us that there is no evidence Dickinson had read Jonathan Edwards (p. 102), and she could not have read Edward Taylor, whose papers were found by his grandson and remained unedited until 1939, though she would have dearly loved his work. See Sewall, *Emily Dickinson*, vol. 2, p. 709.

44. See "The Organic Principle," in F. O. Matthiessen, *American Renaissance: Art and Expression in the Age of Emerson and Whitman* (New York: Oxford University Press, 1941) pp. 133-78. Matthiessen advances the idea, though not with respect to Dickinson's work.

Index of Dickinson
Poems Discussed

General Index

Allegorical structures, 69, 96–98, 101–2, 103, 127–29, 131, 204; compared with symbolic structures, 102, 128–29
Alterity. *See* Landscapes; Loss
"A Lyke-Wake Dirge," 246
Anderson, Charles, 13, 14, 75–76, 109, 113
Aristotle, 19, 56
Auden, W. H., 218–20
Auerbach, Erich, 19–20, 100
Augustine, Saint, 25, 117, 134, 229

Bakan, David, 28, 45, 153, 156, 170
Beckett, Samuel, 20–21, 24, 134, 163
Beginnings and ends: and complete stories, 69; lyrics unconcerned with, 70–71, 196, 247; poetic structures framed by, 69
Benjamin, Walter, 69–70
Benveniste, Emile, 270 n.1
Bergson, Henri, 172–73, 185, 211, 270 n.36
Blackmur, R. P., 13, 14, 32, 44, 150
Blake, William, 21, 166, 179, 198–99, 213–14, 220, 221, 254
Blanchot, Maurice, 223, 245–46
Bloom, Harold, 110, 213
Böll, Heinrich, 153
Bonhoeffer, Dietrich, 194–95
Booth, Wayne C., 64
Boundaries. *See* Identity, as fusion of self and other; Temporal boundaries, collapse of
Browning, Robert, 70
Burke, Kenneth, 28–29

Capps, Jack L., 11
Carew, Thomas, 165
Cavell, Stanley, 22
Center, 18, 74, 151–52, 157, 194–95. *See also*

Death; Time, juxtaposed to immortality
Chase, Richard, 16
Chaucer, Geoffrey, 165
Chronology, in poems. *See* Context; Time
Clark, James D., 41
Cody, John, 11
Coleridge, Samuel Taylor, 128, 216–17, 221, 222, 259
Context: beginnings and problems of, 31, 34–38, 170, 247, 250; middles and problems of, 18, 74–83, 149, 174, 197, 198; conclusions and problems of, 100, 171, 197, 204; coherence of, in poems, 17, 24, 30, 32–38, 44, 52, 56, 57–68, 74–88, 203, 257–58; complete, as necessary for meaning, 31, 44–45, 71–74, 194
Cooper, David, 52
Crane, Hart, 223, 227–33, 236, 238–39
Cullman, Oscar, 116–17
Cunningham, J. V., 97, 171

Death, 87, 89, 92–93, 110, 142, 168, 203, 204–5, 212, 213–14, 238–39; despair and fusion with, 17, 93–103, 134; dialectic between sexuality and, 56–90, 108, 123–24, 253–57; as mystery explained, 103–6, 130–33, 135; of otherness, 112–13, 122–26, 128, 129–31, 134–35, 136–38; and perception, coincidence of, 24, 112–18, 120–21, 124–31; proleptic utterances and, 24, 92, 104–6, 113–15, 118, 122–32, 135, 137, 209–10; reading as providing knowledge of, 69–74, 195–96
Definitions. *See* Names
de Man, Paul, 97–98, 129
Derrida, Jacques, 140–41, 156, 169, 172, 187, 188, 192

277

The Johns Hopkins University Press

This book was composed in Aldine Roman text and Palatino display type by Horne Associates, Incorporated. It was printed on 50–lb. Bookmark Natural Text paper and bound in Holliston Roxite cloth by Thomson-Shore, Inc.

Library of Congress Cataloging in Publication Data

Cameron, Sharon.
  Lyric time.

  Includes index.
  1. Dickinson, Emily, 1830–1886—Criticism and interpretation.
2. Lyric poetry—History and criticism. I. Title.
PS1541.Z5C29 811'.4 78-9983
ISBN 0-8018-2171-1